JESUS AND
VIRTUE ETHICS

JESUS AND
VIRTUE ETHICS

BUILDING BRIDGES BETWEEN
NEW TESTAMENT STUDIES
AND MORAL THEOLOGY

DANIEL J. HARRINGTON, S.J.

JAMES F. KEENAN, S.J.

A SHEED & WARD BOOK

ROWMAN & LITTLEFIELD PUBLISHERS, INC.
Lanham • Boulder • New York • Toronto • Plymouth, UK

SHEED & WARD
Lanham, Maryland
Chicago, Illinois

A SHEED & WARD BOOK

ROWMAN & LITTLEFIELD PUBLISHERS, INC.

Published in the United States of America
by Rowman & Littlefield Publishers, Inc.
A wholly owned subsidiary of The Rowman & Littlefield Publishing Group, Inc.
4501 Forbes Boulevard, Suite 200, Lanham, Maryland 20706
www.rowmanlittlefield.com

Estover Road
Plymouth PL6 7PY
United Kingdom

Scripture quotations are from the New Revised Standard Version of the Bible,
copyright 1946, 1952, 1971, 1989, by the Division of Christian Education of the
National Council of the Churches of Christ in the USA. Used by permission.

☉™The paper used in this publication meets the minimum requirements of
American National Standard for Information Sciences—Permanence of
Paper for Printed Library Materials, ANSI/NISO Z39.48-1992.
Manufactured in the United States of America.

LIBRARY OF CONGRESS CATALOGING-IN-PUBLICATION DATA

Harrington, Daniel J.
  Jesus and virtue ethics : building bridges between new Testament studies and
    moral theology / Daniel J. Harrington and James F. Keenan.
    p.cm.
  Includes bibliographical references and index.
  ISBN 978-1-58051-125-4

  1.Christian ethics—Catholic authors. 2.Christian ethics—History of doctrines.
  3.Bible. N.T.—Criticism, interpretation, etc. 4.Ethics in the Bible.
  I. Keenan, James F. II. Title.

BJ1249 .H37 2002
241'.042—dc21

2002075752

To John W. O'Malley, S.J.
An exemplary Jesuit, Scholar, and Colleague

CONTENTS

INTRODUCTION

In its Decree on the Training of Priests, the Second Vatican Council stated: "Special care should be given to the perfecting of moral theology. Its scientific presentation should draw more fully on the teaching of Holy Scripture and should throw light upon the exalted vocation of the faithful in Christ and their obligation to bring forth fruit in charity for the life of the world" (*Optatam totius* 16). Before Vatican II, Catholic moral theology (the branch of theology dealing with principles of moral or ethical conduct) was based largely on the natural law tradition (principles derived from nature and reason, and regarded as binding for all humans), with Scripture being used primarily as a quarry for prooftexts to bolster positions arrived at on other grounds. However, the council's statement updated and challenged the Church's thinking by recognizing the need to take Scripture on its own terms and by emphasizing the biblical-theological foundations of Catholic moral theology, to make it more explicitly Christian and theological. The statement also recognizes that moral theology should proceed from Christian identity and spell out the ways in which Christians should act in the context of their relations with God, other people, and the whole created universe.

Both biblical scholars and moral theologians have welcomed the council's statement. But for the most part, they have proceeded along their separate ways without doing much to further the integration of Scripture and Catholic moral theology. Biblical scholars write fine books and articles describing the ethical teachings of the various books of Scripture, tracing the development of a pertinent biblical theme or concept, and sometimes venturing opinions on how their findings might impact church doctrine or practice on this or that matter. Moral theologians concern themselves mainly with the several sources (including Scripture) of moral argument, and with trying to shed light on the dizzying array of ethical problems that modern technology poses to our Church and world. But there has been relatively little effort at exploring in a concrete way what modern biblical studies and Catholic moral theology might have to say to one another.

The authors of this book are Roman Catholic theologians. We are members of the Society of Jesus and professors at the Weston Jesuit School of Theology in Cambridge, Massachusetts. Daniel Harrington, professor of

New Testament, has been the general editor of *New Testament Abstracts* for more than thirty years. In this capacity, he sees virtually everything published in the New Testament field, and in recent years he has taken a particular interest in the foundations and applications of New Testament ethical teachings. James Keenan, professor of Moral Theology, has worked extensively on the history of Catholic moral theology (especially Thomas Aquinas), in the revival of interest in virtue ethics (focusing on the question, Who should we become?) and in moral reasoning. He is the editor of the Georgetown University Press "Moral Traditions" series and the coordinator of the "Moral Notes" for *Theological Studies*.

What makes our collaboration unique is its focus on virtue ethics. We believe that this approach is true to both the New Testament emphasis on the human response to God's gracious activity in Jesus Christ and to the ethical needs and desires of Christians in the twenty-first century. However, our work is not simply a book about moral virtues. Rather, we are trying to convey the entire sweep of New Testament ethical teaching from its foundations in the Old Testament and in Jesus' life, death, and resurrection, to its goal or *end* with the full coming of God's kingdom. Likewise, following Thomas Aquinas (1225–1275), perhaps the greatest theologian in the Catholic tradition, we take virtue ethics to be a comprehensive approach to all of Christian life, not simply an exercise in character formation divorced from Christian faith and life.

In every chapter (except in the historical survey in the first chapter) Harrington treats the topic from the perspective of New Testament studies, with particular attention first to a key text in the Gospels of Matthew, Mark, or Luke (context, content, significance) and then to the possibilities and problems that the various "biblical perspectives" might contribute to moral theology. His sections are entitled "Biblical Perspectives" and are presented concisely in a reportorial style. Harrington has adapted (with permission) some material from his "Biblical Studies & Moral Theology," (*Church* 13)[1]; "The Sermon on the Mount: What Is It?" (*Bible Today* 36)[2]; and *Why Do We Suffer? A Scriptural Approach to the Human Condition* (2000).[3] All the biblical quotations are from the New Revised Standard Version, which is the most widely available and used Bible translation in English.

At each point Keenan responds from the perspective of Catholic moral theology and from the wider movements within Christian ethics and theology today. His contributions are entitled "Moral Theological Reflections" and take the form of exploratory essays that try to build bridges between the disciplines of New Testament ethics and moral theology. In most cases Harrington goes first and Keenan second; but in several chapters the order is reversed when Keenan's remarks seem to be foundational for understanding the New Testament material. At the end of the book, under

"Final Thoughts," Keenan draws some general conclusions and points out problems that remain.

Our work is not a comprehensive portrait of Jesus and his teachings or a full-scale survey of New Testament moral teachings or a systematic reflection on how the Bible has been used in moral theology. Rather, it explores some topics in the Synoptic tradition—represented by the Gospels of Matthew, Mark, and Luke—to see where the encounter between biblical studies and moral theology might go. The use of "Jesus" in our title refers to Jesus as he is presented in the Gospels of Matthew, Mark, and Luke. However, since all the main emphases can be traced with relative certainty to the historical Jesus—that is, to the earthly Jesus, before his death and resurrection—we are dealing at least with "the voice of Jesus" as heard through the medium of those Gospels.

This book is intended more as a heuristic probe, or a means toward encouraging further investigation and discovery, than as a definitive statement. It deals with some New Testament texts (mainly from the Synoptic Gospels) and with what biblical scholars of various religious denominations make out of them, and reflects on what they may or may not mean for moral theology today. The focus on the Synoptic tradition is dictated mainly by a desire to be focused and concrete in our probe. Similar probes could be made on the basis of the Johannine writings, the Pauline corpus, and other New Testament writings, as well as various parts of the Old Testament.

Likewise, our essays are not intended as debates or as pleas for the value of one discipline over the other. The word *Bridges* in our subtitle indicates what we are trying to do. We are seeking to make links between two specialized theological disciplines that have seldom been joined together. And we are convinced that the "virtue ethics" approach is a promising start toward opening conversations at even deeper levels between specialists in biblical studies and moral theology.

We dedicate this book to John W. O'Malley, S.J., on the occasion of his seventy-fifth birthday. John has been our colleague, friend, and academic inspiration for many years.

Notes

1. *Church* 13/4 (1997), pp. 13–18.

2. *Bible Today* 36/5 (1998), pp. 280–286.

3. *Why do we suffer? A scriptural approach to the human condition* (Franklin, WI: Sheed & Ward, 2000), pp. 95–100.

Chapter One

THE HISTORIES OF MORAL THEOLOGY AND NEW TESTAMENT ETHICS

To build bridges between the fields of moral theology and New Testament studies, we need to recognize that considerable groundwork has already been established in each of the respective fields. We start with a brief survey of the long history of moral theology and of the more recent work in New Testament ethics. This review can help us to grasp not only the accomplishments that earlier investigations have yielded but also the challenges that lay before us.

Keenan presents a sketch of the history of moral theology through seven periods. He notes that each era has been distinguished by a primary emphasis either on avoiding evil or sin, or on becoming a disciple of Christ. When the latter emphasis prevailed, moral theologians relied on Scripture as their primary text, developed an integrated anthropological profile for the Christian, and pursued a much more positive agenda that accommodated the interests often relegated to ascetical theology (the branch of theology that trains one in holiness).

Harrington then considers the development of New Testament ethics, starting with its more Protestant initiatives and moving into its more comprehensive agenda. Study of the ethical teachings in the New Testament moved from consideration of the character of Jesus to an appreciation of both the underlying eschatologies operative in the Gospels and the significance of historical and hermeneutical concerns in New Testament research.

MORAL THEOLOGICAL REFLECTIONS
J. F. Keenan

The history of moral theology can be divided into seven periods. Three of them (nos. 1, 3, 7) were greatly influenced by Scripture, and four (nos. 2, 4,

1

5, 6) were not. They can be labeled by these terms: 1) patristics; 2) penitentials; 3) scholasticism; 4) confessional manuals; 5) casuistry; 6) moral manuals; and 7) contemporary moral theology.

PATRISTIC PERIOD
(From the New Testament to the Sixth Century)

The great writers of the "patristic" period (from the Latin word *patres*, and referring to the "Fathers of the Church") were primarily commentators on Scripture. The most prolific and prominent among them—Origen (185–254), John Chrysostom (347–407), Augustine (354–430), and Jerome (345–420)—all wrote extensive expositions of biblical texts. And their sermons and other writings were largely concerned with clarifying biblical concepts and applying biblical insights to the practice of Christian life. When they wrote on moral or ethical matters, they generally did so in the language of, and from the perspective of, Scripture. And even their more speculative efforts at Christology and Trinitarian theology had implications for the shaping of Christian morality. And here, too, their language and conceptuality were heavily biblical.

Scholars of early Christianity and late antiquity, such as Peter Brown, Abraham Malherbe, and Wayne Meeks, have written extensively on this period. But few moral theologians attend to this research. Key for early Christians was their effort at developing Christology. Gedaliahu Stroumsa claims that integrating the divinity and humanity of Christ was the major theological task and accomplishment of the early church. He writes: "The unity of Christ, possessor of two natures but remaining nonetheless one single persona, is, of course, in a nutshell, the main achievement of centuries of Christological and Trinitarian pugnacious investigations."[1] This achievement took practical significance in the ascetical imitation of Christ that called Christians to seek a unified self like Christ's. As Christ brought divinity and humanity into one, Christians were called to bring body and soul together. Integration became a key task for all early Christians, to "be an entity of body and soul, a Christ-bearing exemplar."[2]

Thus while the interiority of the believer was stressed, the outward expression of that interiority was equally emphasized: the love of Christ was concretely expressed in the contemporary world through the works of mercy. Similarly, just as much as one's identity was intimately tied to discipleship, so too was that discipleship lived out in the community of the emerging church, where the horizon of expectations was constantly being shaped by the believers' understanding of the kingdom.

The time of the early church was, then, a remarkably innovative period, when the integrated moral life was understood as a central component for living out of one's call to discipleship. The moral life was a response to the Word of God; it was an application of the rhetoric of preaching to the ordinary life. Here we can pause to reflect on one significant innovation described in Peter Brown's *The Body and Society*. In order to provide support to the early church, some wealthy Christian widows did not remarry. Instead of relinquishing their family's income to a second husband, Christian widows used their funds to support church ministry. Eventually their daughters imitated their mothers by committing themselves to perpetual virginity, a completely new state of life. These Christ-bearing exemplars were the embodiment of generosity.

PENITENTIALS
(Early Medieval Times)

The practice of confessing one's sins with some regularity began in the sixth century. Throughout the Celtic lands, local spiritual leaders, usually abbots who had cultivated this practice among their monks, extended the practice to some of the devout laity. By writing penitentials (catalogs compiled for confessors specifying the appropriate penance for various sins), these leaders attempted to assign adequate penance tariffs that took into account the sin, its gravity, and the state of life of the confessing penitent. These writings were loosely organized around the seven deadly sins—pride, envy, anger, sloth, avarice, gluttony, and lust. Eventually, the practice of individual regular confessions spread throughout Ireland and the British Isles and into northern Europe.

During this period, moral theology was shaped predominantly by a concern about the sins one should avoid, and not about the good to be pursued. Similarly, with emphasis on one's own moral state, the Christian's communal self-understanding was less important, and a long period of moral narcissism began, in which Christians became anxious not about the kingdom or the needs of the Church, but rather about the state of their individual souls. Although neither Christian idealism nor innovation was particularly evident in the ordinary moral concerns of the day, and although judgment day loomed not as a day of deliverance but as a day of damnation for the masses, these penitential manuals served as important instruments of social control and stability in a period of considerable chaos and political instability.

SCHOLASTICISM
(Middle Ages)

This phenomenon emerged in the midst of a variety of vigorous movements. The Church began to codify personal rights and procedures through ecclesiastical or canon law. Towns in Europe started to define themselves and to grow into cities, and cathedrals rose up in their centers. Universities began to flourish in Paris, Oxford, Bologna, Cologne, and Montpellier. The twelfth century became a time of enormous spiritual reawakening. A deep fascination with the human as the image of God animated the thought of Richard of St. Victor (d. 1173), Bernard of Clairvaux (1090–1153), and Hildegard of Bingen (1098–1179), among others. These devotional insights inevitably led to charismatic figures like Dominic (c. 1170–1221), Francis (1181/82–1226), Clare (c. 1193–1253), and their followers. Within the context of these evangelical movements celebrating the human as the image of God, painters like Cimabue, Duccio, and Giotto inaugurated the Renaissance.

From the twelfth through the sixteenth century, the schoolmen investigated ways of expressing faith through reason. Inasmuch as theology was seen as a science investigating God and the human, moral theology specifically studied humanity as responding lovingly to the initiative of God. This study was then highly anthropological (that is, concerned with the human condition) and naturally depended on the virtues to outline an appropriate moral identity. Here again the Church's moral agenda was reintegrated, and the natural law was expressed again as the pursuit of the good and the avoidance of evil. As important as this theology was, however, it remained largely academic in its influence.

CONFESSIONAL MANUALS AND THE TEN COMMANDMENTS
(Middle Ages and the Protestant Reformation)

As these academic, canonical, and evangelical movements were underway, Pope Innocent III (1160–1216; pope 1198–1216), convinced that the masses were nonetheless damned, imposed on the entire Church the requirement to annually confess or declare openly sins. The nineteenth-century church historian Henry Lea called this "the most important legislative act in the history of the Church."[3]

To meet this new ministerial task, Innocent charged the newly established Dominican Order to become trained as confessors—those who hear confessions and offer absolution or forgiveness based on appropriate penance, or the prayers or works one performs to atone for sins. They, along with Franciscan companions, in turn developed sophisticated confessional manuals, again based (for the most part) on the seven deadly sins. These became the predominant instruments for forming clergy to help the laity in discerning the moral life. Thus, despite the integrated theology of the scholastics, those involved in the moral lives of ordinary Christians were almost entirely concerned with matters of sin.

Concurrently, for several reasons, the Protestant Reformers such as Martin Luther and John Calvin attacked the confessional manuals and their use of the seven deadly sins, by insisting on the centrality of the Ten Commandments for moral instruction. First, the Ten Commandments enjoyed divine sanction; they, not the seven deadly sins, were biblically based. Second, they were a solid pedagogical tool that resisted any attempt at embellishment. Inasmuch as the seven deadly sins were no more than the name of seven vices, they afforded the medieval mentality the opportunity to elaborate on the vices so as to declare more and more human activity as sinful. But the Ten Commandments were more than a name; they were propositional utterances with a specific text worthy of commentary. Third, unlike the seven deadly sins, they offered not only negative prohibitions but also on occasion positive prescriptions. In fact, in commenting on the Decalogue (= the Ten Commandments), the Reformers always discussed both the prescriptions and the prohibitions for each commandment. Finally, with the possible exception of pride, the deadly sins were primarily offensive to human life, whereas the Ten Commandments began with our relationship to the divine and moved to our relationships with the human. This more integrated, balanced, and Scripture-based ethics remained central to Protestant moral education

CASUISTRY
(Early Modern Times)

European expansionism into the Americas and Asia in the sixteenth century led to the recognition of the inadequacy of contemporary moral guidelines. Professors at the University of Paris were regularly asked to determine new questions. Rather than resorting to a deductive application of principles to these cases, the professors developed a case method or "high casuistry" (from the Latin *casus* meaning "a case") as it has been called. This method, which dominated moral theology until the mid-seventeenth century, used a paradigm or exemplary case instead of a principle as its truth standard. For instance, in cases concerning whether a person could dissemble (meaning to conceal the truth of one's feelings under false appearances), the paradigm case was often Jesus at Emmaus (Luke 24:13–35), who acted both as if he knew nothing of the information the disciples were discussing and as if he had no intention of having a meal with them. Casuistry was then the exploration of the significance of circumstantial differences between the authority of a paradigm case and a new unresolved case. Eventually, seminary professors applied the method for forming fellow priests to hear confessions. As innovative as this method was and as clever as its users were, nevertheless casuistry was almost always about determining what was sinful and what, therefore, needed to be avoided. Casuistry rarely considered the good to be pursued.

At the same time, devotional or ascetical manuals began to appear. Erasmus's (1466–1536) enormously popular *Enchiridion militis christiani* (*Handbook for the Christian Soldier*) appeared in 1503. In its first hundred years, it underwent more than one hundred editions of the original Latin and innumerable translations. Erasmus's influence stemmed from a number of personal factors: his theological vision, emphasis on Scripture, interest in a devotional life that extended beyond monastery walls, desire to shift devotional practices from external actions to internal dispositions, and belief that learning and prayer were together the guiding instruments of our growth in holiness. His *Enchiridion* became the prototype for subsequent popular works by Lorenzo di Scupoli (1530–1610), Luis de Granada (1504–1588), and others. In these works, we find the pursuit of the good and the call to love the neighbor.

MORAL MANUALS
(Up to the Twentieth Century)

By the middle of the seventeenth century, church leaders and members, tired and suspicious of high casuistry because it sometimes became oversubtle and even intellectually dishonest, prompted moral theologians to distill their learning into universal principles and to provide textbooks, or moral manuals as they were called, that could be taught in seminaries around the world. Moral reasoning in this context became deductive again (meaning to move from the universal principle to the individual case), and the principles were about avoiding sins. Inasmuch as they were designed to train confessors, the manuals looked on the conscience as scrupulous, perplexed, doubtful, or erroneous. Not surprisingly, then, moral manualists were rarely interested in the pursuit of the good, and they routinely referred readers to contemporary ascetical literature for such guidance.

One of the most succinct descriptions of these manuals can be found in the preface of the first moral manual to appear in English, Thomas Slater's *A Manual of Moral Theology:*

> [Moral theology] is the product of centuries of labor bestowed by able and holy men on the practical problems of Christian

ethics. Here, however, we must ask the reader to bear in mind that the manuals of moral theology are technical works intended to help the confessor and the parish priest in the discharge of their duties. They are as technical as the text-books of the lawyer and the doctor. They are not intended for edification, nor do they hold up a high ideal of Christian perfection for the imitation of the faithful. They deal with what is of obligation under pain of sin; they are books of moral pathology. They are necessary for the Catholic priest to enable him to administer the sacrament of Penance and to fulfill other duties.

Slater noted the "very abundant" literature of ascetical theology, but added that "moral theology proposes to itself the much humbler but still necessary task of defining what is right and what is wrong in all the practical relations of the Christian life . . . The first step on the right road of conduct is to avoid evil."[4]

CONTEMPORARY MORAL THEOLOGY

To replace the manualist method, which had the long-standing, singular concern of knowing, describing, and parsing sin, twentieth-century moral theologians such as Fritz Tillmann, Gerard Gilleman, Josef Fuchs, and Bernard Häring turned to Scripture, a renewed study of Thomas Aquinas, and ascetical theology to amplify the task of contemporary moral theology. They recognized the love of God as foundational to moral theology, incorporated Scripture's many insights about virtue into a relational anthropological vision, asserted the primacy of the conscience, and challenged the notion of moral truth as universal, eternal, and immutable.

The Second Vatican Council's admonition to moral theology validated the work of these theologians: "Special care should be given to the perfecting of moral theology. Its scientific presentation should draw more fully on the teaching of Holy Scripture and should throw light upon the exalted vocation of the faithful in Christ and their obligation to bring forth fruit in charity for the life of the world" (*Optatam totius* 16). But shortly afterwards, Pope Paul VI's *Humanae vitae* reasserted the manualists' notion of moral truth and their insistence on avoiding certain actions at all cost. By the end of the twentieth century, popes and many bishops identified their moral teachings with the manualist method, and stood in opposition to the approach of many contemporary moral theologians.

This brief historical overview yields two key insights. First, the present tension in moral theology is representative of two dominant trends in moral theology over the past two thousand years. In a manner of speaking, the tradition seesaws back and forth between a singular concern for sin, external actions, and universal claims, on the one hand, and a more inclusive notion of the natural law, the formation of internal dispositions, and an appreciation for concretely specific notions of moral truth on the other. Second, generally speaking, when Scripture becomes the foundation of moral theology, we renew our understanding of the natural law's twofold principle (do good and avoid evil). We turn to ascetical theology to accentuate human growth and to develop a stronger appreciation of the virtues. We look to the virtues as the right realization of Christian's internal dispositions. We cultivate a more integrated view of theology. And animated by love, we look to develop a more relational anthropology.

BIBLICAL PERSPECTIVES
D. J. Harrington

The term *New Testament ethics* refers to the ethical teachings that are found in the twenty-seven books of the New Testament. Although surely influenced by Jewish ethical traditions and Greco-Roman moral teachings, the New Testament books (and the traditions they shaped) are distinctive in their appeal to the Christ event; that is, to the person and teachings of Jesus of Nazareth, his saving death and resurrection, and his continuing influence through the Holy Spirit. Early Christian writers took the coming kingdom of God and the accompanying judgment as the horizon of faith and action, and tried to express what behaviors are consistent with Christian identity and what rewards and punishments might be expected.

New Testament ethics is oriented toward encountering God and doing God's will in the light of the Christ event. It is concerned with God's saving action through Christ and how people of faith may participate in it. It gives relatively little attention to natural law (but see Romans 1:26–27), to virtues as personal character traits only, to defining *happiness*, to seeking the *mean* as Aristotle does, or to doing the *right thing* as its own reward. It uses terms such as *justice* and *freedom,* but almost always in the context of God's action through Christ. It is primarily a religious ethic, an ethic of relationship with God, others, and the world in light of that relationship. It is a historical ethic, in the sense that it takes its direction from a particular person in history (Jesus of Nazareth) and moves its adherents toward the final manifestation of God's kingdom.[5]

THE HISTORY OF THE DISCIPLINE

New Testament ethics in its technical sense refers to what modern New Testament exegetes and biblical theologians have made out of the ethical teachings of the New Testament. It arose as part of the dominance of historical criticism in the late nineteenth century, when scholars came to appreciate better the historical distance between the biblical writings and the present. Since the primary practitioners of historical criticism in the late nineteenth and early-twentieth centuries were Protestants, its early history at least was Protestant, with only a few serious Catholic contributions.

The Liberal Protestant (as opposed to Evangelical or Fundamentalist) approaches of the late nineteenth century viewed Jesus of Nazareth as a model of good character and virtue, and tended to play him off against later credal developments and church practices. The famous German church historian Adolph von Harnack reduced Jesus' teaching to the following basic principles: the kingdom of God and its coming; God the Father and the infinite value of the human soul; and the higher righteousness and the love command. Little or no attention was given to eschatology (the general resurrection, the last judgment, etc.). Rather, the focus was the search for eternal values and ideals, as well as their internalization and universalization.

The Social Gospel Movement (stressing Jesus' social teachings and their applications to public life) was a particular variant of the Liberal Protestant approach that was (and is) especially influential in the United States. Its most prominent proponent was Walter Rauschenbusch in the late nineteenth and early twentieth century. In this approach, dedication to the kingdom of God proclaimed by Jesus meant trying to recreate the social and political structures of the Jesus movement and the earliest church. It viewed Jesus as a social reformer, or at least as a teacher with a social message that involved love, sacrifice, goodwill toward others, desire to cooperate, and so forth. The idea was that the religion of Jesus could cast light on and help to solve present-day social and economic problems.

In the early twentieth century the recognition of the centrality of the kingdom of God in Jesus' teaching and the eschatological nature of that kingdom, especially by Johannes Weiss (1863–1914) and Albert Schweitzer (1875–1965), brought about a new phase in the history of New Testament ethics. In the context of the Judaism of Jesus' day, the kingdom of God referred most obviously to the future display of the sovereignty of the God of Israel over all creation. Therefore the ethical teachings of John the Baptist and Jesus should be regarded as concerned with repentance in preparation for the coming kingdom. The moral behavior urged by these prophets of the coming kingdom was thus an *interim* ("for the time being") ethic until the fullness of God's kingdom will be made manifest. But since the kingdom did not appear as John and Jesus believed it would (according to Weiss and Schweitzer), these ethical teachings had to be either dismissed as part of a tragic mistake or reinterpreted in light of the nonappearance of the kingdom.

One such reinterpretation was made by Rudolf Bultmann (1884–1976), with his program of demythologization. For him, the apocalyptic imagery associated with the kingdom of God in the early Jewish texts and the Gospels was merely a mythological way of speaking about an existential encounter with God and the personal decision that it provokes. Moreover, for Bultmann, even the alleged ethical teachings of Jesus are merely examples of how to respond to God, not timeless truths to be followed in every situation. Jesus teaches us how to relate to God, not ethics.

The Biblical Theology Movement (a return to biblical sources and themes, studied in their historical contexts) of post–World War II period, which was especially influential in Protestant circles in the United States, acknowledged the importance of eschatology in Jesus' teaching. But it looked instead to the larger context provided by the concept of covenant that is prominent in various Old Testament texts and can be taken as a theological assumption in the New Testament. The biblical covenant was based on the dynamics of ancient Near Eastern treaties. In the Bible the word *covenant* was used to express God's relation to Israel as the chosen people. Its starting point is what Yahweh the God of Israel had done on Israel's behalf: leading them out of Egypt and promising them the land of Israel. From this relationship, Israel takes on certain obligations to be carried out in response to God as its covenant lord and accepts that its failures to do so will be punished. In the covenant context, the divine commands scattered throughout the Torah especially become ways of responding to the prior revelation of God's saving love and of fulfilling the will of God, and are not simply free-floating imperatives. In the covenant context, the apocalyptic kingdom of God becomes the vehicle for the perfect fulfillment of God's promises to Israel, and Jesus becomes the messianic lawgiver who shows God's people how to act in anticipation of the coming kingdom.

The approach most commonly adopted today in studying the ethical teachings of the New Testament combines historical and hermeneutical concerns. It seeks to place the New Testament texts in their historical setting within the Roman Empire of the first century. It highlights the differences between that world and the world of the reader today, and challenges the reader to apply the principles of hermeneutical theory to the biblical texts: examining one's prejudices and presuppositions, acknowledging the historical and cultural distance between oneself and the text, attempting to make a fusion with the horizon of the text, and entering into a relationship of communion with the text. The historical-hermeneutical approach is concerned mainly with how Scripture provides a language for doing Christian ethics and how it shapes a person and a community that reasons morally and acts appropriately.

POSITIVE CONTRIBUTIONS

If Scripture is to have a greater place in Catholic moral theology, we must be clear about what we can and cannot expect from Scripture. On the positive side, careful attention to Scripture can allow the word of God to shape Christian character and Christian community. Scripture reminds us constantly of the religious context—the history of salvation—in which Christian ethical teachings took form and are practiced. By making us confront the cultural assumptions of our ancestors in faith from long ago and far away, we come to recognize also our own rootedness in time and place, and to see the continuity and the new developments in salvation history.

The Bible also provides important insights about human conduct and guidelines for responding to God's initiatives through Christ. The Ten Commandments establish the basic framework for Jewish and Christian moral teaching. The Sermon on the Mount (see Matthew 5–7) and the Sermon on the Plain (see Luke 6:20–49) as well as the Johannine Farewell Discourses (see John 13–17) continue to give guidance and challenge to Christians. The ethical implications that Paul draws from the death and resurrection of Christ can offer analogies and directions for people who seek to live out their faith with integrity and fidelity.

The Bible is a primary source of Christian spirituality. The term *spirituality* concerns how we stand before God and how we relate to God, to others, and to all creation in light of that relationship. The Bible tells us how God has intervened in human history, and how the great heroes of our religious tradition, from Abraham and Moses to Jesus and Paul, have related to God. These figures in turn help us by way of example in our relationship with God, especially in viewing our attitudes and actions in the light of our identity as part of God's people in Christ.

PROBLEM AREAS

On the negative side, there are problems with using Scripture in moral theology. The Bible is a huge and varied book. In fact, it is a collection of books. On most topics there is no single biblical position. Rather, there is usually a variety of perspectives, often depending on the historical circumstances. For example, one cannot easily harmonize Paul's directives to respect and cooperate with the officials of the Roman Empire (see Romans 13:1–7) and the scathing critique of Roman officialdom and of the emperor cult in the Book of Revelation.

Moreover, the Bible does not contain a moral treatise, that is, a systematic exposition of biblical morality. Instead, its moral teachings appear in various literary forms (commands, prohibitions, case laws, prophetic exhortations, wisdom sayings, and so forth) and frequently in the course of a narrative (as in Exodus through Deuteronomy and in the Gospels). Can or should an interpreter take these teachings out of their narrative and historical frameworks and treat them as free-floating moral principles? On what grounds?

And of course the Bible can hardly be expected to address problems (e.g., surrogate motherhood, genetic manipulation, biological warfare, saturation bombing) that were never dreamed of in biblical times. Although it may be possible to take from the Bible certain analogies and directions in approaching such issues, one can hardly build a moral argument about them directly on biblical texts. Also, since the New Testament presents a religious ethic, there will be some difficulty in appealing to biblical texts in the context of "secular" ethical or political debates. Likewise, the Bible is frequently interested in issues that no longer pertain to people today or that the Bible itself has solved (e.g., whether non-Jews should be circumcised before becoming Christians).

Moreover, some moral theologians wonder whether the New Testament presents any unique moral teachings at all. Although the Bible does surely supply a distinctive identity and distinctive motivations, does it supply unique content? The command to love one's enemies is sometimes cited as uniquely Christian. But with respect to content, one can find ancient parallels to this and practically every other "ethical" teaching in the New Testament. On most issues there are not entirely new or extreme departures in the New Testament from the noblest social norms of the Jewish and Greco-Roman worlds. And some books (for example, 1 Peter, the Pastorals) deliberately promote good behavior according to the "sound" moral thinking of the day as an effective Christian missionary strategy. The uniqueness of early Christian moral teaching is probably best traced to the use of Jewish and Greco-Roman ethical ideas in the new context created by Jesus and the claims of the community about him. That community embraced the best ideals of contemporary moral philosophy against the horizon of Jewish eschatology, and encouraged their acceptance and practice not merely by a small group of elite intellectuals or by dedicated Jews but rather by a more inclusive religious movement that eventually grew and became very influential in the late Roman Empire.

Finally, there is the problem of discerning the importance of Scripture in an ethical argument. Most New Testament scholars and Christian moral theologians affirm that Scripture should have a place in an ethical argument. But what place? If one does not want to devalue reason, tradition, and experience and to exalt the role of Scripture alone, the question remains, How does one discern among the voices? Can one construct a kind of "calculus" or theological "computer program" that would facilitate the process of discernment?

PROSPECTS FOR THE FUTURE

At present, biblical studies and moral theology continue to operate largely in isolation from each other. Biblical scholars produce marvelous historical studies, literary-theological analyses of texts with great ethical significance, and investigations of biblical themes. But these are largely unread by moral theologians. Likewise, moral theologians make honest attempts to use Scripture along with right reason, tradition, and experience in forming moral arguments. But few biblical scholars have the interest or the ability to enter into the conversation.

There is on both sides a strong sense for the need of interdisciplinary cooperation and some practical efforts toward such collaboration. But an even greater commitment to dialogue is needed if Scripture is to assume its role as the "soul of theology," including moral theology. Moreover, the dialogue cannot be limited to exegetes and moral theologians. The issues that emerge in this conversation embrace fundamental theology (reason and revelation, the authority of Scripture, hermeneutics), systematic theology (the nature of God, anthropology, the Church), and pastoral theology (liturgy, religious education).

What is needed especially is cooperation at the level of interpretation or hermeneutics. Biblical scholars must try to learn the language and conceptuality of moral theology, and moral theologians need to learn the language and conceptuality of biblical studies (exegesis and biblical theology). Such cooperation can help rescue biblical exegesis from falling into antiquarianism and irrelevancy, and can at the same time help to enrich and enliven moral theology precisely as a Christian theological discipline.

Questions for Reflection and Discussion

1. What do you think are the major effects of Scripture's influence on moral theology?

2. Why is Scripture's influence so remarkable?

3. Moral theology animated by Scripture has many differences from moral theology not so animated. Name some of them.

Notes

1. Gedaliahu Stroumsa, "*Caro Salutis cardo:* Shaping the Person in Early Christian Thought," in *History of Religions* 30 (1990), pp. 25–50.

2. Ibid., pp. 35, 39–40.

3. Henry Lea, *The History of Auricular Confession and Indulgences in the Latin Church*, vol. I (Philadelphia: Lea Brothers, 1896), p. 230.

4. Thomas Slater, *A Manual of Moral Theology,* vol. I (New York: Benziger Brothers, 1906), pp. 5–6.

5. See Leander E. Keck, "Rethinking 'New Testament Ethics,'" *Journal of Biblical Literature* 115 (1996), pp. 3–16.

Select Bibliography

Barton, John. *Ethics and the Old Testament.* Harrisburg, PA: Trinity Press International, 1998.

Birch, Bruce C. and Larry L. Rasmussen. *Bible and Ethics in Christian Life.* Rev. ed. Minneapolis: Augsburg, 1989.

Black, Peter and James F. Keenan. "The Evolving Self-Understanding of the Moral Theologian: 1900–2000." *Studia Moralia* 39 (2001), pp. 291–327.

Bretzke, James T. *Bibliography on Scripture and Christian Ethics.* Lewiston, NY: Mellen, 1997.

Brown, Peter. *The Body and Society: Men, Women, and Sexual Renunciation in Early Christianity.* New York: Columbia University Press, 1988.

Carter, Philippa. *The Servant-Ethic in the New Testament.* New York-Bern: Lang, 1997.

Daly, Robert J. et al. *Christian Biblical Ethics.* New York: Paulist, 1984.

Gallagher, John. *Time Past, Time Future: An Historical Study of Catholic Moral Theology.* New York: Paulist, 1990.

Houlden, Leslie. *Ethics and the New Testament*. Rev. ed. Edinburgh: T&T Clark, 1992.

Lea, Henry. *The History of Auricular Confession and Indulgences in the Latin Church*. Philadelphia: Lea Brothers, 1896.

Lohse, Eduard. *Theological Ethics of the New Testament*. Minneapolis: Fortress, 1991.

Long, Edward L. *To Liberate and Redeem: Moral Reflections on the Biblical Narrative*. Cleveland: Pilgrim, 1997.

Mahoney, John. *The Making of Moral Theology*. Oxford: Clarendon Press, 1987.

Malherbe, Abraham. *Social Aspects of Early Christianity*. Baton Rouge: Louisiana State University, 1977.

Marxsen, Willi. *New Testament Foundations for Christian Ethics*. Minneapolis: Fortress, 1993.

McNeill, John T. and Helena Gamer (trans.), *Medieval Handbooks of Penance*. New York: Columbia University Press, 1938.

Meeks, Wayne. *The First Urban Christians*. New Haven: Yale University Press, 1983.

Osborn, Eric. *Ethical Patterns in Early Christian Thought*. Cambridge, UK: Cambridge University Press, 1976.

Poschmann, Bernard. *Penance and Anointing of the Sick*. New York: Herder and Herder, 1964.

Sanders, Jack T. *Ethics in the New Testament. Change and Development*. Philadelphia: Fortress, 1975.

Schnackenburg, Rudolf. *The Moral Teaching of the New Testament*. New York: Seabury, 1979.

Schrage, Wolfgang. *The Ethics of the New Testament*. Philadelphia: Fortress, 1988.

Slater, Thomas. *A Manual of Moral Theology*. New York: Benziger Brothers, 1906.

Stroumsa, Gedaliahu. "*Caro salutis cardo*: Shaping the Person in Early Christian Thought." *History of Religions* 30 (1990), pp. 25–50.

Tentler, Thomas. *Sin and Confession on the Eve of the Reformation*. Princeton: Princeton University Press, 1977.

Vereecke, Louis. *De Guillaume D'Ockham Saint Alphonse de Liguori.* Rome: Collegium S. Alfonsi de Urbe, 1986.

Verhey, Allen. *The Great Reversal: Ethics and the New Testament.* Grand Rapids: Eerdmans, 1984.

_____. *Remembering Jesus: Christian Community, Scripture, and the Moral Life.* Grand Rapids: Eerdmans, 2002.

Chapter Two

METHODS: THE NEW TESTAMENT AND MORAL THEOLOGY

I n constructing bridges between New Testament studies and moral theology, we need to turn now from their histories to the more immediate concerns regarding methodology and application. Harrington first explains methodological issues in biblical exegesis (an explanation of the literary, historical, and theological features of biblical texts) and hermeneutics, and examines the approaches and contributions of biblical theologians in treating New Testament ethics. The debate revolves about which horizon gets priority or greater emphasis: the horizon of the text or the horizon of the interpreter. While some biblical scholars are content to describe the world of the Bible, others, such as Richard Hays, Elisabeth Schüssler Fiorenza, and various liberation theologians have introduced normative criteria for mediating the claims of biblical revelation today.

From among various methods used in moral theology, Keenan proposes virtue ethics as especially suitable for bridging the concerns of New Testament studies and moral theology. He extends this claim to show how virtue ethics can help moral theology engage effectively with ascetical theology, liturgy, and church life. Exploring the promise of virtue ethics, he concludes by demonstrating how this approach provides a context for exploring moral theological reflection on New Testament ethical teachings.

BIBLICAL PERSPECTIVES
D. J. Harrington

New Testament ethics is based on the careful study of written texts. Such study has historical, literary, and theological components. Each of the biblical sections that follows begins with a close reading of a specific text in the Synoptic Gospels (Matthew, Mark, and Luke). This analysis takes account of the historical and literary contexts, the content, and the theological significance of the text. The close reading of the text then leads into a wider consideration of biblical perspectives and to reflections on the implications for moral theology today.

To illustrate the process of textual interpretation (biblical exegesis) that is foundational for all aspects of New Testament ethics, we focus now on a short and famous passage that appears both in Matthew 6:24 and in Luke 16:13.

YOU CANNOT SERVE GOD AND WEALTH
(Matthew 6:24; Luke 16:13)

No one can serve two masters; for a slave will either hate the one and love the other, or be devoted to the one and despise the other. You cannot serve God and wealth.

The *historical context* presupposes the institution of human slavery. In such a situation (which was common in ancient societies, including that of the Old and New Testaments), one person could be regarded as the property of another, and was obligated to do what the master ordered. People became slaves by going into debt, by being captured in war or kidnapped, or by being born into slavery. To a large extent, the Roman Empire was built upon and sustained by a slave-based economy, and so the institution of slavery was familiar to the first readers of the New Testament books. Indeed some early Christians were slaves and slave owners.

The very strong language of "love" and "hate" in the New Testament saying is rooted in such Old Testament texts as Deuteronomy 21:15. The word translated here as "wealth" is *Mammon* in the Greek original. Although the Gospels of Matthew and Luke were both composed in Greek, they have preserved *Mammon* as a loanword taken over from Hebrew and Aramaic. It is based on the Semitic root *'aman* meaning "to be true or faithful," which is the origin of our word *Amen*. When we say "Amen," we affirm that we believe and that we put our trust in something or someone. In this saying, *Mammon* refers to money or wealth in general as something in which people place their faith or trust, and so it assumes a God-like status. Here Mammon is portrayed as a rival to the one and only God, Yahweh the God of Israel and Father of our Lord Jesus Christ, the only Lord who is truly worthy of our service.

The *literary context* refers to the textual setting in which the passage now appears. The teaching about God and Mammon now occurs in Matthew 6:24 and Luke 16:13. Thus it occurs in the larger contexts of Matthew's Sermon on the Mount (see 5:1–7:29) and Luke's Journey Narrative (see 9:51–19:44). For both Evangelists, these sections were important occasions for conveying large amounts of traditional teaching materials attributed to Jesus. The God-and-Mammon text seems to have been originally part of the anthology of Jesus' sayings known among modern biblical scholars as the Sayings Source Q, the collection of sayings used by Matthew and Luke to supplement Mark's narrative. It has been incorporated by each Evangelist in a different context and with a different emphasis.

Both Matthew and Luke used the God-and-Mammon saying as part of their narratives about Jesus' life, death, and resurrection, in which Jesus appears as a wise teacher and a powerful and compassionate healer. In Matthew's Sermon on the Mount (see our chapter 5 for a full treatment) the immediate context in 6:19–34 is the general theme of total commitment to the service of God. There it is one of several short units in a wisdom instruction that are connected by their emphasis on single-hearted service of God. In the Matthean context, the key word is *serve*, and what is at stake is the Lord whom one chooses to serve. In Luke's Journey Narrative, the immediate context is the parable of the dishonest manager (see 16:1–8) and a collection of short units about the proper and improper uses of money (see 16:9–13). The Lukan context places the emphasis on "money" and on the choice between serving God or money as one's master.

The *content* of the saying in Matthew 6:24 (and Luke 16:13) is best uncovered by literary analysis. The meanings of the key words and images—*slavery*, *love* and *hate*, and *Mammon*—have already been treated with reference to the historical context. The teaching takes the form of a parable or similitude that purports to concern slaves and masters but moves to another level of our relationship to God and other "masters." The progress of thought unfolds first with a general statement ("No one can serve two masters"), then a reason ("for . . ."), and finally an application ("You cannot serve God and wealth"). In the Matthean context of teachings about total commitment to God, the passage emphasizes the message to serve God as the only true Lord. When placed in the context of Matthew's narrative of Jesus and in Jesus' first great speech (the Sermon on the Mount), it becomes part of the larger story of Jesus and his teachings.

For those interested in the New Testament and moral theology, Matthew 6:24 (and Luke 16:13) has a double *significance*. On the general level, it concerns the fundamental choice or option that everyone must make: Who is your lord? Is it God or someone (or something) else? On the more specific level, it is a warning not to make wealth or material possessions into the object of one's faith or trust (Mammon).

The task of drawing out the significance of a biblical text is called *hermeneutics*. It is what theologians, preachers, and those who pray on Scripture do. In *Truth and Method*,[1] German philosopher Hans-Georg Gadamer describes the process of interpretation or hermeneutics as the fusion between the horizon of the text (in its historical setting) and that of the interpreter (here and now). Gadamer also emphasizes the role of the reader's pre-understandings or prejudices, the character of a "classic" text that retains continuing validity beyond its original historical context, interpretation as the sharing of common meanings, and the need for application. By sharing horizons with a text (or a piece of music, a work of art, etc.), we do not remain exactly what we were.

Among hermeneutical theorists there is a debate about where the emphasis should lie. Should it be with the horizon of the text or with the horizon of the interpreter? For example, American literary theorist and critic E. D. Hirsch distinguishes between what the text said in its original horizon or setting (meaning) and what it might say to people in a different horizon (significance). For French philosopher Paul Ricoeur, however, the text once put in written form becomes an object and gains a certain autonomy, and so may be appropriated in different ways by different interpreters. The approach taken in this book is more along the lines set forth by Gadamer (fusion of horizons) and Hirsch (meaning and significance), without denying entirely the validity of Ricoeur's insights.

APPROACHES TO NEW TESTAMENT ETHICS TODAY

Where does the study of New Testament ethics stand today? The following approaches are indicative of how New Testament scholars and theologians carry out their task. No one of them is adequate in itself, and elements from all of them are taken up in the presentations that follow. The purpose here is to provide a current map of the field and so to sensitize readers to different methods and perspectives.

Historical description: In *The Origins of Christian Morality: The First Two Centuries,*[2] Wayne A. Meeks of Yale University presents an "ethnography" of early Christian morality within the larger complex culture of the Roman Empire. Using parallel literature from all over the Greco-Roman world, Meeks deals with the following topics: the moral consequences of conversion; city, household, and people of God; loving and hating the world; the language of obligation; the grammar of Christian practice; knowing evil; the body as sign and problem; a life worthy of God; senses of an ending; and the moral story.

Meeks's approach is strictly historical. And he demonstrates that almost all the moral teachings in the New Testament are paralleled in form and content by writings from the Greco-Roman world. But his observation that "context was everything"[3] has theological significance. His point is that while much in the content of the New Testament moral teaching is commonplace, what is peculiar or distinctive is the theological context in which it is set: doing God's will in view of the last judgment, the appeal to the Old Testament Scriptures, and (most importantly) the focus on Jesus' life, death, and resurrection.

Descriptive biblical theology: In *New Testament Ethics: The Legacies of Jesus and Raul,*[4] Frank J. Matera of the Catholic University of America offers descriptions of the ethical teachings of each Gospel and of the Pauline and Deuteropauline epistles in the context of their overall theological visions. His method is descriptive, and the focus is literary and theological. From his individual analyses, Matera then draws some general conclusions about the shape of New Testament ethics: The moral life of believers is a response to God's work of salvation (present and future), is lived within a community of disciples (church), is instructed and sustained by the example of Jesus and Paul, consists in doing God's will, shows itself in love (for God, neighbor, and enemy), and is an expression of faith.

Making moral decisions informed by Scripture: In *The Moral Vision of the New Testament,*[5] Richard B. Hays of Duke Divinity School seeks to go beyond description, and to articulate a framework within which New Testament ethics might be pursued as a normative theological discipline, that is, one that yields standards or rules for Christian conduct. He first describes some visions of the moral life in the New Testament (Paul, the Pauline tradition, Mark, Matthew, and so forth). Next he proposes three focal images for synthesizing the moral vision of the New Testament: community, cross, and new creation. Then he examines how theologians have used Scripture and offers hermeneutical proposals for using biblical texts in an ethical argument. Finally he applies his method to five ethical issues: violence, divorce and remarriage, homosexuality, anti-Judaism and ethnic conflict, and abortion. Hays admits the value of the four traditional sources (Scripture, reason, tradition, and experience) in ethical discernment. But he consistently regards Scripture as of higher value and greater clarity than the other three sources, and gives it more attention and credence in developing his positions.

Hays is especially interested in how to move from the biblical texts to making normative ethical judgments or decisions today. He proposes a three-step process. First, one gathers all the biblical texts pertinent to the theme (e.g., God and wealth) and confronts the full range of witnesses that such an inventory yields. The biblical texts must be allowed to speak in their own voice and as part of the larger biblical story. The second step is a theological evaluation of these texts in light of what Hays regards as the three major images or master themes in the New Testament: the church as the countercultural community of disciples, Jesus' death on the cross as a paradigm of God's fidelity, and the new creation in the context of an "already but not yet" eschatology. The third step brings the biblical synthesis to bear on a concrete issue (abortion) or plan of action (combating homelessness). For Hays, the Bible's perspective on moral issues is privileged and offers the best guidance in Christian decision-making.

Christian community and character: In *A Community of Character*, Stanley Hauerwas, also of Duke Divinity School, contends that the Bible taken as a whole and the community shaped by it provide the context for appreciating and acting upon biblical morality. He states: "The moral use of Scripture, therefore, lies precisely in its power to help us remember the stories of God for the continual guidance of our community and of individual lives."[6] In this approach the ethical teachings of the Bible are not so much laws or rules as they are part of the Christian community's story of faith and have been found crucial to a people formed by the Bible's story of God and his people. Hauerwas's approach is important for establishing the community context in which the Bible is to be read and for highlighting the role of the Bible and the community in shaping Christian character throughout the ages and today.

Feminist and liberationist perspectives: While not primarily concerned with New Testament ethics, Elisabeth Schüssler Fiorenza, of Harvard Divinity School, in *In Memory of Her: A Feminist Theological Reconstruction of Christian Origins*,[7] interprets the early Christian movement and the New Testament from a feminist and liberationist perspective. She takes as her starting point and interpretive criterion the experience of women as an oppressed group. She works on three levels: exposing the patriarchal assumptions of the biblical world (suspicion), recovering the Bible's positive portrayals of women (retrieval), and drawing attention to the Bible's many liberating themes that have significance for women today (liberation).

There are many links between feminist theology and liberation theology. In the liberationist approach, the Bible is read from the perspective of the economic poor, and the experience of the poor provides the hermeneutical criterion for faithful and fruitful interpretation. The approach is based on the insight that since the biblical texts were produced from the poor, they are best understood by the poor today. In the liberationist reading, the Bible serves as a help toward interpreting life and promoting the fusion of the Bible's horizons (especially the Exodus event and Jesus as good news for the poor) with those of the economic poor as they struggle for justice and freedom today.

Using Scripture in theology: In *Scripture and Ethics: Twentieth-Century Portraits,*[8] a Protestant New Testament scholar, Jeffrey S. Siker of Loyola-Marymount University in Los Angeles, provides descriptive analyses of how Scripture has been used and interpreted in the theology and ethics of eight prominent and influential Christian theologians. To each theologian, Siker poses five questions: What biblical texts are used? How does the author use Scripture? How is the authority of Scripture envisioned? What kind of hermeneutic is employed in approaching the Bible? What is the relationship between the Bible and Christian ethics?

Siker deals with the works of the eight Christian theologians under headings that express the essence of their approach to Scripture: Reinhold Niebuhr (Scripture as symbol), H. Richard Niebuhr (confessing with Scripture), Bernard Häring (the freedom of responsive love), Paul Ramsey (obedient covenant love), Stanley Hauerwas (the community story of Israel and Jesus), Gustavo Gutièrrez (liberating Scriptures of the poor), James Cone (Scripture in African American liberation), and Rosemary Radford Ruether (Scripture in feminist perspective). The survey highlights the pivotal significance of how theologians view the authority of Scripture and the value they give Scripture in shaping their theology.

MORAL THEOLOGICAL REFLECTIONS
J. F. Keenan

There are various methods in moral theology today: responsibility ethics, personalist ethics, an ethics of care, feminist ethics, natural law ethics, and so on. Most of these ethical approaches overlap with one another in their concerns, scope, and particular method. Whereas advocates of any of these methods could probably develop a robust argument for why their method would serve New Testament ethics well, we stand with virtue ethicists like William Spohn who claims that *virtue ethics* provides a suitable framework for expressing a New Testament ethics.

Virtues are characteristic ways of behaving that make both persons and actions good, and also enable persons to fulfill the purpose of their lives. Virtue ethics focuses on the question, Who should we become? Indeed, virtue ethicists expand that basic question into three key, related questions: Who are we? Who ought we to become? and How do we get there?

VIRTUE ETHICS AS A METHOD FOR BUILDING BRIDGES
BETWEEN SCRIPTURE AND MORAL THEOLOGY

When the Scottish philosopher Alasdair MacIntyre presented his case for virtue ethics in *After Virtue*[9], he argued that contemporary ethics had fragmented and disintegrated, and that we now live in a state of "moral disagreement." Each person has a moral position and dismisses any other position by simply saying, "Well that's your opinion."

MacIntyre claimed that this "disintegration" occurred because ethicists had depersonalized ethics. The ethics of Aristotle, Plato, Augustine, and Aquinas was the ethics of character, virtue, and being, whereas contemporary ethics is an ethics of action. If action follows being (*agere sequitur esse*), where was being? Without an ethics of being, ethicists were left only to comment on isolated actions.

MacIntyre offered an insightful agenda. In summoning ethicists to look at persons and not just their actions, he suggested that ethics should address the question: What type of people ought we to become? Instead of asking whether an action is right, MacIntyre re-personalized ethics and proposed that we start discussing not only what we are now doing, but more importantly, who we are now becoming?

Christian ethicists immediately recognized the importance of this question. Who more than Jesus beckons us to consider the question about the people we can become? In Scripture, Jesus invites us to become his disciples, children of God, and heirs of the kingdom. Christian ethicists saw, then, in the virtues an enormous opportunity for answering the challenge of Vatican II (*Optatam totius* 16), which admonished moral theologians to draw more fully on the teaching of Scripture and to throw light upon the exalted vocation of the Christian.

The Lutheran theologian Gilbert Meilaender developed an argument to show that the virtues were naturally congruent to living out a life of sanctification, or growth in holiness. Likewise, the Mennonite pastor Joseph Kotva established the suitability of virtue ethics for Christian moral theology by making specific appeals to Matthew's Gospel and Paul's letters as written with specific concerns to summon people to commit to a lifetime journey of personal growth, love, and service in response to the merciful love of God in Jesus Christ. From his Greek Orthodox tradition, Joseph Woodill investigated the Eastern patristic writings to demonstrate that the early church developed personal and communal goals for intimacy with the Lord.

Christian ethicists are discovering, then, that virtue ethics can offer more resources than we ever imagined. It provides bridges between moral theology and a variety of other fields, such as spirituality, worship, church life, and Scripture. In this way, virtue ethics unites fields of theology that have long been isolated from one another. This bridging function means that through virtue ethics Christian ethicists are able to integrate a variety of concerns that face not only Christian ethicists as they write and teach but also ordinary Christians and their pastors as they try to live the life of the gospel. In fact, the greatest bridge that virtue ethics provides is the direct connection between theologians and pastors and their communities as they try to respond to the call of Christ.

After twenty years of talking about the virtues, however, there has also emerged an important critical stance toward the virtues. Not all talk of the virtues is necessarily good. For instance, whenever we hear someone talking about the virtues, we should know which ones and for what end. In order to make us sensitive to those questions, we will consider four bridges that virtue ethics has recently provided to the contemporary Church: the bridge between ascetical and moral theology; the bridge between liturgy and moral theology; the bridge between church life and moral theology; and the bridge between Scripture and moral theology.

The Bridge between Ascetical and Moral Theology

We saw in the previous chapter that over the last four centuries moral theologians separated their work from ascetical theology. Today, moral theologians, following the leads of Bernard Häring and Norbert Rigali, are working to reintegrate the two fields. For instance, a few years ago, *The Supplement to the Way* dedicated an entire issue to the relationship between ethics and spirituality. Not surprisingly most of the essays appealed to the virtues. Why?

For nearly fifteen centuries, that is, from the end of the fourth century to the beginning of the twentieth century, Christians understood their lives to be divided into three stages of growth: the beginners, the proficient, and the perfect. This division was based on the premise that the majority of Christians were in the first stage (the beginners), which really was a rather simple one: avoid sin; don't fall out of grace; and if you do sin, properly confess and amend your life with the firm purpose never to sin again. Moral theologians took care of this first stage. They wrote about sin and the occasions of sin and helped priests to be good confessors. The second stage (the proficient) was for those who were more serious about their baptism and who sought to grow into a deeper experience of discipleship through ascetical or devotional manuals and through the corporal and spiritual works of mercy. Ascetical writers provided these persons with guidance. When we look at these first two stages, we can say that moral theology was concerned with avoiding evil whereas ascetical theology attended to doing the good. The final third stage (the perfect) was for the very few. It focused on the practice of contemplative prayer and on the mystical experience of God. It concerned union with God, and it is what we all hope will be ours in the next life.

The virtues were alive and well on the second and third stages, and were treated in the ascetical texts. Readers of these texts sought to become better disciples. They read about charity, patience, humility, fidelity, and a host of other virtues. When contemporary moral theologians began to appropriate these virtues from the works of ascetical theology, they created a bridge to help people move from the first to the second stage of Christian growth.

By using the virtues, these moral theologians implicitly abandoned their agenda of solely considering the avoidance of evil. By talking about the virtues they could also talk about something positive: the types of characters that we could develop and about the people we could become. In a manner of speaking, by using the virtues, moral theology crossed the bridge between avoiding evil and doing good, and united these two halves of the first principle of the natural law.

This recognition—that the virtues flourished in ascetical literature as they were dormant in moral theology for centuries—helps us to reread history. For instance, many philosophers have claimed that Thomas Aquinas developed the virtues for the *Summa Theologiae* after reading Aristotle. But that no longer seems to be the case. The enormous charismatic movements of the twelfth century developed into organized religious movements in the thirteenth century, among them the Franciscan and Dominican orders. The language of those orders predominantly focused on the virtues. Not surprisingly, then, having already encountered the virtues in religious life, Aquinas was already disposed to Aristotle's interest in virtue.

Our enthusiasm for restoring a bridge between moral and ascetical theology (or, what we today call spirituality) ought to be tempered, however, by a realistic assessment of the virtues we use. Although ascetical literature from the twelfth to the sixteenth century was scripturally rich and theologically insightful, for the last four centuries it was not generally so. From the seventeenth century until Vatican II, ascetical literature was often used to invite readers not to become more energetic, creative, and animated disciples of Christ, but rather to become conforming Christians. The virtues functioned not as a guide to human flourishing, but rather as a restraint. The virtue of prudence, for instance, served from the twelfth to the sixteenth century as the practical, self-directing wisdom for consistently moving forward. From the seventeenth century on, however, it became the virtue of caution, reluctance, and self-restraint.

The christological images that these ascetical writings offered also contributed to this inhibiting vision. They were hardly depictions of an imaginative, extroverted, and loving Jesus Christ. From the humble one born in a manger, to the pietistic one who sought prayerful places, to the obedient one in the garden or the patient one on the cross, the humble, obedient, pietistic, and patient Christ offered plenty of virtuous images in Catholic devotional literature for the pious reader. But those images did not include the Jesus who fed, taught, healed (on the Sabbath!), served, welcomed the stranger, was a friend to women and the poor, and so on.

Virtues dealing with the imagination, justice and fairness, friendship, love, and personal growth appeared almost exclusively in the earlier ascetical texts from the twelfth to the sixteenth century. With those virtues there was a richer and more active Christological vision. But later writers gave us the obedient Jesus who became the reigning Christ the King, and also gave us virtues that were ancillary ones, like patience, chastity, meekness, steadfastness, and temperance. These virtues made us obedient to carry out "Christ's" commands, which were often no more than the commands of these moralists' imaginations. Through these virtues, these writers controlled the human spirit, harnessed the human passions, and sublimated any sense of personal uniqueness.

Let us consider an illustration. Our school of theology was once located on a campus in Weston, Massachusetts, that now serves as a renewal center and infirmary. It features a cavernous granite chapel designed for the Jesuit students who studied there from 1930 to 1970. Each window is dedicated to a virtue: chastity, long-suffering endurance, temperance, courage, patience, meekness, obedience, and hope. Nowhere do we see joy, love, imagination, friendship, gratitude, justice, magnanimity, and so on. Imagine a young Jesuit praying there fifty years ago. Every one of his affective urges would have been tempered and channeled by the virtues depicted on the windows. The message in the chapel was "Subdue! Submit! Submerge!" There was no encouragement to see oneself as unique yet relational, and as invited to promote the gospel creatively. This setting helps us to see that we cannot promote just any virtue. Rather, we need to ask ourselves, What type of people ought we to become? From that answer we can begin to determine the appropriate virtues.

THE BRIDGE BETWEEN
LITURGY AND MORAL THEOLOGY

In his book on virtue ethics entitled *The Fellowship of Life: Virtue Ethics and Orthodox Christianity*,[10] Joseph Woodill not only examines the writings of earlier Orthodox writers but contemporary ones as well, like

Stanley Harakas and Vigen Guroian, who have been describing the moral life of their communities in the key of virtue. They have written about how liturgy is itself effective in forming us as God's people.

Catholic moralists have appropriated this insight. The Greek word *eucharistia* means "thanksgiving." By the Eucharist, we are formed into a grateful people—grateful for the mercy of God. From the first signing of the cross in baptism, by which we are saved, to the communion by which we receive and become with one another the body of Christ, the liturgy begins with a recognition of the need for mercy and weaves mercy throughout the narrative of the eucharistic prayers. In the light of that mercy, we are invited into reconciliation with God and one another, a prayer that is repeated as we pray the Our Father.

The more we look at the eucharistic liturgy, the more we recognize that the liturgy calls us through a variety of processes to become true disciples of Christ in the context of a narrative and a communal practice. The liturgy invites us into the kingdom and provides us with true spiritual exercises of gratitude, mercy, reconciliation, and hope so that we may become the people that Christ wishes us to become. Bruce Morrill examines the moral formative role of liturgy in his book, *Anamnesis as Dangerous Memory.*[11]

These virtues again reiterate the communal call of discipleship. Because the entire context for liturgy is gratitude, we are forced to recognize the pure gratuity of God's grace. The liturgy keeps us from any pride, continually alerts us to the giftedness of our vocation and our response, and forms us as a people who follow our God who beckons us forward.

THE BRIDGE BETWEEN CHURCH LIFE AND MORAL THEOLOGY

Inasmuch as the Eucharist is really the center of parish life, it reminds parish members that through a variety of other practices they can be disciples of Christ. For instance, we find in many parishes Twelve Step programs that promote the attitude of gratitude as well as a sense of humility, accountability, and honesty. Whether it be Alcoholics Anonymous, Over-Eaters Anonymous, or any other responsible self-help organization, each one promotes a set of virtues to help its members live more ordered lives. Moreover, they provide a context in which, through the virtues of trust and mutual respect, members can learn from one another. It is not surprising, then, that most of these organizations seek the parish church as their proper venue.

The parish itself tries to promote a context so that through religious instruction, for instance, children and adults may learn effective ways for developing Christian understanding and character. Any parish that turns to the virtues for the formation of children, young adults, and older adults inevitably finds a helpful resource for providing much-needed direction.

My own book *Virtues for Ordinary Christians* provides an accessible introduction not only to virtue ethics in general but also to specific virtues, allowing readers to discover the varied ways in which we can become more the people God calls us to be. The moral formation of ordinary parishioners inevitably leads to questions about the formation of ordinary pastors and their parish communities. Thus, with Joseph Kotva, I edited *Practice What You Preach*,[12] a collection of essays by twenty-five virtue ethicists from different churches across the United States who examined issues in their own congregations and discerned how the virtues could be used to lead communities to greater integrity in living out the gospel.

THE BRIDGE BETWEEN
SCRIPTURE AND MORAL THEOLOGY

In this book, we shall put virtue ethics to use in building bridges between moral theology and Scripture. But here let us consider just one particular benefit that this approach could bring by reflecting on the significant work by Richard Hays, *The Moral Vision of the New Testament*.[13]

Hays proposes three focal images for synthesizing the moral vision of the New Testament: community, cross, and new creation. These serve as master lenses through which we move from an examination of a variety of texts on a particular theme, through a theological evaluation of the texts, and finally to a biblical synthesis. But Hays, unlike the feminists and liberationists, ignores the social location of the one using these master lenses. It is as if any of us could look at the texts through these lenses and see the same thing in the same way for the same end. But since Aristotle, we have recognized that the ability to recognize the good depends on the ability of the agent—the one looking. Whatever we see depends in part on our own particular ability to see.

Hays's three lenses have three virtues correlative to them: reconciliation, mercy, and hope. And these virtues, because they engage the very person of the one who is reading Scripture, serve to guide us more accurately in our biblical evaluations and syntheses. The community we envision is a reconciled one in that Christ reconciles us to God and to one another through Christ. The cross is always for us a symbol of God's mercy and the eternal willingness of God to be merciful; that is, to enter into the chaos of another. By the cross, we are called to be merciful as God is merciful. The new creation is that for which we are a community of hope. Thus not only should we be attentive to the lenses through which we read the texts, but more importantly we must recognize that insofar as reconciliation, mercy, and hope constitute us as disciples, to that extent we will grasp the meaning of Scripture.

Questions for Reflection and Discussion

1. Virtue ethics is a person-oriented ethics. What benefit does that insight provide us in reading Scripture?

2. Name some virtues that you think are appropriate for being a disciple of Christ. Why are they important?

3. Consider three reasons why an ethics that addresses who we ought to become could help someone in preparing to preach the gospel.

Notes

1. Hans-Georg Gadamer, *Truth and Method* (New York: Continuum, 1982).

2. Wayne A. Meeks, *The Origins of Christian Morality: The First Two Centuries* (New Haven, London: Yale University Press, 1993).

3. Ibid., p. 3

4. Frank J. Matera, *New Testament Ethics: The Legacies of Jesus and Paul* (Louisville: Westminster John Knox, 1996).

5. Richard B. Hays, *The Moral Vision of the New Testament: Community, Cross, New Creation: A Contemporary Introduction to New Testament Ethics* (HarperSanFrancisco, 1996).

6. Stanley Hauerwas, *A Community of Character: Toward a Constructive Christian Social Ethic* (Notre Dame, IN: University of Notre Dame Press, 1981), pp. 53–71, p. 66.

7. Elisabeth Schüssler Fiorenza, *In Memory of Her: A Feminist Theological Reconstruction of Christian Origins* (New York: Crossroad, 1983; rev. ed., 1998).

8. Jeffrey S. Siker, *Scripture and Ethics: Twentieth-Century Portraits* (New York-Oxford: Oxford University Press, 1997).

9. Alasdair MacIntyre, *After Virtue: A Study in Moral Theory* (Notre Dame, IN: Notre Dame University Press, 1981).

10. Joseph Woodill, *The Fellowship of Life: Virtue Ethics and Orthodox Christianity* (Washington, D.C., Georgetown University Press, 1998).

11. Bruce Morrill, *Anamnesis as Dangerous Memory: Political and Liturgical Theology in Dialogue* (Collegeville, MN: Liturgical Press, 2000).

12. James F. Keenan and Joseph Kotva (eds.), *Practice What You Preach: Virtues, Ethics and Power in the Lives of Pastoral Ministers and Their Congregations* (Franklin, WI: Sheed & Ward, 1999).

13. See footnote 5.

Select Bibliography

Bretzke, James T. "Scripture: The 'Soul' of Moral Theology?—The Second Stage." *Irish Theological Quarterly* 60 (1994), pp. 259–271.

Cates, Diana Fritz. *Choosing to Feel: Virtue, Friendship, and Compassion for Friends*. Notre Dame: University of Notre Dame Press, 1997.

Curran, Charles E. *The Catholic Moral Tradition Today: A Systhesis*. Washington, D.C.: Georgetown University Press, 1999.

Curran, Charles and Richard A. McCormick (eds.). *The Use of Scripture in Moral Theology*. New York: Paulist, 1984.

Gorgulho, G. da Silva. "Biblical Hermeneutics," in *Mysterium Liberationis*, eds. Ignacio Ellacuria and Jon Sobrino. Maryknoll, NY: Orbis, 1993, pp. 123–133, 139–149.

Harrington, Daniel J. "Biblical Studies & Moral Theology." *Church* 13/4 (1997), pp. 13–18.

Hauerwas, Stanley. "Scripture as Moral Authority." *A Community of Character: Toward a Constructive Christian Social Ethic*. Notre Dame, IN: University of Notre Dame Press, 1981.

Hays, Richard B. "The Church as a Scripture-Shaped Community: The Problem of Method in New Testament Ethics." *Interpretation* 54 (1990), pp. 42–55.

_____. *The Moral Vision of the New Testament*. San Francisco: HarperCollins, 1996.

Keck, Leander E. "Rethinking 'New Testament Ethics.'" *Journal of Biblical Literature* 115 (1996), pp. 3–16.

Keenan, James F. *Virtues for Ordinary Christians*. Kansas City: Sheed & Ward, 1996.

Keenan, James F. and Joseph Kotva (eds.). *Practice What You Preach: Virtues, Ethics and Power in the Lives of Pastoral Ministers and Their Congregations.* Franklin, WI: Sheed & Ward, 1999.

Kelsey, David H. *Proving Doctrine: The Uses of Scripture in Modern Theology.* Harrisburg, PA: Trinity Press International, 1999.

Kotva, Joseph. *The Christian Case for Virtue Ethics.* Washington, D.C.: Georgetown University Press, 1996.

Lee, Dorothy A. "Scripture, Ethics and Spirituality." *Supplement to the Way* 88 (1997), pp. 16–25.

MacIntyre, Alasdair. *After Virtue: A Study in Moral Theory.* Notre Dame, IN: University of Notre Dame Press, 1981.

Matera, Frank J. *New Testament Ethics: The Legacies of Jesus and Paul.* Louisville: Westminster John Knox, 1996.

McDonald, J. I. H. *Biblical Interpretation and Christian Ethics.* Cambridge, UK: Cambridge University Press, 1993.

_____. *The Crucible of Christian Morality.* London-New York: Routledge, 1998.

Meeks, Wayne. *The Moral World of the First Christians.* Philadelphia: Westminster, 1986.

_____. *The Origins of Christian Morality: The First Two Centuries.* New Haven: Yale, 1993; paper, 1996.

Meilaender, Gilbert. *The Theory and Practice of Virtue.* Notre Dame, IN: University of Notre Dame Press, 1984.

Morrill, Bruce. *Anamnesis as Dangerous Memory: Political and Liturgical Theology in Dialogue.* Collegeville, MN: Liturgical Press, 2000.

Ogletree, Thomas W. *The Use of the Bible in Christian Ethics.* Philadelphia: Fortress, 1983.

Parker, D. "Virtue Ethics and the New Testament," *Studies in Christian Ethics* 10/2 (1997), pp. 39–57.

Pieper, Josef. *The Four Cardinal Virtues.* Notre Dame, IN: University of Notre Dame Press, 1966.

Porter, Jean. *The Recovery of Virtue.* Louisville: Westminster John Knox, 1990.

Schüssler Fiorenza, Elisabeth. "Discipleship and Patriarchy: Early Christian Ethos and Christian Ethics in a Feminist Theological Perspective." In *Feminist Ethics and the Catholic Moral Tradition*, eds. Charles Curran and Margaret Farley. Mahwah, NJ: Paulist, 1996, pp. 51–65.

Siker, Jeffrey S. *Scripture and Ethics: Twentieth-Century Portraits*. New York-Oxford: Oxford University Press, 1997.

Soelle, Dorothee. "The Use of the Bible." In *Thinking about God: An Introduction to Theology*. Philadelphia: Trinity Press, 1990, pp. 32–41.

Spohn, William C. *Go and Do Likewise: Jesus and Ethics*. New York: Continuum, 1999.

_____. "The Return of Virtue Ethics." *Theological Studies* 53 (1992), pp. 60–75.

_____. *What Are They Saying about Scripture and Ethics?* Rev. ed. New York: Paulist, 1996.

Supplement to the Way: Spirituality and Ethics 88 (1997).

Woodill, Joseph. *The Fellowship of Life: Virtue Ethics and Orthodox Christianity*. Washington, D.C.: Georgetown University Press, 1998.

Chapter Three

THE KINGDOM OF GOD AS HORIZON AND GOAL: WHO OUGHT WE TO BECOME?

Having reviewed historical and methodological issues in New Testament studies and moral theology, we now turn to the kingdom of God as the horizon for Jesus' ethical teachings and their goal. Harrington provides the biblical perspectives by first examining the parables of the kingdom found in the Synoptic Gospels. After looking at the Jewish backgrounds to the kingdom of God, he considers the significance of Jesus' resurrection as a decisive turning point in understanding the kingdom. Then he divides interpretations of the nature of God's kingdom into four categories: eschatological, individual-spiritual, political, and ecclesiastical. Finally after looking at various motivations for right acting, he discusses the relevance of the virtue of vigilance in the light of the kingdom of God.

Keenan offers his moral theological reflections by turning first to the notion of end or goal in virtue ethics to establish a corollary with the kingdom of God. Then he asks whether the kingdom provides motivations for right acting only or actual substantive guidance. Arguing in favor of the latter, he demonstrates how the virtue of mercy informs the ethical teachings associated with the kingdom. Noting the significance of the kingdom as both here and not yet, he proposes the notion of "Christian idealism" as a framework for understanding and articulating the type of people that the kingdom of God requires us to become.

BIBLICAL PERSPECTIVES
D. J. Harrington

The kingdom of God serves as the horizon for Jesus' ethical teachings and their goal. According to the parables in the Synoptic Gospels, the kingdom belongs to God, is future, and marks a decisive change from the present.

Some sayings in the gospel tradition (for example, Mark 9:1; 13:30; Matthew 10:23) suggest that Jesus and his early followers thought that the fullness of God's kingdom would come very soon. This topic is sometimes called *eschatology* (the doctrine of the "last things"), which is the study of the final destiny of humankind and, indeed, the whole created world at the end of this age in human history and in the fullness of God's kingdom that is yet to come. Other texts (for example, Luke 11:20; 17:21; Matthew 11:12) indicate that the kingdom is enough of a present reality so that one can speak of its "already" being here, as anticipated or inaugurated in and through Jesus' ministry.

PARABLES ABOUT GOD'S KINGDOM
(Matthew 13:44–50)

44. The kingdom of heaven is like treasure hidden in a field, which someone found and hid; then in his joy he goes and sells all that he has and buys that field. 45. Again, the kingdom of heaven is like a merchant in search of fine pearls; 46. on finding one pearl of great value, he went and sold all that he had and bought it. 47. Again, the kingdom of heaven is like a net that is thrown into the sea and caught fish of every kind; 48. when it was full, they drew it ashore, sat down, and put the good into baskets but threw out the bad. 49. So it will be at the end of the age. The angels will come out and separate the evil from the righteous 50. and throw them into the furnace of fire, where there will be weeping and gnashing of teeth.

A parable is a story taken from everyday life or ordinary experience. It uses figurative speech (similes or metaphors) to compare one thing to another. There is usually a strange or unusual feature, leading the hearer to suspect that this is no ordinary story and to try to discover what the story is really about.

The Synoptic Gospels contain many parables, with clusters of them in Mark 4, Matthew 13 and 24–25, and Luke 8. Many of the parables are prefaced with the notice "the kingdom of God (or heaven) is like (or may be compared to)." The kingdom of God seems to have been the central theme of Jesus' preaching and to have provided the theological context for his healings (as signs of the kingdom, see Luke 11:20). In these parables, many biblical scholars contend, one can hear the "voice" of Jesus.

Matthew 13 is a revised and expanded version of Mark 4. The early parts of Matthew 13 make clear various dimensions of the kingdom of God: the mixed reception of Jesus' proclamation of the kingdom (see 13:3–9, 18–23), the contrast between the kingdom's small beginnings in the present and its great conclusion (see 13:31–33), and the attitude of patient tolerance in expectation of its fullness and the accompanying final judgment (see 13:24–30, 36–43).

The discourse in Matthew 13 comes to a close with three short parables (see 13:44–50). These texts can provide an entry to Jesus' teaching about the kingdom and about the conduct appropriate to those who seek after it.

The parables of the treasure buried in the field (see Matthew 13:44) and the fine pearl (see 13:45–46) have the same basic structure and message. The one who comes upon them recognizes their surpassing value, makes a total commitment to obtaining them, and takes every means toward that goal. The parable of the net thrown into the sea consists of the story proper (see 13:47–48) and an explanation (see 13:49–50). Whether the interpretation circulated originally with the parable or was added later (which is more likely), it serves to underscore the theme of divine judgment as part of God's coming kingdom.

All three parables fit the context of first-century Palestine and would have been intelligible (although intriguing and a little puzzling) to persons taught by Jesus. People buried valuables in fields to avoid their being stolen; some merchants dealt in precious stones; and commercial fishermen (like Jesus' first disciples) regularly used large dragnets. All three parables begin with the notice "the kingdom of heaven is like . . . ," thus alerting us to their real topic—a topic that was very important at least in some Jewish theological and religious circles in Jesus' day.

The parables of the treasure and the pearl bring out the surpassing value of God's kingdom and the total commitment that it deserves and demands. The parable of the net (and its explanation) suggests that the full coming of God's kingdom will be accompanied by a universal judgment in which the righteous will be vindicated and rewarded, and the wicked will be condemned and punished (or annihilated).

JEWISH BACKGROUNDS

In the New Testament the "kingdom of God" refers to God's future display of power over all creation and the acknowledgment of it by all created things. The Lord's Prayer (see Matthew 6:9–13; Luke 11:2–4) is preeminently a call for the full coming of God's reign, when God's will is to be done perfectly on earth as it is in heaven.

The idea has its roots in the Old Testament concept of God's reign over all the earth (see Psalms 93, 96–97, 99), perhaps celebrated annually in ancient Israel to mark the beginning of the new year. In early Judaism, the focus shifted from the present reign of God to the future display of God's reign. The shift was very likely associated with the political subjugation of

Israel after the return from exile in the sixth century B.C. to A.D. 70—in turn to the Persians, the Egyptian Ptolemies, the Syrian Seleucids, and the Romans. God's ancient promises to Israel remain in effect but are put off to the future "Day of the Lord." When the course of Israel's history has been accomplished (and that should be soon), God will intervene to vindicate the faithful within Israel by destroying evil and evildoers and by creating a new heaven and a new earth where God's will prevails. It is the task of God to bring about this kingdom and to make it visible to all. There are many scenarios as to how this will come about (see Daniel 12:1–3; 1 Enoch 91:12–17; Assumption of Moses 10; Qumran *Rule of the Community* 3–4). Not all involve a messiah figure.

JESUS' RESURRECTION

The resurrection of Jesus is a decisive turning point in the New Testament doctrine of the kingdom of God. Resurrection was regarded in many Jewish circles as part of the scenario of end-time events (eschatology). The claim that an individual should be raised from the dead before and apart from all the other end-time events was quite extraordinary. Jesus' resurrection made it possible, according to Paul and other early Christians, for persons in the present to enjoy the benefits traditionally associated with the fullness of God's kingdom (salvation, justification, redemption, reconciliation, and so forth).

The classic expression of belief in "realized" eschatology appears in John 5:24: "Whoever hears my word and believes in the one who sent me has eternal life and will not come to condemnation, but has passed from death to life." Certain Deuteropauline texts (see Colossians 2:12; Ephesians 2:6) suggest that some early Christians were convinced that their own resurrection had already taken place—a position that the New Testament writers felt obliged to nuance and even correct.

THE NATURE OF GOD'S KINGDOM

Throughout Christian history, the kingdom of God has been identified in various ways. The saying in Luke 17:21 ("the kingdom of God is among you") has historically led many to an individual and spiritual interpretation ("the kingdom of God is within you") that is not true to the social and indeed cosmic dimensions of the kingdom according to Scripture. When Christianity under the emperor Constantine became an officially approved religion in the Roman Empire, it was inevitable that God's kingdom would be identified with the dominant political structure. And this identification has been repeated many times over. But this approach ignores the transcendent aspect of kingdom; it is God's kingdom to bring, and what God will bring will surpass any earthly kingdom. It has also been tempting to identify the kingdom as the Church. While the Church bears witness to God's kingdom, tries to live out its values, and hopes and prays for its full coming, it is not really identical with the kingdom of God in Scripture.

Each of these three interpretations of the kingdom—the individual-spiritual, the political, and the ecclesiastical—has some truth to it. Nevertheless, no one of them is entirely true to the eschatological kingdom proclaimed by Jesus and witnessed in the Synoptic Gospels. If we want to be faithful to the biblical tradition, we need to recover the transcendent, future-present, and eschatological dimensions of the kingdom of God. If we want to use the biblical teachings about the kingdom of God in the renewal of moral theology, we need to recognize the kingdom of God as the horizon against which we live our Christian lives. It is not something we bring about; rather, God brings it about. In the meantime we await it with hope for the fullness of that kingdom and try to act in a way that is appropriate to its claims. The kingdom is the horizon against which Christian life is be lived, and it is the goal toward which all must point.

WARRANTS FOR GOOD ACTIONS

The Synoptic Gospels offer many motivations for doing "the right thing." Some texts appeal to the authority and example of Jesus (see Matthew 10:37–39) and others urge us to imitate the example of God who shows love for evildoers (see Matthew 5:43–48) and to fulfill God's will made manifest in the Scriptures and interpreted by Jesus (see Matthew 5:17–20). But idealistic modern readers sometimes ignore the many appeals for right action based on the promise of rewards in the future and the present (see Mark 10:29–31).

Many parables (see especially in Matthew 24–25) urge a constant vigilance in the present against the horizon of the coming kingdom. The kingdom's coming is certain. But the precise time of its coming is known only to God (see Mark 13:32; Matthew 24:36). Therefore, the proper response is to be prepared always, to act as if the kingdom with its final judgment were to come in the very next moment. If one wants to be ready for the last judgment, then one should live always in its shadow. One's attitude, however, should be hopeful rather than fearful: "But when these signs begin to happen, stand erect and raise your heads because your redemption is at hand" (Luke 21:28). The last judgment will be a time of vindication rather than condemnation for the righteous faithful.

It is not adequate to the biblical tradition to ignore the eschatological dimensions of God's kingdom or to explain them away as simply primitive religious imagery. Rather, in the context of New Testament theology, the kingdom of God is the place where God the creator and lord of all and Jesus as the proclaimer and sign of the kingdom of God join together.

MORAL THEOLOGICAL REFLECTIONS
J. F. Keenan

In major ethical writings, the end in the sense of "goal" is where we begin. Not surprisingly, New Testament ethics starts with the kingdom of God, which is the "end" for us all. From an ethical viewpoint, the end is the quintessential point of departure, since strong ethical systems always start with the end. The goal always defines the agenda being pursued. The agenda, from start to finish, is shaped by the end.

We can see the role that the end plays in Thomas Aquinas's *Summa Theologiae* (*Summary of Theology*), which is generally regarded as his greatest work and surely one of the most influential in the history of theology. Aquinas divides the *Summa* into three parts. Each part is comprised of questions, and each question has several (one to sixteen) articles which begin in the form of a question. In the second part, Aquinas raises 180 questions (i.e., more than one thousand articles) regarding the virtues we ought to have in order to be moral. When we read these "questioning" articles, then we realize that the *Summa* is primarily a work of theological investigation.

Aquinas has a particular subject matter in each of the three parts of his investigation. The first part is dedicated to matters pertaining to God, and is called the *exitus* ("going forth") because it concerns how God reveals God's self to us. The second part is dedicated to humanity and is considered the *reditus* ("return"), because it narrates how we can, by God's grace and the virtues, return to God. The third part is dedicated to Christ and the sacraments, and that is where divinity and humanity meet.

In a manner of speaking, in each part Aquinas is investigating *mystery*. *Mystery* can be understood in two ways. First, *mystery* can act as an answer (or non-answer) to a question. For instance, when we were younger, we may have asked, "How are three persons in one God?" When our teachers answered, "It's a mystery," they really meant, "You'll never be able to understand it." This is "mystery" as the "conversation-stopper," as when we ask why someone did something and we are told, "It's a mystery" meaning "Don't bother asking."

The second meaning of *mystery* is the theological one, and its meaning is just the opposite of the first. This use of *mystery* is like its use in describing the fiction genre, "mystery." *Mysteries,* like good detective stories, are about discovering more and more. Rather than being a conversation-stopper, *mystery* here is an invitation into a continuous act of learning.

Not surprisingly, many good mysteries begin with the end. The mystery, then, is to figure out how we arrive at the end. Aquinas just does that in the second part of his *Summa* as he investigates the human condition. In the very first question, he asks about our last end. To probe this question further, he introduces a list of eight articles:

1. whether it belongs to human nature to act for an end;

2. whether this is proper to the rational nature;

3. whether a human's actions are specified by their end;

4. whether there is any last end of human life;

5. whether a person can have several last ends;

6. whether a person ordains all to the last end;

7. whether all humans have the same last end;

8. whether all other creatures concur with the human in that last end.

Through the next four questions, Thomas continues investigating the end. In trying to understand the human, Aquinas asks the fundamental question: What is it that humans ought to aim at? Among the three questions that MacIntyre gave us—Who are we? Who ought we to become? and How do we get there?—Aquinas begins with the second question, the end at which we aim, the final person we ought to become. Aquinas answers that the end is charity, union with God, which is, in effect, the kingdom of God, where we all find our happiness.

THE MODERN DEBATE

After a long hiatus, the awareness and appreciation of the *telos* (the goal toward which a movement is being directed) or the "end" of moral systems has recently been restored to ethics. In order to understand this, let us return to the days when we ignored the end and let us consider the approach of the famous French sociologist Emile Durkheim (1858–1917). He argued that even though the Christian religion was now, as he claimed, dead, it still was important to preserve its moral tradition, since the new secular society needed a moral fabric. Christianity had supplied that fabric but now, without God or the Church, Durkheim called for moral educators to take the moral stuff of Christianity without its *telos*; that is, the kingdom or union with God.

Durkheim could make the claim that moral educators would be able to weave the moral fabric of society completely on their own, in part, because he believed that the end of moral systems was detachable from the contents of such systems. But in *After Virtue*, the philosopher Alasdair MacIntyre argued just the opposite: every ethical system must have its own end.[1] While Durkheim sought to take the substance of Christian ethics without the end of Christian ethics, MacIntyre claimed that such truncated systems eventually rediscover their original ends or they fade away.

What did Durkheim want to do? Having removed the religious purposes of moral teachings, he supposed that the stuff of the moral tradition could be kept intact. Thus religious tradition taught us to treat all people equally either because God commanded it, because God would reward or punish us if we do not, because we share in God as being images of God, or because it was our destiny to be one with God and every human. Durkheim effectively deleted the clauses beginning with the word *because*.

What differentiates Durkheim from MacIntyre concerns the function of the end in each thinker's explication of moral theory: Does the end simply motivate us, or does it actually shape the contents of morality? Does union with God simply move us to assume a virtuous life, or does it shape the contents of Aquinas's virtues? Is the kingdom of God the end, the *because* that prompts us to live rightly, or is it also that which determines the content of the Christian agenda? Durkheim basically claimed the former, while MacIntyre claims the latter in all these cases.

This debate is not much different from one that occurred among Catholic moral theologians in the 1970s and 1980s about the distinctiveness of Christian ethics. Then many Jesuit Catholic moralists such as Richard McCormick, Bruno Schüller, and Josef Fuchs, suggested that while the end or motivation of Christian ethics was distinctive, the content of Christian morality was no different from any humanist morality. Their claim is no longer widely accepted among Catholic moral theologians.

CHRISTIAN ETHICS

We can understand that the end is more than a motivator and that it determines the content of its system if we look at whether the kingdom or union with God squares with an Aristotelian ethics. This is a reasonable question.

The Greek philosopher Aristotle (384–322 B.C.) developed his version of virtue ethics entirely within the human sphere, with only occasional mention of the gods. For him, happiness consisted in cultivating the virtues and avoiding the vices at their extremes, so as to insure a life with the greatest possible happiness and without much pain and trouble. (It was, of course, the genius of Thomas Aquinas to try to integrate Aristotelian philosophy and Christian theology.)

Aristotle believed in human flourishment or happiness as do all Christians. In a manner of speaking, such flourishment is the end of virtue ethics, and for that matter of all ethics. But in what does that flourishment consist? Is the content of Christian ethics really the same as Aristotelian ethics? Or does the end of Christian ethics, that is, the kingdom, distinguish the content of Christian ethics from non-Christian ethics?

In Scripture, we see that Jesus teaches that, although God's kingdom will establish the right order, it will not be simply based on human standards of justice and on strict reward and punishment. The parable of the laborers in the field who enter the work force at different times (see Matthew 20:1–16) makes clear that the eschatological celebration will not be a simple *quid pro quo*, since, because of the owner's generosity, all are paid the same, even though some worked only a short time. Aristotle would never be able to understand such a parable; rather, he would have insisted on strict justice.

In like measure, Aristotle could never understand the story of the "good thief" (see Luke 23:39–43). The idea that at the end of one's otherwise disreputable life, one could enter, by Christ's mercy and forgiveness, the kingdom of God contradicts Aristotle's notion of a life dedicated to virtue that alone yields the good life. For Aristotle, human logic based on strict justice, and not the logic of unmerited mercy, singularly governed the moral life. Thus Aristotle would be repulsed by the crucifixion of Jesus and what Christians make out of it. Yet, for the Christian who believes that the end of human existence is the kingdom, the cross is essential. By the cross, the kingdom was won. The cross is the symbol of God's merciful love for us in that while we were still sinners, God loved us and saved us (see Romans 5:8). In fact, for Aristotle any attempt to identify mercy with God would be preposterous. Mercy was a practice only for those who did not know otherwise.

But without mercy we do not have Christian ethics. Mercy is constitutive of the kingdom, and therefore, inasmuch as it pertains to the end, mercy precedes and shapes the content of Christianity. Thus the kingdom does not simply provide a motivation for morality. As morality's end, it also gives shape to the contents of Christian ethics. In short, all ethical systems have an end, and that end is defining.

There is one major problem, however, with the kingdom of God as the end of Christian ethics defining the agenda of Christian living. The kingdom is both "now" and "not yet," both realized and outstanding, and therefore challenges Christian morality to be more aware of the relevance of history in the face of its transcendental claims in determining right conduct. Because the end is not yet fully realized, it is not fully recognized, articulated, or understood. In a manner of speaking, the kingdom as end is at times barely discernible. It beckons us to discover it, proclaim it, and enter it. But it remains on the horizon of our expectations.

The kingdom as the horizon makes the kingdom a heuristic (something that serves to discover and reveal) for Christian ethics inasmuch as it gives us a general, although not patently clear, focus or direction to our lives. The Irish moral theologian Enda McDonagh uses the phrase "signposts" to capture how the kingdom provides both a Christian symbol and the moral imperative for Christian living.

CHRISTIAN IDEALISM

Here we return to the insight we saw in the last chapter. We cannot present a biblical-theological synthesis on the kingdom unless we have been personally shaped and formed by God and God's kingdom. Our ability to understand the kingdom depends in part then on whether we are actually in union with God. But, conversely, our union with God deepens as we respond to the call of the kingdom. In this interim period, the period of our sanctification, we see better as we become more charitable. In turn, as we see better, we long for greater union. The two go hand in hand. The kingdom as the horizon of our expectations calls us, by God's invitation and grace, to go beyond ourselves. And the more we do so, the more we fathom the nature of the kingdom.

One way of capturing this tension is through the notion of idealism. Idealism in the moral schema means seeing the end through the realistic context of history. History, our familiarity with the real world and the way reality unfolds, keeps idealism from being utopian; that is, perfectly ideal. Without history, the end becomes a utopian dream, not at all subject to the constraints of reality. But with history, that is, the accumulated evidence of our experience, we are able modestly but credibly to articulate the ideal as a legitimate expectation. The older we get, the more we may mature, and the more we may see in our faith what the kingdom of God actually is.

Our vision, the *telos*, the kingdom, our ideal, is a "beyond" point for which to strive. In providing that out-there-horizon, the kingdom offers a dynamic context for developing higher insights into right activity.

This notion of idealism, then, does not mean that all moral law ought to be seen as unattainable. It does mean, however, that we must take note of where we are in the course of human and personal history in determining right conduct. We must take into account not only the fact that the kingdom is now but not yet, but also that just as it is being realized, so are we. Human growth, then, needs to be considered in determining what the kingdom requires of us.

Paul considered the significance of human growth when he spoke about the difficulty of feeding solid food to those who could only digest milk (see 1 Corinthians 3:2). Using this very passage, Brazilian moral theologian Leonard Martin has tried to develop an ethics sensitive to the different ways that we each grow. Paul showed the same sensitivity to the stages of a person's growth in faith and morals when he enjoined the Corinthian community to observe their younger members' vulnerability as they bought and ate the food offered to the idols (see 1 Corinthians 8:1–11:1). In a similar way, Belgian moral theologian Roger Burggraeve has developed an ethics of mercy that is based on a realistic ethics of growth in Christians seeking the kingdom. With a similar interest, American moral theologian Phillip Keane has analyzed the relevance that human growth bears on moral norms. In sum, from Paul to contemporary moral theologians, we see a need for a realistic ethics of growth, an ethics of growing into the kingdom that is willing to discuss the ideals which, as we advance, may themselves need to be reformulated.

The not-yet-realized kingdom and not-yet-realized child of God are nonetheless realities within history. History then makes real our moral claims by at once grasping at what we can legitimately expect, while acknowledging what also remains to be done. The tension that arises from recognizing and realizing ideals in history presents a dynamic view of moral theology.

These same dynamic claims are applicable to our life in the Church, for the Church anticipates in its life what it perceives as the kingdom of God. For this reason, several Christian ethicists, most importantly Methodist Stanley Hauerwas, have argued that the ethical challenge for today is not to make the world ethical but rather to make the Church ethical. The Church must get the narrative of the kingdom right not only in its proclamation to its members but also in the way it witnesses to its understanding of the kingdom. The Church must, in its practices, be faithful to the kingdom. In a similar way, two Jesuit liberation theologians, Jon Sobrino and the martyred Ignacio Ellacuria, in light of their many years in El Salvador, developed arguments that the Church must be measured by the cross, by the kingdom, and by the principle of mercy. The measure of the Church's integrity is the kingdom itself.

Questions for Reflection and Discussion

1. How does the kingdom of God shape your understanding of right moral living?

2. How is the mercy of Jesus a normative standard for all Christians?

3. How might the Church actualize the kingdom in its life?

Notes

1. Alasdair MacIntyre, *After Virtue: A Study in Moral Theory* (Notre Dame, IN: Notre Dame University Press, 1981).

Select Bibliography

Burggraeve, Roger. "From Responsible to Meaningful Sexuality: An Ethics of Growth as an Ethics of Mercy for Young People in This Era of AIDS." In James F. Keenan et al. (eds.). *Catholic Ethicists on HIV/AIDS Prevention.* New York: Continuum, 2000, pp. 303–316.

Burke, Kevin. *The Ground Beneath the Cross: The Theology of Ignacio Ellacuria.* Washington, D.C.: Georgetown University Press, 2000.

Chilton, Bruce D. (ed.). *The Kingdom of God in the Teaching of Jesus.* Philadelphia: Fortress, 1984.

Durkheim, Emile. *Moral Education: A Study in the Theory and Application of the Sociology of Education.* New York: Free Press, 1961.

Fuellenbach, John. *The Kingdom of God: The Message of Jesus Today.* Maryknoll: Orbis, 1995.

Harrington, Daniel J. "Kingdom of God." In *The New Dictionary of Catholic Social Thought,* ed. Judith A. Dwyer. Collegeville, MN: Liturgical Press, 1994, pp. 508–513.

Himes, Michael. "The Human Person in Contemporary Theology." In Ronald Hamel and Kenneth Himes (eds.), *Introduction to Christian Ethics.* Mahwah, NJ: Paulist Press, 1989, pp. 49–62.

Keane, Phillip. "The Objective Moral Order: Reflections on Recent Research." *Theological Studies* 43 (1982), pp. 260–278.

Martin, Leonard. "'I Fed You with Milk': Missionary Morals in Brazil in a Time of AIDS." *Catholic Ethicists on HIV/AIDS Prevention,* pp. 128–134.

McDonagh, Enda. "The Reign of God: Signposts for Catholic Moral Theology." *Catholic Ethicists on HIV/AIDS Prevention*, pp. 317–323.

Sobrino, Jon. *The Principle of Mercy: Taking the Crucified People from the Cross.* Washington, D.C.: Georgetown University Press, 2000.

Viviano, Benedict. *The Kingdom of God in History.* Wilmington: Glazier, 1988.

Wilder, Amos N. *Eschatology and Ethics in the Teaching of Jesus.* New York-London: Harper, 1939.

Willis, William (ed.). *The Kingdom of God in 20th-Century Interpretation.* Peabody, MA: Hendrickson, 1987.

Chapter Four

DISCIPLESHIP AS CONTEXT: WHO ARE WE?

I f the answer to the second question of a Scripture-based virtue ethics (Who ought we to become?) is "a member of the kingdom of God or one in union with the risen Jesus," then the answer to the first question (Who are we?) is "a disciple of Jesus, made in the image and likeness of God." Being a disciple establishes a primary identity for the Christian subject. In that identity, Christians define themselves not only in relationship to Jesus but also in relation to fellow Christians, because following Jesus has always been a communal activity and is never a solitary action.

In this chapter, Harrington presents New Testament perspectives on discipleship through an examination of one of the several missionary instructions in the Gospels. While noting the difficulties in transferring the first-century expression of "discipleship" to twenty-first-century Christian self-understanding, he insists that in every era the Christian disciple is one who wants to be with Jesus and to share in his mission. The disciple belongs to a new family, takes on a simple lifestyle, and learns to subordinate personal needs for the sake of the mission itself. Keenan reflects on "discipleship" as the foundation of Christian ethics, using the work of Fritz Tillmann and Klaus Demmer. He concludes by commenting on the christological significance of the parable of the Good Samaritan.

BIBLICAL PERSPECTIVES
D. J. Harrington

The instructions to disciples in the Synoptic Gospels fit the context of first-century Palestine and of the Greco-Roman world in general. There philosophies were spread by traveling missionaries who either begged for food and support or relied more subtly on help and hospitality from others along the way. What is distinctive about Luke 9:1–6 and other such texts in the Synoptic Gospels is the specific religious context—sharing in Jesus' mission of teaching and healing—in which the instructions are set. The truly important tasks are proclaiming the kingdom of God and healing as a sign of its presence. The simple lifestyle is entirely in the service of the mission, subordinate to it, and useful only as a help toward preaching God's kingdom in word and deed.

THE MISSION OF THE TWELVE
(Luke 9:1–6)

> 1. Then Jesus called the twelve and gave them power and authority over all demons and to cure diseases, 2. and he sent them out to proclaim the kingdom of God and to heal. 3. He said to them, "Take nothing for your journey, no staff, nor bag, nor bread, nor money—not even an extra tunic. 4. Whatever house you enter, stay there, and leave from there. 5. Wherever they do not welcome you, as you are leaving that town, shake the dust off your feet as a testimony against them." 6. They departed and went through the villages, bringing the good news and curing diseases everywhere.

The "mission of the Twelve" (see Mark 6:7–13) appears toward the end of Luke's account of Jesus' ministry in Galilee (see 4:14–9:50). Based on various sources (Mark, the Sayings Source Q, special Lukan material), this part of Luke's Gospel presents Jesus as a teacher especially in the Sermon on the Plain in Luke 6:20–49 and in the parables discourse in Luke 8:1–18, as well as a powerful healer (see 5:12–26; 7:1–10) who is able even to restore the dead to life (see 7:11–17; 8:49–56) and to have control over a storm at sea (see 8:22–25), demons (see 8:26–39), and chronic illness (see 8:40–56).

Luke 9:1–6 describes the mission of the Twelve Apostles as the extension of Jesus' own mission of teaching and healing. A similar passage appears in Luke 10:1–12 in which a group of seventy (or seventy-two) disciples is appointed to prepare the way for Jesus as he and his followers make their way to Jerusalem in the Journey Narrative (see 9:51–19:44). The fact that the two instructions are so much alike suggests that they were intended for a larger circle than that constituted by the Twelve Apostles.

The "mission of the Twelve" consists of a narrative framework (see Luke 9:1–2, 6) and an instruction (see 9:3–5). In the first part of the narrative (see 9:1–2) Jesus determines to share his powers as a teacher and healer, and in the concluding section (see 9:6) the Twelve are sent out on their mission. In Luke's two-volume narrative, the Twelve Apostles serve as an important principle of continuity between the ministry of the earthly Jesus and the early days of the church in Jerusalem after Jesus' resurrection and ascension (see Acts 1–9). Here they are called to do what Jesus does in his ministry and to share actively in his mission from God.

The instruction (see Luke 9:3–5) assumes that the Twelve Apostles will be on the move as they carry forward Jesus' mission. According to 9:3, they are to avoid all unnecessary baggage ("no staff, nor bag, nor bread, nor money . . .") and to place their trust totally in God to provide for their needs. On the practical level (see 9:4), they are to rely on the hospitality and generosity of those whom they encounter and accept them into their households. Rather than spending time and energy on seeking better accommodations, the Twelve Apostles are told to be satisfied with what is first given to them by their hosts. If and when they meet opposition and rejection (see 9:5), the proper response is for them to move on peacefully, with only a symbolic gesture of leave-taking: "shake the dust off your feet as a testimony against them."

THE SHAPE OF DISCIPLESHIP

In the Synoptic tradition, the first disciples called by Jesus have an exemplary significance, both positive and negative. The first four are fishermen: Simon and Andrew, James and John (see Mark 1:16–20; Matthew 4:18–22; Luke 5:1–11). As such they would have enjoyed a relatively stable existence in the present and decent prospects for the future, since commercial fishing in the Sea of Galilee was (and is) a fairly prosperous business enterprise. There is no indication that they had met Jesus or even knew anything about him. This serves to highlight the extraordinary power of Jesus' call and the attractiveness of his person. Moreover, the usual Jewish pattern by which students became associated with a master teacher was by their seeking out the teacher. However, by the power of his word alone ("follow me and I will make you fish for people") Jesus chooses and gathers to himself the disciples who will be with him throughout his public ministry.

The essence of discipleship is to be with Jesus and to share his mission (see Mark 3:14). The simple lifestyle recommended in the various missionary discourses (Mark 6:7–13; Matthew 10:1–42; Luke 9:1–6; 10:1–12) is in the service of sharing in Jesus' proclamation of God's kingdom and healing those in need.

The absolute and radical claims involved in following Jesus may demand separating from one's natural family and becoming part of the "new family" of Jesus (see Mark 3:31–35). At the very beginning of Luke's Journey Narrative, Jesus refuses the requests of prospective disciples to bury a father or to say farewell to those at home (see 9:59–62). In a culture in which family ties and obligations are enormously important, this is power-ful teaching. Indeed, Jesus promises division within the household (see Luke 12:51–53), and even urges prospective disciples to "hate" their family members (see 14:26).

These family tensions are illustrated by the case of Jesus himself. According to Mark 3:21, members of his own family try to restrain him on the grounds that people were saying "He has gone out of his mind," thus bringing shame upon the entire family. In response, Jesus redefines his family as "whoever does the will of God" (Mark 3:35). His disciples—those dedicated to his ideals and mission—now constitute the family of Jesus.

The disciples, especially the Twelve Apostles but also presumably the wider circle, are promised rewards not only in the future but also "in the age to come" (see Mark 10:28–31). During Jesus' public ministry, disciples have the benefit of receiving Jesus' wisdom and even his foreknowledge of the suffering that awaits him and them. Nevertheless, in all the Synoptic Gospels they are more or less obtuse, and instead of growing in spiritual insight they regress on the way from Galilee to Jerusalem. Then, in Jerusalem, when Jesus is arrested, they scatter, and Peter denies Jesus three times. By contrast, the women followers emerge as the faithful ones when they witness Jesus' death and burial, and go to his tomb on Easter Sunday.

Transfer Value

The major problem posed by these Synoptic Gospel texts is their applicability or transfer to Christians beyond the first century and outside the Land of Israel. Or to put the same point in another way, Can we use Jesus' instructions to his disciples in Christian moral theology today?

In the Christian tradition there has been a long-standing debate on this issue. Some contend that the discipleship teachings are incumbent on all Christians. Others make a distinction between a Christian elite and ordinary Christians.

From the perspective of biblical studies, the question is often posed and treated in a historical framework. Some would argue that the extreme teachings about discipleship—especially the simple lifestyle and the separa-tion from family—pertain only to the mission of the historical Jesus in first-century rural Palestine. Others argue that the teachings about lack of family, possessions, and stable abode best fit the rural conditions of the earliest days of the post-Easter Christian mission. In both periods, those who proclaimed the kingdom of God went from place to place, dependent upon the hospitality and generosity of the local population.

The link between the very concrete instructions most at home in first-century Palestine and the generalizing tendency in the Christian theological tradition is best found in the editorial work of the Synoptic Evangelists. Each gospel writer used traditional materials in a new urban context outside the land of Israel: Mark in Rome around A.D. 70; Matthew in Antioch around A.D. 85–90; and Luke perhaps in Greece around A.D. 85–90. They all faced the challenge of translation or transfer, and each of them gave distinctive emphases to the discipleship tradition: success and failure along the way (Mark), learning from Jesus the teacher (Matthew), and carrying on the message and work of Jesus (Luke). It seems that the very process of interpretation and development as illustrated by the Evangelists provides the bridge between discipleship in Jesus' time and in other times and places.

It is neither possible nor useful to imitate Jesus' lifestyle in all its details, or to try to put into practice all the concrete instructions that he gave to his first followers. But one can and should discern some core values in the discipleship passages in the Synoptic Gospels—absolute dedication to God's kingdom, sharing in Jesus' mission, a simple lifestyle, a willingness to subordinate or forgo human ties and physical comforts, and the assurance of opposition and suffering for the sake of the gospel—that can give shape to Christian discipleship in any age and place. These core values can serve as the starting points for reflecting on the use of Jesus' discipleship teachings in moral theology today.

MORAL THEOLOGICAL REFLECTIONS
J. F. Keenan

In developing the theme of following Christ, we turn to two moral theologians who have brought the notion of discipleship to the fore in Christian ethics: Fritz Tillmann and Klaus Demmer. Each provides a significant link between Scripture and ethics, via the notion of discipleship.

FRITZ TILLMANN

Tillmann (1874–1953) was originally a Scripture scholar. From 1905 to 1931, he wrote on a variety of biblical themes: Jesus' self-disclosure as the Son of Man, the future coming of Christ, the self-understanding of the Son of God, and personality and community in the sermons of Jesus. Because the study of Scripture was then so restricted by Vatican pressure, from fear of what was called *modernism*, Tillmann left for the relative freedom to study moral theology, which was then regarded as a more stable and safe field.

By his crossing over, Tillmann constructed the first major bridge between the studies of Scripture and Catholic moral theology, as his writings in moral theology followed from his studies in Scripture. Because Tillmann's interests there revolved around the personal effect that Jesus' self-understanding had on the community of disciples, he naturally developed the belief that the Christian pursuit of the good had to be within the framework of being a disciple of Jesus. Tillmann held that moral theology was the scientific presentation of following Jesus in the life of the individual and the community: Catholic moral theology finds the source of its search for moral truth in the person of Jesus as the original image and the eventual goal for all of us.

In order to appreciate the innovation that Tillmann brought to moral theology, we should first consider the terrain that Tillmann entered when he began writing in moral theology. We saw in the first chapter that from the seventeenth century, Catholic moral theologians developed moral theology solely to study the nature and species of sin; that is, what sin is, and what kinds of actions constitute sins. They specifically denied any relationship between moral and ascetical theology. When the twentieth century began, the only significant innovation that moral theologians made was to produce their manuals of moral theology in the vernacular rather than in Latin.

Tillmann's approach to moral theology was completely different. In 1937 he wrote *Der Meister ruft* (later translated into English as *The Master Calls*),[1] which was divided into four parts. The first part ("principles") was a striking departure from those principles in the contemporary manuals of moral theology which determined the relevance of sinful actions. Among Tillmann's principles, the first was the following of Jesus. This principle was an ideal, because Jesus himself is an unsurpassable goal of an unattainable value who is always before us and who, in inviting us to follow him, calls us into a dynamic moral life. By following Jesus, we become children of God and share his relationship with God as Father ("Abba").

Here Tillmann turned to ascetical theology and the pursuit of spiritual perfection through the virtues realizing inner dispositions. His rather demanding ethics was completely Scripture based. Tillmann provided no other sources for his claims. He offered a vision of human existence marked by piety, compassion, a reconciling spirit, mildness, humility, and faithfulness. He argued that the pursuit of Jesus was never separated from either the love of neighbor or a concern for the needs of the world. For Tillmann, Jesus is the soul of every Christian community.

In developing the theme of discipleship, Tillmann claimed that the primary sacrament for moral theology was not penance but rather baptism, which alone supplied the call that is freely given by Christ. By baptism, we enter into a new creation; we are not the old Adam, but we are regenerated, liberated, and elevated by Christ. Tillmann wrote that by the Holy Spirit "we are made free to share in the magnificent liberty of the children of God."[2] Such joyful effusiveness was never expressed in Catholic moral theology, at least not since the seventeenth century.

By baptism, then, we have a new relationship with God whose will makes possible, and therefore is the foundation of the moral life. This new relationship calls us to take notice of the imprint of God's self within ourselves. There, within, we are called to allow the work of God to continue in the development of our interior dispositions and consciences. Tillmann added that we should not give excessive attention to external actions.

The call to the moral life is a call to walk on the way of the Lord, which is the summons for union with Jesus, or what ascetical theology called perfection: "the attainment of perfection is the task and goal of every Christian."[3] By bringing the call to spiritual perfection into the moral life *and* by insisting that this call is for everyone, Tillmann effectively democratized ascetical theology. Moreover, as such, this perfection is a call not to flee the world, but rather to grow within it.

The subsequent three parts of Tillmann's *The Master Calls* constitute a parsing of the love command—to love God, neighbor, and self. Throughout his treatment of the three loves, Tillmann regularly invoked Jesus himself as the model and motive of the possibility for our following him. The entire moral life is organized and shaped by our following of Jesus.

KLAUS DEMMER

The link between Jesus' self-understanding and its normative relevance for his disciples is brought out by Klaus Demmer, a German moral theologian who teaches at the Gregorian University in Rome. Demmer asserts that the word of Jesus is the person of Jesus. When Jesus says something, we understand who he is, and to understand revelation is to understand Jesus.

With regard to morality, the New Testament, according to Demmer, gives us a new self-understanding rather than new norms. Like Jesus of Nazareth, our self-understanding must be situated in history. Thus, just as Jesus reveals to us his self-understanding in history, so too we must work out in history that self-understanding of ourselves in Jesus.

Demmer writes that Jesus brings to us a new knowledge of God.[4] This is not a deductive knowledge but a knowledge of God that derives from Jesus' self-understanding, which is really an understanding of his relationship to God. If Jesus calls God *Father*, then those whom he calls to be his brothers and sisters can share in that relationship. The knowledge of God is always personally mediated.

Furthermore, Jesus expresses his self-understanding as the Son of Man, which is the eschatological expression of our end and of the means to that end. Jesus is thus our model, our forerunner, our *Alpha*. He makes possible both our inclination to him and our ability to pursue him. In Jesus all things are possible, and through Jesus all things happen.

Demmer describes Jesus' self-understanding as a radical openness of his will to God's will. Our participation in Jesus' self-understanding, then, is a call to us to that same radical openness. Stanley Hauerwas makes a similar connection when he insists that the role of the disciple is to get the narrative of Jesus right. Hauerwas points out that Peter repeatedly demonstrated an inability to get it right. Peter was able to recognize that Jesus was the Messiah, but refused to acknowledge that this identity required Jesus to die and that the cross was constitutive of Jesus' radical openness to the will of God. Hauerwas adds that by getting the narrative of Jesus right we are transformed in the process. He concludes by noting that that transformation and the ability to get Jesus' narrative right are dialectically dependent. The more we understand the narrative, the more we are transformed, the more we are able to understand, and so on.

Demmer also likes to play with two movements of discipleship. On the one hand, we are invited to participate *in* the self-understanding of Jesus. In Jesus we accept his lot, for being *in* Jesus the cross is inevitable; the cross is not extrinsic, but intrinsic to the self-understanding. But while we see ourselves *in* Jesus, we still see ourselves as *following* Jesus. Like Tillmann, Demmer insists that Jesus is our model and animator, our goal and our cause. But Demmer adds that while Jesus is unsurpassable, he is still always before us, never invisible. Jesus is in history, admittedly on the horizon of our history, but never beyond it.

Therefore, Demmer also stresses the "effective history" of the Christ event. We are called to discipleship precisely in light of the fact that Jesus has died for our sins and, in that redemption, we are capable of hearing and responding to the call of discipleship. Thus we are not to be trapped by the history of our guilt. Jesus' redemption offers the tangible assistance of freeing us from that guilt. Our "ability" to follow Jesus, that is, to be disciples, has been made possible or "effective" by Jesus himself.

Concretely, Demmer argues that freedom from guilt (not only of past sins, but of those to come) is one of the two effective gifts of the redemption. When we allow ourselves to be haunted, oppressed, or weighed down by guilt arising from our sins, then we are implicitly, if not explicitly, rejecting the merciful, forgiving, and reconciling offer of Jesus' own redemption of us from sin.

The great German Lutheran martyr Dietrich Bonhoeffer (1906–1945), who was killed by the Nazis for resisting their regime, would say that this freedom from our guilt is hardly "a cheap grace." Rather, because our guilt was so dearly paid for in Jesus' death, we are all the more aware of the call of Jesus. Rather than trying to save ourselves, we are called to respond to the redemptive offering of freedom from guilt and, as sinners, to move forward along the way of the Lord. When we protest in our sinfulness that we are not worthy or that we are full of guilt, then we remain isolated as prisoners of our own history, and neither participate in the self-understanding of Jesus nor follow in his footsteps.

Demmer proposes that the second "effective" gift of the redemption is freedom from the effects of death. This means that we are freed from our own fear of death as well as from the power of death to end absolutely our lives and our relationships with God and one another. In short, by the redemption, we are in our histories as disciples of Jesus free from the sting of death.

If we are called to participate in Jesus' self-understanding of radical openness to the will of God, this means inevitably recognizing that the cross and death are constitutive of the self-understanding of children of God. This recognition and the acceptance of our call is what Bonhoeffer calls the cost of discipleship.[5] Yet, we should see here that our ability to follow Jesus is made effective by Jesus defeating the claims of death.

Following Jesus

As disciples then, we participate in the self-understanding of Jesus. What does that mean, specifically? We have seen that by his self-understanding Jesus entered into a radical openness to the will of God, and that in that openness he freed us from sin and death; in turn, Jesus made possible our ability to hear and respond to his call to follow in his footsteps. But what does following in his footsteps look like?

In director/writer Pier Paolo Pasolini's famous movie, *The Gospel According to Matthew*, the person of Jesus is preaching and teaching while he is busy hurrying to Jerusalem for his encounter with history. Pasolini's Jesus never stops, sits, or rests. Rather, he is always walking at a fast pace, and the disciples are trying to keep up with him. When he preaches, even in parables, he does not pause. Rather, he keeps moving forward toward Jerusalem, occasionally looking back to let his disciples know that he realizes they are trying to follow him. He is the unsurpassable goal who always goes before us, making our call to follow him a dynamic movement.

That image of Jesus on the road is, of course, a dominant one in understanding the call to imitate Jesus. Nowhere is it more emphatic than in Jesus' answer to the question, "And who is my neighbor?" Here Jesus responds with the parable of the Good Samaritan (see Luke 10:25–37).

The parable is an odd one because its end is, unless we are not attentive, a reversal of the beginning. As the story unfolds, the neighbor seems to be the wounded man on the road. But by the end, the scribe tells us that the neighbor is the one traveling on that road, the Good Samaritan, the one who shows mercy. In a way, Jesus is telling us not to look for a neighbor to love but rather to *be* a neighbor who loves.

As we saw in the second chapter, in virtue ethics we are first instructed to appreciate that *being* precedes *doing*. That is exactly the lesson that we are taught in the parable of the Good Samaritan. The parable is in the end a lesson about imitating the Good Samaritan. Moreover, although often forgotten today, the Good Samaritan has traditionally been interpreted as first a narrative of Jesus' redemptive work and *then* a call to imitation. The parable reveals the mercy of Jesus.

Throughout history, preachers and theologians have used the parable to tell the story of Jesus. They told it this way: The wounded man was Adam, wounded by original sin and now exiled outside of the gates of the city, which is Paradise. Neither the Law nor the Prophets (the priest and the Levite) was able to help Adam. Then one not from the land of Adam, Jesus the Good Samaritan, found Adam, tended to him, and carried him on his mule to the inn, which is the church. There Jesus paid an initial price, our redemption, which will be paid in full when Jesus returns again at the end of time to take Adam into the kingdom.

According to this traditional allegorical reading of Luke 10:25–37, Jesus is the neighbor who has entered our chaos to rescue and save us. The incarnation, passion, death, and resurrection of Jesus—that is, the saving mission of Jesus—was understood as a life of mercy. That life of mercy is what the disciples of Jesus are to live as they follow the one who goes before them; the one who challenges his disciples to "go and do likewise" (Luke 10:37b).

Questions for Reflection and Discussion

1. Why does the topic of discipleship follow the topic of the kingdom of God?

2. Explain how Jesus is the source and the end (or goal) of our call to discipleship.

3. If we are to get the story of Jesus right, what factors in the narrative of Jesus must we know?

Notes

1. Fritz Tillmann, *The Master Calls: A Handbook of Christian Living* (Baltimore: Helicon Press, 1960).

2. Ibid., p. 23.

3. Ibid., p. 47.

4. Klaus Demmer, *Shaping the Moral Life: An Introduction to Moral Theology* (Washington, D.C.: Georgetown University Press, 2000).

5. Dietrich Bonhoeffer, *The Cost of Discipleship* (New York: Macmillan, 1958).

Select Bibliography

Bonhoeffer, Dietrich. *The Cost of Discipleship*. New York: Macmillan, 1958.

_____. *Ethics*. New York: Macmillan, 1955.

_____. *Letters and Papers from Prison*. New York: Macmillan, 1971.

Demmer, Klaus. *Shaping the Moral Life: An Introduction to Moral Theology*. Washington, D.C.: Georgetown University Press, 2000.

Donahue, John R. "Growth in Grace." *Southwestern Journal of Theology* 28 (1986), pp. 73–78.

Fischer, Georg and Martin Hasitschka. *The Call of the Disciple: The Bible on Following Christ*. New York: Paulist, 1999.

Longenecker, Richard N. (ed.). *Patterns of Discipleship in the New Testament*. Grand Rapids: Eerdmans, 1996.

McDonagh, Enda. *Doing the Truth: The Quest for Moral Theology*. Notre Dame, IN: University of Notre Dame Press, 1979.

Theissen, Gerd. *Sociology of Early Palestinian Christianity*. Philadelphia: Fortress, 1978.

Tillmann, Fritz. *The Master Calls: A Handbook of Christian Living*. Baltimore: Helicon Press, 1960.

Wilder, Amos N. *Eschatology and Ethics in the Teaching of Jesus*. New York: Harper, 1939, pp. 200–220.

Wilkins, Michael J. *Discipleship in the Ancient World and Matthew's Gospel*. Grand Rapids: Baker, 1995.

Chapter Five

THE SERMON ON THE MOUNT AND CHRISTIAN VIRTUE ETHICS: HOW DO WE GET THERE?

W e have seen that discipleship provides us with a context for answering the question of who we are, and that the kingdom of God gives us a profile of who we are called to be. Now in answering the third of MacIntyre's questions (How do we get there?), we turn to the Sermon on the Mount and see the personal characteristics that Christians need to develop so as to be called into the fullness of God's kingdom.

As Harrington points out, the Sermon on the Mount is a summary of Jesus' wise teachings. A study of the sermon requires us to know not only the text itself but also its origin and context, content, genre, and theological significance. He argues that the sermon is best understood as part of an ethics of virtue. Keenan elaborates on the nature of virtue ethics. By referring to the work of Mennonite theologian Joseph Kotva, he makes a specific case that virtue ethics is a worthy medium for translating the ethical teachings of the New Testament into a contemporary context. He then offers a Christian anthropological profile using the virtues of mercy, a reconciling spirit, and hope as the defining characteristics of the Christian life.

BIBLICAL PERSPECTIVES
D. J. Harrington

The Sermon on the Mount is Matthew's composition on the basis of earlier sources that allows us to hear the voice of Jesus the wise teacher. The first of the five great discourses in Matthew's narrative of Jesus, it deals with true happiness, the proper interpretation of the Law and the Prophets, genuine piety, wise attitudes and behavior in everyday life, and the need to translate wisdom into action. As a Jewish wisdom instruction, it expresses the wisdom of Jesus. Today it is best taken as proposing an ethics of Christian character or a Christian virtue ethics. It is foundational for Christian life but always requires interpretation, adaptation, and application.

TRUE HAPPINESS
(Matthew 5:3)

Blessed are the poor in spirit,
for theirs is the kingdom of heaven.

Jesus' first discourse in Matthew's Gospel (see chapters 5–7) takes place on a mountain (a traditional place for revelation), and addresses both the crowds and his disciples. The sermon begins with nine "beatitudes" (see 5:3–12) in which Jesus declares as "happy" or "blessed" (see Psalm 1 for an example of the literary form) those who practice certain virtues, and promises them an eternal reward in the fullness of God's kingdom.

The first beatitude (see Matthew 5:3) calls "happy" those who are "poor in spirit." Compare Luke 6:20 ("Blessed are you poor, for yours is the kingdom of God"), which is generally regarded as the earlier (Q) form. The first beatitude questions the assumption that money and possessions can buy happiness. It should be read against the Old Testament background of God's special care for the poor (see Isaiah 61:1–3; Exodus 22:25–27, 23:11; Leviticus 19:9–10; Deuteronomy 15:7–11). Matthew's qualification "in spirit" serves to define the poor as those who recognize their own poverty in the face of the greatness of God and the gift of God's kingdom. The first beatitude promises that the poor in spirit will be part of God's kingdom in the future, and suggests that those who are truly poor in spirit have entered it in the present.

The nine beatitudes in Matthew 5:3–12 give a sample of virtues and actions that will be rewarded in the fullness of God's kingdom and therefore are to be cultivated in the present. Their way of life promises true happiness. But Jesus' list of values, character traits, and attitudes calls into question much conventional human wisdom about happiness and how to achieve it. They declare as happy the poor in spirit (not the rich), those who mourn (not those who laugh), the meek (not the tough), those who hunger and thirst for righteousness (rather than for power), the merciful (not the hard-minded), the "pure in heart" (not the clever pragmatists), the peacemakers (not the warriors), and those who are persecuted for the sake of righteousness and reviled on Jesus' account (not those who are universally praised and honored). The beatitudes promote a vision of Christian character that was perfectly embodied and exemplified by Jesus. The future fullness of their reward is expressed in various ways: "theirs is the kingdom of heaven ... they will be comforted ... they will inherit the earth ... they will be filled . . . they will receive mercy . . . they will see God . . . they will be called children of God."

ORIGIN AND CONTEXT

Matthew wrote in the late first century A.D. for a largely Jewish Christian community, perhaps at Antioch in Syria. His work was a revised and expanded version of Mark's Gospel, in which he integrated material from the Sayings Source Q and from a special tradition (or traditions) found only in Matthew's Gospel and commonly referred to as M. Matthew sought to give a larger sample of Jesus' teaching than what was included in Mark, and to present Jesus as the authoritative representative and interpreter of the Jewish tradition in the crisis facing all Jews after the destruction of Jerusalem and its Temple in A.D. 70 by the Roman army in response to a Jewish revolt.

In composing the Sermon on the Mount, Matthew used the block of Jesus' teaching in Q that also appears in Luke as the Sermon on the Plain (see Luke 6:20–49). He supplemented this foundational piece with other sayings that are either concerned with Jewish life or breathe the air of Jewish wisdom literature. Since Matthew assembled and edited these traditions, it is fair to call the composition Matthew's Sermon on the Mount.

Nevertheless, Matthew lets us hear the voice of Jesus, even though it is unlikely that Jesus delivered this sermon as such, word for word, at one time and in one place. Jesus taught in Aramaic, and Matthew wrote in Greek on the basis of Greek sources. Moreover, the content of the sermon is so rich that an audience would struggle to absorb it all at one hearing. And yet, the Sermon on the Mount contains many teachings that modern scholars attribute with confidence to the historical Jesus: the beatitudes, the prohibitions of divorce and oaths, love of enemies, the Lord's Prayer, and so on. In that sense, Matthew's Sermon on the Mount allows us to hear the voice of Jesus.

The Sermon on the Mount is the first of five great speeches by Jesus in Matthew's Gospel. The other discourses deal with discipleship (see chapter 10), the kingdom of heaven (see chapter 13), community life (see chapter 18), and preparation for the full coming of the kingdom (see chapters 24–25). Placed first in the series, the Sermon on the Mount (see chapters 5–7) serves as a summary or compendium of Jesus' most important and distinctive teachings.

The sermon appears in the context of Matthew's narrative of Jesus' birth and his emergence from the circle of John the Baptist (see 1:1–4:16). As readers we know that Jesus is not only the Son of Abraham and Son of David but also the Son of God. We know that Jesus burst on the public

scene proclaiming the coming kingdom of heaven (see 4:17) and summoning disciples (see 4:18–22). The audience for the sermon includes not
only his small circle of disciples but also the crowds gathered from all the
surrounding regions (see 4:24–5:2, 7:28–29).

The sermon is followed in Matthew 8–9 by a series of miracle stories
in which Jesus appears as a healer, an exorcist, and a miracle worker. The
one who is powerful in word (as shown in the Sermon on the Mount) is
also powerful in deed (as shown in his mighty acts). Then in the second
great discourse (see chapter 10), Jesus invites his disciples to do what he
does—to teach, to proclaim the kingdom of God, and to heal the sick (see
4:23; 9:35; 10:1, 7–8). Thus, the sermon is part of the story of Jesus, not a
self-standing ethical treatise.

CONTENT

Matthew's Sermon on the Mount consists of five major sections. The
introductory part (see 5:3–16) presents in 5:3–12 the beatitudes ("Blessed
are the poor in spirit . . ."), which set forth the personal characteristics,
values, attitudes, and actions that will be rewarded in the fullness of God's
kingdom and are therefore to be cultivated in the present. The importance
of those who follow Jesus' teaching and the service that they perform for
the world is expressed with the help of three images in 5:13–16: the salt of
the earth, the light of the world, and the city built on a hill.

The second part (see Matthew 5:17–48) concerns Jesus and the Jewish Law. The fundamental assertions in 5:17–20 are that Jesus came "not to
abolish but to fulfill" the Law and the Prophets, and that his approach is
superior to that of the scribes and Pharisees. That Jesus offers deepening
and intensification rather than abolition is then illustrated by the six
"antitheses" about murder and anger (see 5:21–26), adultery and lust (see
5:27–30), marriage and divorce (see 5:31–32), oaths (see 5:33–37), retaliation and nonviolence (see 5:38–42), and love of enemies (see 5:43–48).

The third part (see Matthew 6:1–18) deals with acts of piety: almsgiving
(see 6:2–4), prayer (see 6:5–6), and fasting (see 6:16–18). The wrong way to
perform acts of piety is to make a public spectacle in the hope of getting a
good reputation for holiness. The right way is to seek to serve and please
God alone. Also included are teachings about brevity in prayer (see
6:7–8), how to pray—the Lord's Prayer (see 6:9–13)—and forgiveness (see
6:14–15).

The fourth part (see Matthew 6:19–7:12) provides wise advice about
various topics: treasures (see 6:19–21), eyes (see 6:22–23), masters (see 6:24),
anxiety (see 6:25–34), judgments (see 7:1–5), dogs and pigs (see 7:6), prayer
(see 7:7–11), and the Golden Rule (see 7:12).

The concluding exhortation (see Matthew 7:13–27) uses short parables about gates and ways (see 7:13–14), trees and fruits (see 7:15–20), saying and doing (see 7:21–23), and houses and foundations (see 7:24–27) to highlight the challenges involved in practicing Jesus' teachings and the need for integrity and spiritual depth. It is not enough to know Jesus' teachings and to call him "Lord" (see 7:21–23). One must also do what he says. His wisdom is practical rather than purely speculative.

GENRE

The Sermon on the Mount is a summary of Jesus' wise teachings. Some scholars compare it to the epitomes or compendia (concise or condensed treatises) that were used in antiquity to summarize the doctrines of philosophers. However, given Jesus' (and Matthew's) roots in Judaism and the Jewish character of his teachings, a better analogy can be found among the wisdom instructions in Proverbs, Ecclesiastes, Sirach, and the Wisdom of Solomon.

In a wisdom instruction, the sage addresses those in search of wisdom. The sage uses various literary forms: beatitudes, proverbs, commands and prohibitions often accompanied by reasons ("for . . ."), general principles, parables, and so on. While there is sometimes an architecture or external framework in wisdom instructions, there is no extended argument or logical development of an idea. Instead, the sage moves rapidly from topic to topic, often only on the basis of keywords or catchwords. The content embraces general principles, attitudes, and actions. All these features appear in Matthew 5–7, and to that extent, it is fair to call the Sermon on the Mount a wisdom instruction.

THEOLOGICAL SIGNIFICANCE

It is probably easier to say what the Sermon on the Mount *is not* rather than what it *is*. It is not an elitist or perfectionist ethics, intended only for a few individuals or a small group. Indeed, it addresses not only Jesus' inner circle but also the crowds. It is not an impossible ethic—as Martin Luther (1483–1546) proposed—designed mainly to make us recognize our sinfulness and our need for God's grace. Rather, it is presented as something that people can and should put into practice (see Matthew 7:13–27). And it is not an interim ethics (at least in the narrow sense suggested by Albert Schweitzer), put forward by Jesus who mistakenly imagined that God's kingdom would come in a very short time. Matthew wrote some sixty years after Jesus' death.

Neither is the Sermon on the Mount a law code. Instead, it freely mixes general principles such as love of enemies (see Matthew 5:43–48) and the Golden Rule (see 7:12) with parables, exhortations, examples, declarations, and so on. Nor is it the new Torah. Instead, it presents Jesus as the authoritative interpreter of the Law of Moses and puts forward as his basic principle "not to abolish but to fulfill" (see 5:17).

The Sermon on the Mount presents the wisdom of Jesus. In his initial wisdom instruction according to Matthew, Jesus lays out his teachings on true happiness, the interpretation of the Law and the Prophets, the service of God, and wise attitudes and actions in various spheres of human life. He concludes with a reminder about the practical nature of his wisdom. In form and content, Matthew 5–7 is a Jewish wisdom instruction.

What significance does the Sermon on the Mount have for us? What do we do with it? The sermon is best understood today as part of an ethics of Christian character or Christian virtue ethics. The kingdom of God is the horizon and goal. The sermon tells us how to prepare to enjoy its fullness and to act appropriately in the present. The search for "perfection" takes God as its model and criterion: "Be perfect, therefore, as your heavenly Father is perfect" (Matthew 5:48). Its ethical teachings appear as part of a narrative in which Jesus is not only the master teacher but also the best example of his own teaching.

Being a student in Jesus' wisdom school involves formation in character and commitment to certain ways of acting. Rather than providing a complete code of conduct, the Sermon on the Mount shapes Christians to discern wisely and to act correctly. The sermon presupposes life in community and its positive impact for the common good as the salt of the earth, the light of the world, and the city on a hill.

The sermon makes no sharp distinction between law and love. Rather, law and love work together. The body of the sermon begins with Jesus' claim that he came "not to abolish but to fulfill" the Law and the Prophets (see Matthew 5:17). It ends with the Golden Rule: "In everything do to others as you would have them do to you; for this is the Law and the Prophets" (see 7:12).

Various motives are offered for why one should act wisely and do good: entering the kingdom of heaven, imitating the example of God, going to the root of a divine (Old Testament) commandment, behaving in a wise and appropriate manner, avoiding punishment in the present or in the world to come, and so on. There is no single motive to the exclusion of all others.

Another way to approach the present significance of the Sermon on the Mount is to compare it with the American Declaration of Independence and the Bill of Rights. These foundational documents express the vision of the Founding Fathers and the commonly accepted principles on which the United States is built. They contain the basic attitudes, ideals, and stances that serve as norms for legislation and behavior. They also set limits or parameters. And yet these documents, since they are well over two hundred years old, reflect a very different social and historical situation from our own. And they do not address issues that either were not regarded as imperative or practical in the late eighteenth century (abolition of slavery, women's suffrage, and so on) or that have been raised by modern technology (cloning, surrogate motherhood, weapons of mass destruction, and so on), while devoting great energy to matters that we now happily regard as resolved (freedom of assembly, of the press, of religion, and so on). Like the Sermon on the Mount, these documents need continuing interpretation, adaptation, and application. And yet they remain foundational, normative, and meaningful.

MORAL THEOLOGICAL REFLECTIONS
J. F. Keenan

At this point we can begin to perceive a particular affinity between virtue ethics and Scripture. But now we need to do two things. First, we must demonstrate that our preliminary perceptions are valid: that there is a strong congruency between the concerns of Scripture and the concerns of virtue ethics. Here we turn to the work of Mennonite theologian Joseph Kotva, who makes the case that there is a correlation between Scripture and virtue ethics by specifically examining Matthew's Gospel and Paul's letters. Second, inasmuch as we claim that the Sermon on the Mount is well understood through the lens of virtue ethics, we should see whether a particular anthropological profile emerges specifically from the sermon.

JOSEPH KOTVA'S WORK ON
SCRIPTURE AND VIRTUE ETHICS

In recognizing the compatibility between Scripture and virtue ethics, Kotva first notes an emphasis on internal qualities, and to make the point he turns to the beatitudes that concern "the poor in spirit" (Matthew 5:3) and "the pure of heart" (see 5:6). Likewise, the sermon's antitheses (see 5:21–48) move us to recognize the internal dispositions that eventually find expression in external actions: Jesus warns against anger and lust, recognizing that our conduct flows from our inner character (see 5:21–22, 27–28). Kotva also reminds us that Matthew frequently reiterates the comment that good or evil trees yield correspondingly good or evil fruit (see 3:8, 10; 7:15–20; 12:33), and that the measure of a person is found in whatever comes out of the person (see 15:10–11, 17–20).

Second, Kotva highlights Matthew's summons to aim for ideals. For instance, we hear the call to be more righteous than the scribes and Pharisees (see Matthew 5:20) and to be perfect as God is perfect (see 5:48; 19:21). But Matthew's idealism is neither destructive nor unrealistic. While he often emphasizes the ideal, he constantly proffers the need for reconciliation and forgiveness, which is a recognition of human frailty and finitude (see 5:21–26; 6:12, 14–15; 18:15–35). This balance between striving for a goal and recognizing human limitations develops, then, into a healthy tension. This tension embodies, moreover, the challenge that we saw in the last chapter, wherein discipleship requires us to articulate constantly the goal or end that remains outstanding on the horizon of our expectations.

Third, Aristotle held that we could learn what virtue was by acting *as* the prudent person does. Similarly, Thomas Aquinas recognized that one grows in the virtues only to the extent that one is accompanied by a prudent mentor. Thus, an interpersonal tutoring from a practically wise person is a constitutive component of virtue ethics. Why? Because in order to rightly realize or, as the scholastics of medieval theology would say, to perfect one's dispositions, one needs to understand oneself adequately, to articulate the personally appropriate goals for the right realization of those dispositions, and to determine the suitable means for achieving these goals. These three tasks correspond to the three questions that MacIntyre raised in *After Virtue*: Who are we? Who ought we to become? and How do we get there?[1] But here we see that these are hardly abstract questions but rather are fundamentally personal and concrete ones that can be answered only with the help of someone who is wise enough to understand both life itself and the person seeking to grow in virtue.

Precisely here we recognize the Jesus who trains his disciples throughout Matthew's Gospel. Certainly his instructions themselves are critically important for the formation of his disciples (see 4:23; 5:1–2; 9:35; 11:1; 13:36; 13:54; 26:55). But his method is profoundly intimate. He is a master teacher or a tutor, a personal guide. He claims to know his disciples, who they are and what they (privately) think. He sends them out on apprenticeships, so that they may learn to teach, preach, heal, and minister. He wants them to know themselves, their desires, and their capabilities. In short, he trains them. Moreover, he is different from other tutors. He wants them to share not only in his life and mission but also in his suffering and deliverance (see 10:24–25, 38; 16:24).

For that reason, Jesus is not only trainer but also a model, paradigm, and image. He is the prudent one, the virtuous one. In answer to the question, Who is the virtuous one? the answer is Jesus. We are to be like him.

Fourth, Kotva insists that the concerns of virtue ethics and Matthew's Gospel are both individual and corporate. Jesus calls particular persons to be disciples (see 4:18–22; 9:9), interacts with very specific individuals (see 8:2–15), discusses the individual's feelings (see 5:21–24), and is willing to leave the group of ninety-nine to rescue the one who is lost (see 18:12–14). Yet in Matthew 18, Jesus carefully treats the need for humility, forgiveness, and respect in the community. Whether addressing the person or the community, Jesus never sacrifices the concerns of the one for the other. He is the master teacher not only for individual disciples but also for the community of disciples. The tasks that we saw above for the individual are effectively the same for the community.

Fifth, we have learned from Stanley Hauerwas, among others, how narrative affects virtue. The gospel narratives form us. They provide the context wherein pilgrims encounter the possibility of understanding their own condition as sinners, as broken, as forgiven, as redeemed, as healed, and/or as welcomed. The Gospels are what Klaus Demmer calls effective histories. They are not only written or read, proclaimed or heard; they are also to cause a transforming change in their preachers and in their listeners. They are the material by which we become what we otherwise could never become.

There is a discernible inclination to virtue ethics in Matthew's Gospel, then, and it is an inclination that revolves very much around the central figure of Jesus. Unlike other teachers, it is not only his teaching that we are predominantly interested in. Jesus is not like Karl Marx (1818–1883) or Immanuel Kant (1724–1804) or Thomas Aquinas. For each of these persons, we seek to understand their teachings and not their very own person. But Jesus is himself the lesson we seek to know: we seek virtues so as to be more like him, so as to follow him, so as to arrive at God's kingdom, which is life with Jesus Christ.

The emphasis on the person of Jesus reflects in turn a healthy preoccupation with the person of the disciples and their communities. This overall preference to focus on the formation of the person rather than on the morality of specific actions has prompted many, who confuse ethics with solely being concerned with the latter, to overlook the ethical significance of the former.

We need here to see that, as Kotva argues, the concern about the right formation of the person is not exclusively a Matthean concern. Rather, it pervades Scripture, and a simple turn to the Pauline letters can establish the validity of that claim. In Paul's letters we see again an affinity with virtue ethics. For instance, Paul views himself as the model to be imitated (see 1 Corinthians 4:16; Philippians 3:17) as he imitates Jesus (see 1 Corinthians 11:1). Eventually, Paul's underlying concern is recognized:

we are all to be like Christ (see Romans 15:1–7). Moreover, we too are to be models for one another (see 2 Corinthians 8:1–15; Philippians 2:15). The moral standard is found not in particular types of actions but rather in particular types of persons, Christ-bearers.

Paul frequently turns to internal qualities. For instance, he proposes several lists of virtues to be pursued and vices to be avoided (see Romans 1:29–31; 13:13; 1 Corinthians 5:10–11; 6:9–10; 2 Corinthians 12:20–21; Galatians 5:19–23; Philippians 4:8). More importantly, he often focuses on the Spirit transforming our hearts (see Romans 5:5; 8:27; 2 Corinthians 1:22; 3:3; Galatians 4:6). And he insists on the primacy of love (see 1 Corinthians 13:4–8, 13).

Similarly, the Christian life is expressed in terms of both individual and corporate concerns. The Church as a living body is a dominant metaphor for Paul (see 1 Corinthians 12:12–31; Romans 12:4–5). In these passages, Paul manages to emphasize the importance of both the individual's gifts and the Church's needs. Elsewhere, Paul expresses his concern for the community as it celebrates the Lord's Supper (see 1 Corinthians 11:17–34), as it is called to practice hospitality (see Romans 12:13; 1 Corinthians 16:5–7, 10–11), and as it responds to the collection (see Romans 15:25–31; 2 Corinthians 8:1–9:15; Galatians 2:10). Paul's concern for the personal never compromises his concern for the communal.

Similarly, prudential discernment governs many of the Pauline texts. Paul frequently is preoccupied with the question, Who will we become by the actions we perform? (and not, What should we do?). Thus discerning who should lead the community becomes a question of what the community will become by that leadership (see Romans 12:3–8; 1 Corinthians 12–14). The clearest example of Pauline discernment is found in the matter of meat sacrificed to idols (see 1 Corinthians 8:1–11:1). Here the rightness of the action is derived not by considering the action itself. Paul discards, if you will, the intrinsic value or disvalue to the eating of idol meat. Rather, the singular issue is whether by our actions we further forge our newly constituted relationship of being siblings in the Lord. Paul is always interested in the question of who we will become by the actions that we perform.

Here Paul's discernment is like Thomas Aquinas's distinction between transient and immanent actions, which corresponds to the difference between making and doing.[2] In the former case, action proceeds outward from the agent and primarily affects the object being made as when a carpenter makes a table. The latter case, however, concerns human action where the action redounds to the agent, further forming the agent by the doing of the action as when a person plays the piano, becoming by the action, a better pianist. Paul is invariably concerned with actions that we do, those that redound to us as agents.

In addition to the many similarities with Matthew, Paul provides a distinctive contribution that furthers the congruency between Scripture and virtue ethics: the variety of images that convey a journey of moral growth. "Walking," for instance, conveys a pattern of moral behavior from which we discern whether or not a person is living the life of a Christian (see Romans 6:4; 8:4; 13:13; 14:15; 1 Thessalonians 2:12; 4:1, 12; Galatians 5:16; 1 Corinthians 3:3). "Racing" emphasizes a struggle and an urgency in pursuing the end or goal of Christian living (see 1 Corinthians 9:24–27; Philippians 3:11–17; Galatians 2:2). For Paul, the Christian life is dynamic, not static. There is always room for growth, a call to perfection, a summons to strive, an invitation to increase (see Philippians 1:9–10, 25; 1 Corinthians 3:1–2; 2 Corinthians 6:13, 10:15). The theological notion of sanctification is easily analogous to these various images about the need to progress in the life of the Spirit.

If the centrality of the person of Jesus shapes the distinctive virtue ethics in Matthew's Gospel, then grace defines the distinctiveness of virtue ethics in Paul's letters. God is the source of everything (see Romans 8:28; 1 Corinthians 3:21–23; 8:6; Philippians 1:6; 2:13). Kotva notes, for instance, that the collection itself is attributed to God's grace (see 2 Corinthians 8:1; 9:8, 14) as is Paul's own ministry (see Romans 15:15; 1 Corinthians 3:5–7; 15:10; 2 Corinthians 3:5–6; 4:7; Galatians 1:15–16). Kotva writes: "In short, Christian living flows from God's act in Christ and is empowered by the Spirit's continuing presence."[3]

Like the centrality of Jesus, grace is a distinguishing and necessary condition of any Christian ethics. Without grace, notions of moral progress or growth are fraught with strong Pelagian (by willpower alone) designs. But the gratuitousness of grace preserves Christian virtue ethics from being anything more (or less) than the appropriate response to God's initiatives and gifts.

A CHRISTIAN APPROACH
TO THE HUMAN CONDITION

We saw earlier how certain presuppositions of Scripture regarding human flourishment were not compatible with Aristotle's philosophy: the crucifixion, mercy, and the gratuitousness of grace. These differences between Aristotle and Scripture are not unique, however. Every culture has a way of defining their expectations of human fulfillment, and therefore every culture has its own concept of the virtuous person.

Certainly, as we shall see later in this book, every culture in a way shares certain bottom-line or "thin" expectations for what is minimally speaking a virtuous person, but that "thin" profile is "thickened" by other concerns that distinguish individual cultures. For instance, some understanding of a virtue like justice (that is, the willingness to be impartial and to give to each their due) is presumably present in every culture. Justice in the United States, however, is affected considerably by the American esteem of personal autonomy, and this differentiates American justice from justice in the Philippines, where an emphasis on "smooth interpersonal relationships" governs most social relationships. Likewise, the justice promised to the "good thief" in Luke 23:43 is very different from the justice Aristotle would have accorded him, since Jesus does not demand retribution but simply assures him a place in God's kingdom.

We shall see in the next chapter the primacy of love in Scripture, and to that extent we now simply acknowledge love as a distinctive Christian virtue. Here we want, instead, to propose three other virtues that emerge from the Sermon on the Mount as specifically Christian virtues: mercy, a reconciling spirit, and hope. By "specific" we do not mean that they are not practiced by non-Christian people. Rather, we mean that the Christian tradition promotes several virtues, and these are prominent among them. Finally, we need to recognize that the sermon promotes a great variety of virtues, for instance, vigilance against false prophets (see Matthew 7:15). But we choose these three because they enjoy a certain priority in Scripture.

Mercy: We saw earlier the enormous influence of the Good Samaritan parable (see Luke 10:25–37) in presenting at once the mercy of Jesus that we have already received and the mercy that, in turn, we are called as neighbor to practice. Likewise in Matthew's Gospel, judgment is rendered solely on the basis of the works of mercy; no other virtuous practice is required to enter the kingdom of God (see 25:31–46). Mercy occurs in the Sermon on the Mount as well. In the sermon, mercy appears often with reference to the nature of God who gives the kingdom to the poor in spirit (see 5:3), comforts those who mourn (see 5:4), takes care of all of our needs (see 6:25–33), and gives us all good gifts (see 7:11–12). Mercy is also a virtue for those who follow Christ. It is, for example, at the heart of the beatitudes (see 5:7). It implicitly recurs in the statement on judgment: The judgment of mercy that we render unto others in turn will be rendered unto us (see 7:1–2). Mercy is the righteousness that we hunger for (see 5:6), that distinguishes our righteousness from that of the scribes and Pharisees (see 5:17–20), and that motivates us to respond to those in need (see 5:42).

Mercy pervades Scripture. God's covenant with us is dominated by one fundamental disposition: *hesed* or mercy. Mercy appears often in the Gospel of Luke, not only in the Good Samaritan parable but also in the triple parables of rescuing the lost coin, sheep, and son (see 5:1–32). Likewise it characterizes Jesus' stance to the sinful woman (see 7:36–50), Zacchaeus (see 19:1–10), and the good thief (see 23:39–43). Not surprisingly, then, Luke exhorts us to be merciful as our heavenly Father is merciful (see 6:36).

In the *Summa Theologiae* Thomas Aquinas asks whether mercy is the greatest of the virtues.[4] He responds by writing: "Mercy is accounted as being proper to God and therein His omnipotence is declared to be chiefly manifested." Although charity is the greatest virtue when we consider that it unites us to God, still "of all the virtues that relate to our neighbor, mercy is the greatest." In fact, regarding actual activity, Aquinas writes that "the sum total of the Christian religion consists in mercy."

A reconciling spirit: A reconciling spirit is extraordinarily visible in the Sermon on the Mount. It appears among the peacemakers (see Matthew 5:9), at worship (see 5:23–24), on the way to court (see 5:25), in reinterpreting the *lex talonis*, or the law of retaliation (see 5:38–41), in love of enemy (see 5:43–48), and in the Our Father (see 6:12).

We saw earlier that forgiveness is integral to community life. The reconciling spirit that brought us into the kingdom is the same spirit that helps us remain within it. Thus, Paul makes reconciliation the hallmark activity of Jesus' life. By Jesus we are reconciled to God (see Romans 5:1, 10–11; Colossians 1:20–21; 2 Corinthians 5:18–20), and in turn we are called to be ambassadors of reconciliation (see 2 Corinthians 5:20–21).

Hope: Finally, hope is present throughout the Sermon on the Mount, for in many ways it is the foundation by which we are called to understand the sermon. Hope grounds the beatitudes. Our happiness can only be felt in our hope (see Matthew 5:1–12). Likewise, hope animates us to trust that our almsgiving and other good deeds, prayer, and fasting are seen by God alone (see 6:2–4, 5–6, 16–18). Hope allows us to seek treasures in heaven rather than on earth (see 6:10, 19–21), to believe in God's providence (see 6:25–34), and to ask for whatever we need (see 7:7–12).

Inasmuch as human flourishment is in the kingdom of God, as an end that is here though not yet fully realized, then Christians necessarily live in hope. Hope is the virtue that allows us to walk or run on the way of the Lord, for without hope we could not be Christians. "In hope we were saved," says Paul (Romans 8:24; 1 Corinthians 2:9; 2 Corinthians 5:7).

Together with love, these three virtues—mercy, reconciliation, and hope—characterize Christian virtue ethics. We shall apply these virtues to many of the concerns that we raise later in this work. Here we see that they provide an image or profile for those persons who are called to belong to the community of Jesus' disciples. But in keeping with the overall theme of this chapter, they are first attributes of the one in whose image we are made and through whom we are saved. By mercy and in hope we were reconciled through and in Christ.

Questions for Reflection and Discussion

1. What are key features in Scripture that highlight for you the relevance of virtue ethics?

2. Mention certain features in Mark's or Luke's Gospel that might highlight a correlation with virtue ethics.

3. Aside from mercy, a reconciling spirit, and hope, what other virtues would you propose as specifically or characteristically Christian? Why?

Notes

1. Alasdair MacIntyre, *After Virtue: A Study in Moral Theory* (Notre Dame, IN: Notre Dame University Press, 1981).

2. See Thomas Aquinas, *Summa Theologiae*, I–II. 1.2 ad 3; 57. 4c.

3. Joseph Kotva, *The Christian Case for Virtue Ethics* (Washington, D.C.: Georgetown University Press, 1996), p. 129.

4. See Thomas Aquinas, op. cit., II.II. 30.4.

Select Bibliography

Allison, Dale C. *The Sermon on the Mount: Inspiring the Moral Imagination.* Minneapolis: Fortress, 1999.

Betz, Hans D. *The Sermon on the Mount.* Minneapolis: Fortress, 1995.

Cahill, Lisa Sowle. "The Bible and Christian Moral Practices." In Cahill and James F. Childress (eds.), *Christian Ethics: Problems and Prospects.* Cleveland: Pilgrim Press, 1996, pp. 3–17.

Carter, Warren. *What Are They Saying about Matthew's Sermon on the Mount?* New York: Paulist, 1994.

Connors, Russell B. and Patrick T. McCormick. *Character, Choices and Community.* New York: Paulist, 1998.

Curran, Charles and Richard McCormick (eds.). *The Use of Scripture in Moral Theology.* New York: Paulist Press, 1984.

Hall, Pamela. *Narrative and the Natural Law: An Interpretation of Thomistic Ethics.* Notre Dame, IN: University of Notre Dame Press, 1994.

Harrington, Daniel J. "The Sermon on the Mount—What Is It?" *Bible Today* 36/6 (1998), pp. 280–286.

Jung, Patricia Beattie. "Sanctification: An Interpretation in Light of Embodiment." *Journal of Religious Ethics* 11 (1983), pp. 75–94.

Keenan, James F. "Proposing Cardinal Virtues." *Theological Studies* 56 (1995), pp. 709–729.

_____. "Virtue Ethics." In Bernard Hoose (ed.), *Christian Ethics.* London: Cassell, 1998, pp. 84–94.

_____. "Virtue and Identity." *Concilium* 2000/2, pp. 69–77.

Kotva, Joseph. *The Christian Case for Virtue Ethics.* Washington, D.C.: Georgetown University Press, 1996.

Lambrecht, Jan. *The Sermon on the Mount: Proclamation and Exhortation.* Wilmington: Glazier, 1985.

McGinn, Bernard. "The Human Person as Image of God." In Bernard McGinn and John Meyendorff (eds.), *Christian Spirituality.* New York: Crossroad, 1985, pp. 312–330.

Patrick, Anne. "Narrative and the Social Dynamic of Virtue." In Dietmar Mieth and Jacques Pohier (eds.), *Changing Values and Virtues.* Edinburgh: T & T Clark, 1987, pp. 69–80.

Swinburne, Richard. *Responsibility and Atonement.* Oxford: Oxford University Press, 1989.

Verhey, Allen. "Scripture and Ethics: Practices, Performances and Prescriptions." *Christian Ethics: Problems and Prospects*, pp. 18–44.

Chapter Six

LOVE AS THE PRIMARY VIRTUE

Having answered in part each of MacIntyre's three questions (Who are we? What do we want to become? and How do we get there?), we can now elaborate some specific moral concerns, beginning with the love command. Harrington notes that in the Bible, love is not so much an ethical principle as it is a response to the experience of God's love for us. Therefore, throughout the New Testament, we see love as the foundation for our relationships with God and with neighbor. God's love makes these relationships possible.

Keenan describes how ethicists and moral theologians have looked to find that which first motivates all subsequent moral dispositions. He turns then to Gerard Gilleman who named charity as the Christian's fundamental source for all subsequent morality. Keenan concludes by reflecting on the threefold love of God, neighbor, and self.

BIBLICAL PERSPECTIVES
D. J. Harrington

As Creator and Lord, as Yahweh the God of Israel, and as the Father of our Lord Jesus Christ, the God of the Bible is the origin, source, and goal of love. The proper response to God's love for us according to Jesus' double love commandment is to love God and to love one's neighbor. According to Jesus, the term *neighbor* is broad enough to include even enemies.

LOVE OF GOD AND NEIGHBOR
(Matthew 22:34–40)

34. When the Pharisees heard that he had silenced the Sadducees, they gathered together, 35. and one of them, a lawyer, asked him

a question to test him. 36. "Teacher, which commandment in the law is the greatest?" 37. He said to them, "'You shall love the Lord your God with all your heart, and with all your soul, and with all your mind.' 38. This is the greatest and first commandment. 39. And a second is like it: 'You shall love your neighbor as yourself.' 40. On these two commandments hang all the law and the prophets."

The pericope about the double love commandment—love God and love the neighbor—appears in somewhat different forms in Matthew 22:34–40; Mark 12:28–34; and Luke 10:25–28. The historical context for Jesus' teaching is the question about the greatest commandment in the Jewish Law (Torah). The rabbis counted 613 commandments—248 positive ("You shall . . .") and 365 negative ("You shall not . . .")—in the first five books of the Hebrew Bible. Some teachers distinguished between "heavy" (serious) and "light" (not so serious) commandments, while others sought the one commandment that might provide the key for perfect observance of all the others.

When asked for a short summary of the Torah (to be given while standing on one foot), Shammai, a famous Jewish teacher of Jesus' time, refused to answer what he apparently regarded as a foolish request. However, his rival, Hillel, replied: "What is harmful for you, do not do to your neighbor; that is the whole Torah, while the rest is commentary; go and learn it."[1] Hillel's response is close to Jesus' Golden Rule (see Matthew 7:12; Luke 6:31) and because of its negative formulation, it is sometimes called the "Silver Rule."

The shortest and least complicated version of Jesus' double love commandment appears in Matthew 22:34–40. The literary context (taken over from Mark) is the final series of controversies in Jerusalem shortly before Jesus' death. Unlike Mark, Matthew presents this episode as a hostile confrontation. The Matthean version very likely reflects the hostility between Matthew's Jewish-Christian community and certain other Jews around A.D. 90 as they competed for spiritual leadership among Jews after the destruction of Jerusalem and its Temple in A.D. 70. The opponents are identified in 22:34 as "Pharisees," who were at least in part the spiritual progenitors of Matthew's rivals. Their spokesman is a "lawyer," an expert in the Jewish Law or Torah. The reason for his question is to "test" Jesus (see 22:35).

Jesus' answer to the lawyer's question in Matthew 22:36 ("Which commandment in the law is the greatest?") is thoroughly biblical and orthodox. Unlike Hillel, Jesus offers as his response two Old Testament quotations, indeed two of the 613 laws in the Torah.

The first quotation (see Matthew 22:37) is from Deuteronomy 6:5:

"You shall love the Lord your God with all your heart, and with all your soul, and with all your mind." This text was (and still is) part of the Jewish daily prayer known as the Shema ("Hear, O Israel"), and so was among the most familiar biblical passages to Jews in Jesus' time. The commandment to love God with the whole of one's being is labeled "the greatest and first commandment" (22:38).

The second quotation (see Matthew 22:39) is from Leviticus 19:18: "You shall love your neighbor as yourself." This is part of the Holiness Code in Leviticus 18–20. The assumption behind it is that humans naturally love themselves, certainly to the extent that they seek to preserve their lives and to find happiness (however they may define it). The challenge is to show the same kind of concern for others. Another problem comes in defining who the neighbor is (see Luke 10:29).

Matthew's version of the double love commandment ends in 22:40 with a statement that fits well in his Jewish-Christian context: "On these two commandments hang all the law and the prophets" (22:40). In his polemical context the Evangelist affirms Jesus' double love commandment as Jesus' authoritative pronouncement on observing God's will as revealed in the Torah. It is part of Jesus' program announced in Matthew 5:17: "I have come not to abolish but to fulfill." The idea is that the remaining 611 commandments depend ("hang") upon the two love commandments, and that those who observe them will do everything that God wills. Matthew's theme of Jesus as God's authoritative interpreter of the Torah began with the Sermon on the Mount (see chapters 5–7) and reaches its climax in Jesus' next-to-last controversy in Jerusalem. Jesus' double love commandment provides the key to understanding God's will and to living in accord with it.

OTHER VERSIONS

While the content of Jesus' double love commandment remains the same, the settings in Mark 12:28–34 and Luke 10:25–28 are different. In Mark 12:28–34, a scribe asks the question in a respectful manner (see 12:28), makes Jesus' answer his own (see 12:32-33a), takes it a step further by observing that love of God and love of neighbor are more important than the sacrificial system (see 12:33b), and wins high praise from Jesus ("You are not far from the kingdom of God," 12:34). The Markan version is more a scholastic dialogue than a controversy. Nevertheless, it is part of the block of passages in Mark 11–12 that describe growing opposition to Jesus in Jerusalem during Holy Week.

The Lukan version (see 10:25–28) appears early in the long Journey Narrative (see 9:51–19:44). Here a lawyer asks Jesus a more general question: "What must I do to inherit eternal life?" When Jesus challenges the lawyer to answer his own question in light of the Scriptures, he does so in the form of Deuteronomy 6:5 and Leviticus 19:18, taken as one commandment (see 10:27). Jesus in turn (see 10:28) approves the lawyer's response ("You have given the right answer") and challenges him to put it into practice: "Do this, and you will live."

LOVE OF ENEMIES

It is said that wise lawyers do not ask questions to which they do not already know the answers. But the lawyer in Luke 10:29 asks: "And who is my neighbor?" His question prompts Jesus' parable of the Good Samaritan (see 10:30–35) in which a Jew, beaten and left for dead by the road between Jerusalem and Jericho, is ignored first by a Jewish priest and then by a Levite (an assistant to the temple priests). What looks like an anticlerical tale in which it is expected that the helper will be a Jewish layman takes a surprising twist when the helper turns out to be a Samaritan—someone whose Jewishness was suspect and who was regarded as naturally inferior and threatening to Judeans and Galileans. When Jesus asks about who proved to be a neighbor to the injured man, the lawyer is forced to answer, "The one who showed him mercy" (see 10:37a).

The assumption is that if you as a listener were to identify yourself with the injured man by the roadside, you would not refuse help from any quarter, even from a Samaritan. People in desperate situations quickly shed their prejudices and are willing to regard as their neighbor anyone who is willing to offer help. Thus, Jesus forces the lawyer to broaden his definition of "neighbor" to include persons outside his narrow ethnic and social parameters. Indeed, the compassion that the Samaritan displays toward the Jewish stranger is presented to the lawyer as an example to be imitated: "Go and do likewise" (10:37b).

Perhaps the most difficult and challenging element in Jesus' ethical teaching concerns love of enemies: "Love your enemies, do good to those who hate you, bless those who curse you, pray for those who abuse you" (Luke 6:27–28; see Matthew 5:44). To illustrate what this principle might involve, Jesus offers four examples: turning the other cheek when struck; giving up your shirt when your coat is taken; going a second mile when forced to go one mile; and giving to all who beg from you (see Luke 6:29–30; Matthew 5:39–42). These are extreme cases in which love of enemies might be practiced. What is recommended is not passivity in the face of evil but rather nonviolent resistance ("Do not resist in kind, violently"; see Matthew 5:39a) used so effectively in the twentieth century by Mohandas Gandhi and Martin Luther King, Jr. The goal is to break the cycle of hatred and violence, and to make possible a new set of human relationships in which former enemies might become neighbors. In this context, love of enemies may be an effective sociopolitical strategy (restorative or redemptive justice). There is, however, no guarantee of its practical success.

Jesus' teaching about love of enemies is also associated with the Golden Rule: "Do to others as you would have them do to you" (Luke 6:31; see Matthew 7:12). As Hillel's response to the question about the greatest commandment shows, this ethical principle is not unique to Jesus. Indeed, Immanuel Kant used it as the basis for his ethics of duty (deontology) and his categorical imperative: one must do only what one can will that all others should do under similar circumstances. Its humanistic value is illustrated in Luke 6:37–38 by various examples: "Do not judge, and you will not be judged . . . give and it will be given to you." The Golden Rule is founded ultimately on reciprocity and mutual self-interest. If everyone acted according to the Golden Rule, human society would presumably function very well and to the benefit of every individual.

Love of enemies may require an even higher ethical stance or principle than nonviolent resistance and the Golden Rule. That higher morality involves the imitation of God: "Be merciful, just as your Father is merciful" (Luke 6:36); and "Be perfect, therefore, as your heavenly Father is perfect" (Matthew 5:48). God cares for both the good and the evil, for both the righteous and the unrighteous. God's love extends even to the enemies of God. The highest form of love goes beyond human self-interest and reciprocity ("Do not even the Gentiles do the same?") and takes the example of God's superabundant love as its model and criterion. Paradoxically such extravagant and unbounded love is promised as the greatest reward: closeness to God. Those who love their enemies and expect nothing in return will find themselves to be "children of the Most High, for he is kind to the ungrateful and the wicked" (Luke 6:35).

THEOLOGICAL SIGNIFICANCE

In the Bible, love is not so much an ethical principle as it is a response to the experience of God's love for us. The closest thing to a definition of God in the Old Testament appears in Exodus 34:6: "A God merciful and gracious, slow to anger, and abounding in steadfast love and faithfulness." And the New Testament stresses God's love for us revealed in Jesus: "In this is love, not that we have loved God but that he has loved us and sent his Son to be the atoning sacrifice for our sins" (1 John 4:10). The persistent message of the Bible is that God has loved us first, and the proper response to God's love for us is to love God and to love the neighbor.

In this theological framework it is possible to describe love not as one virtue among many others but as "the bond of perfection" as in Colossians 3:14: "Above all, clothe yourselves with love, which binds everything together in perfect harmony." Love embraces and holds together all the other virtues. So Paul in his marvelous description of love in 1 Corinthians 13 gives love pride of place among the charisms and ranks it as superior even to faith and hope: " . . . and the greatest of these is love" (13:13). And in his "ethical" advice to the Romans, Paul declares that "the one who loves another has fulfilled the law" (Romans 13:8), and gives as his reason that "love does no wrong to a neighbor; therefore, love is the fulfilling of the law" (13:10).

MORAL THEOLOGICAL REFLECTIONS
J. F. Keenan

In his work on the love command, New Testament exegete Victor Furnish examines the deeply interior role that this command plays in Christian ethics. On the spectrum between the depths of a person and the external actions that one does, Furnish locates the claim of the love command at the most fundamental stage of a person's moral development; that is, as foundational and prior to any other command or disposition.

AIMING TO UNDERSTAND
THE FUNDAMENTAL MOTIVATION

The philosopher-ethicist Stephen Toulmin explains this foundational point of departure for the moral life by calling it the "limiting question"; that is, the question that when answered, yields no other question. Think, for instance, if we were to ask you, "Why are you reading this book?" You might give the answer, "Because I thought it might be interesting." Then we could ask you, "But why did you think you would find it interesting?" You might answer, "Because I am attracted to New Testament studies." Then we still could ask, "But why are you attracted to New Testament studies?" You might respond with yet another answer that discloses an even deeper desire that motivated you toward the action that you performed. And yet we still could ask you "why" again, and you might answer with yet an even deeper disclosure, and so forth. Eventually our "why" questions would lead you to encountering the limiting question, the question that answers all the other "why" questions, the foundational question that explains or motivates you to pursue the variety of your life's activities.

Of course, we could ask those "why" questions for quite a long time before we would reach the limiting question. Moreover, as you try earnestly to provide another, deeper disclosure of yet an even deeper inclination, your ability to articulate those motivating desires might become progressively more difficult, simply because you would be revealing the deepest dimensions of your spirit. When (and if!) we got to the limiting question and you responded with the final answer, inevitably we would realize that we had arrived at a very profound revelation about yourself that would hopefully prompt not another "why" but rather a respectful silence.

That limiting question is then extraordinarily distinctive, since it provides an explanation for the foundation of our moral lives. The answer to this limiting question reveals our most basic moral orientation, what we have heard described as the "fundamental option" or what the Germans call the *Urentscheidung*. When the Germans use *Ur* as a prefix to a word they mean it to be the absolutely first or primary or original expression of the word. For instance, *Urinstinkt* would be a person's most fundamental instinct just as *Urheimat* would be one's original homeland. Inasmuch as *Entscheidung* means decision, an *Urentscheidung* means a decision that is the foundation of all other decisions. It is the very ground to our way of proceeding, and it is prior to every other motivation.

In scholastic Latin we find the same type of expression when we talk about the last "end" (*finis*) out of which we act. As we saw in the third chapter, Thomas Aquinas helps us to recognize that we each have only one last end and that is the foundational motivation out of which we each act. The last end can be ourselves or God or family or money or power and so on. But inevitably there is one last end or fundamental concern that is foundational to all others.

GERARD GILLEMAN
AND THE PRIMACY OF CHARITY

In the middle of the twentieth century, moral theologians made a decisive move by recognizing charity as the appropriate last end for Roman Catholic ethics. This was predominantly based upon the research of Gerard Gilleman, a French Jesuit moral theologian teaching in India, whose dissertation was later published as *The Primacy of Charity in Moral Theology*.[2] Through Gilleman's work, charity became recognized again as the point of departure for all of Catholic morality.

Gilleman was not looking to make new assertions. Rather, he was interested in acknowledging that biblical and traditional claims to the primacy of charity ought to be made similarly for moral theology. By attempting to recover charity from the writings of Thomas Aquinas, Gilleman wanted to show that moral theology was primarily about the interior life. Thus, his work deals with the deeper desires that we have for interior fulfillment.

By pursuing charity, Gilleman brought us to the deepest and yet most animating level of Christian life, for charity is not only the last end, the limiting question, the fundamental option, but it is also that which thrusts us into the center of things. Because of charity, we love God, neighbor, and self. Charity is then the constitutive mover for all the activities of the righteous.

With this charity-based ethics, Gilleman argued that the human person has a profound spiritual tendency and that profound spiritual tendency is charity-love. The moral action seeks to mediate that tendency. But the tendency reveals to us just how deep the source of our moving, our craving, our deepest desires, actually is. It is an ever operating actuation.

This tendency is infused by charity—that is, as a gift from God. The gift from God alone establishes our union with God. Of course, that union or love cannot be fully realized in this life, and that inability to realize it fully is not unlike our own predicament as disciples for a kingdom that is also not yet fully realized or realizable.

By being in union with God, this love of God constitutes us more than even our love for ourselves. This union with God becomes the principle of our communion with others. God not only calls us, then, to love God. But by charity God effects our union with God, ourselves, and all others. Through charity, God makes all things possible. This gift is then grace itself or, as Thomas Aquinas states so clearly, no less than the divinity itself living in us (*Ipsa essentia divina caritas est*).[3]

In Thomas Aquinas's writings we find charity described in a variety of different ways. For the moment we will look at only two. First he calls charity the "mother" of the virtues, and writes that "charity is called mother because she conceives within herself from another, and here hungering for the last end, she conceives the acts of other virtues by commanding them."[4] Here Aquinas captures the deeply generative function of charity as animating all successive acts of virtue.

Aquinas also uses the "heart" to convey charity. Thus, the commandment from Deuteronomy 6:5 becomes pivotal: "Love the Lord your God with your whole heart." Aquinas cites it to affirm our call to love God completely, to argue that God is loved as the end in loving one's neighbor, and to indicate the totality by which God is loved.[5]

For Aquinas then, we are divinized by charity. We are not simply commanded to love. We are given the possibility to love, and we are given that possibility in the deepest, most animating dimensions of our personhood.

Together with the work of Fritz Tillmann, Gilleman's study of Thomas Aquinas gave Catholic moral theology a stronger scriptural foundation and by doing so, a reason to explore and develop the interior moral life.

While Furnish, like Gilleman, describes the love command as prior to all other commands, Furnish joins Gilleman in insisting nonetheless that the love command has an immediate effect on our lives. Furnish does not let love stand as one command among others; rather, he regards it as foundational to all *and* yet he still wants it to emerge from the depths of our lives to express itself in the concrete and the ordinary.

A THREEFOLD LOVE

The love command calls us to express love on three fronts (God, self, neighbor), with the first being a concrete manifestation of our love for God. Rightly, in theology, this love, the love of God, supersedes all other realities. For instance, love expresses our understanding of God, for God is love (see 1 John 4:8). Moreover, because God is love, God needs to express that love within God's self and therefore needs to be triune. Because of that love, moreover, God loves more than God's self and so God desires creation. God wills into being new participants for the love of God. Furthermore, John tells us that our redemption is based on this love, for God so loved the world (see John 3:16). Love of God is also the foundation of our sanctification which is to love God, ourselves, and our neighbor. Our deliverance, too, is completely aimed at our ultimate union with God. All of theology depends, therefore, fundamentally on the love of God.

This love of God cannot be understood as an abstract foundation to the moral life. Both Gilleman and Furnish make clear that our love of God must be immediate, actualized, and expressed. For this reason the love of God is the first commandment of the Decalogue. In understanding the Ten Commandments, we never can underestimate the centrality of the first commandment, which is not an abstraction but rather the first of ten very specific commands about living our lives. The first commandment insists on the sovereignty of God as the foundation of our own well being.

Moreover, we need to see that the Decalogue is not something imposed on us for God's pleasure, but rather it is there for our benefit, for our flourishment. By insisting on God's sovereignty, the first commandment makes our dependency on God the very foundation of our happiness.

Jesuit moral theologian Edward Vacek takes the love of God further.[6] He insists that inevitably every human being must respond to God's command. He argues that the only way we can understand this command is that it is the foundation of everyone's well being and that the commandment to love God cannot be restricted only to those who are believers in God. Nor will he accept the so-called *anonymous Christian* solution (the title given by some Christian theologians to those non-Christians who seem to act in ways that are consistent with the principles of Christianity) that basically claims that by loving our neighbor we implicitly love God, even if we do not acknowledge (or if in fact we deny) the existence of God. Rather, Vacek insists that the love of God is the root and guarantor of the happiness of all humanity.

Vacek's claim means that nonbelievers are not necessarily bad, but rather they are wrong. Although they heed their consciences, they are still in error. By their error about God, they remain incomplete in understanding what ultimately constitutes human happiness (see Romans 1:18–32 for Paul's elaboration of the same idea).

Finally, we cannot lose sight of the fact that we encounter the love of God in what God effects or accomplishes in us. The love of God is not an idea or concept, but a reality that dwells in us. We encounter the love of God not first as a task or as a commandment, but as a gift. God accomplishes God's love in us, as we have seen, in the depths of our being. This is the reality and the place where we begin moral theology: the love of God dwelling in us as gift and therein needing to be realized in our lives. For just as that love was in Jesus of Nazareth and was realized in him, no less are we in his image called to realize that same love by which Jesus calls us his brothers and sisters and God our father and mother.

While we recognize the priority of the love of God, we are also commanded to love our neighbors. Essential to understanding this command is that we love our neighbors not as objects of our devotion, but rather as subjects; that is, as persons. Thus, we cannot love others only because God wants us to do so, since then we would love them as means or as objects and not as persons. We can only love one another as subjects, just as God loves us.

This notion of subject helps us to understand further the Good Samaritan parable (see Luke 10:25–37). We have already seen that many look at the parable and think that the neighbor in the parable is only the wounded man. In fact, most preachers have unfortunately translated the parable in just this way by calling us to respond to our neighbor in need. But Jesus specifically asks us who the neighbor is so as to elicit the response, "The one who showed mercy." Love of neighbor calls us not to love someone in need as much as it calls us to be neighbor. The parable is not a definition of the neighbor as the object of neighborly love, but rather the turning of the question to the subject of neighborly love.

How broadly must we construe our neighbor? Paul Ricoeur, a French philosopher with a strong interest in biblical interpretation, suggests that we can only understand the Golden Rule through the command to love the enemy.[7] We can only grasp that perspective, however, when we first understand ourselves as loved by God *when* we were still sinners (see Romans 5:8). From that perspective we understand ourselves as reconciled to God precisely when we were estranged. From that perspective of gift, from what Ricoeur calls the "economy of gift," we are called to participate in the love of God which is ultimately reconciling. The command to love our enemy is the ultimate decree that brings down every boundary.

For Ricoeur, the love of enemies transforms the logic of equivalence, which so often dominates our ethical thought, into the logic of the economy of gift. The command basically insists that we become reconciled and that we love no one as enemy.

Again we need to see this command first as effective. It can only be grasped when we first understand that Christ has reconciled ourselves to God and that the call to reconciliation is a grace-filled extension of the presence of God in our lives. God effectively makes us ambassadors of reconciliation (see 2 Corinthians 5:18–21), and as ambassadors we are then evidently called to love our enemies as subjects and not as enemies.

In a manner of speaking, the love commandment has, then, many of the same characteristics of the kingdom itself and rightly so, since effectively love and the kingdom are the same last end. Like the kingdom, the love command is realized already by the presence of charity dwelling in us. But it seeks its realization in our love for God and neighbor, a love that in itself will always lead us forward until that love is fully realized in the kingdom. Our limited condition keeps us, however, from being able to love God or humanity absolutely. But the command keeps that call to love always on the horizon of our expectations. It can only remain on that horizon, however, to the extent that we seek its constant realization regardless of our limitations. In a manner of speaking, then, to the extent that we love God and neighbor, to that extent we transcend the very limits of our situation.

Here, then, we begin to understand better what love of self really is. Love of self is loving how it is that God loves us. Love of self is recognizing, then, that God's love for us is very specific and very precious, and that God recognizes us individually as lovable. God's love for us is again the effective love for our love for ourselves. Like the other loves, it is quite clearly called to be realized in tangible expressions of ordinary life. And like the other loves, the love of self is at once realized and yet always an outstanding command. In this way, the love command only has meaning for those who stand in hope.

Similarly it is a reconciling love. Anyone with even the most modest self-understanding would recognize how fundamentally conflicted we are. No less than Paul testifies to this (see Romans 7:7–25). And therefore we must see the love of self as an ongoing reconciliation, of trying to bring together the many ways in which all of us live fragmented lives.

Likewise the love of self is also an act of mercy, because by love of self we become, like the Good Samaritan, willing to enter into the chaos of our own lives. Here then we realize why Jesus calls us to remove the beam from our own eyes (see Matthew 7:5). Jesus recognizes the chaos that rules our lives. By commanding us to love ourselves, however, he motivates and makes possible the merciful disposition to face our own chaotic lives and the reconciling attitude of bringing those lives into a more grace-filled balance.

These movements are only made possible by the initial love of God who makes all things possible. And therein we see that all three loves—of God, neighbor, and self—are fundamentally cooperative with the movement of God, who creates, redeems, sanctifies, and delivers us. It is in this way that we understand the love command then as the summation of the whole Law (see Romans 13:8).

Questions for Reflection and Discussion

1. How does the love of God find concrete expression in your life?

2. What does love of enemies mean specifically in terms of the way you live your life?

3. How would you explain the love of self to a group of high school students?

Notes

1. *Babylonian Talmud Shabbat*, 31a.

2. Gerard Gilleman, *The Primacy of Charity in Moral Theology* (Westminster, MD: Newman Press, 1959).

3. Thomas Aquinas, *Summa Theologiae*, II.II.23.2 ad 1.

4. Ibid., II.II.23.8 ad 3.

5. Ibid., II.II.44.5c.

6. Edward E. Vacek, "The Eclipse of Love for God," *America* (March 9, 1996), pp. 13–16.

7. Paul Ricoeur, "The Golden Rule: Exegetical and Theological Perspectives," *New Testament Studies* 36 (1990), pp. 392–397.

Select Bibliography

Dianich, Severino. *L'Opzione Fondamentale nel Pensiero di S. Tommaso.* Rome: Gregorian University Dissertation, 1968.

Fuller, Reginald H. (ed.). *Essays on the Love Commandment.* Philadelphia: Fortress, 1978.

Furnish, Victor P. *The Love Command in the New Testament.* New York: Abingdon Press, 1972.

Gilleman, Gerard. *The Primacy of Charity in Moral Theology.* Westminster, MD: Newman Press, 1959.

Keenan, James F. *Commandments of Compassion.* Franklin, WI: Sheed & Ward, 1999.

Kinerk, Edward. "Eliciting Great Desires." *Studies in the Spirituality of the Jesuits* 16 (1984).

Marshall, Christopher D. *Beyond Retribution: A New Testament Vision for Justice, Crime and Punishment.* Grand Rapids: Eerdmans, 2001.

Outka, Gene. *Agape: An Ethical Analysis.* New Haven: Yale University Press, 1973.

Perkins, Pheme. *Love Commands in the New Testament.* New York: Paulist, 1982.

Piper, John. *Love your enemies: Jesus' Love Command in the Synoptic Gospels and in Early Christian Paraenesis.* Cambridge, UK: Cambridge University Press, 1979.

Pope, Stephen. "Expressive Individualism and True Self-Love: A Thomistic Perspective." *Journal of Religion* 71 (1991), pp. 384–399.

Reiser, Marius. "Love of Enemies in the Context of Antiquity." *New Testament Studies* 47 (2001), pp. 411–427.

Ricoeur, Paul. "The Golden Rule. Exegetical and Theological Perspectives." *New Testament Studies* 36 (1990), pp. 392–397.

Spicq, Ceslas. *Agape in the New Testament.* St. Louis-London: Herder, 1963–1966.

Toulmin, Stephen. *An Examination of the Place of Reason in Ethics.* Cambridge, UK: Cambridge University Press, 1950.

Vacek, Edward C. "The Eclipse of Love for God." *America* (March 9, 1996), pp. 13–16.

_____. *Love, Human and Divine.* Washington, D.C.: Georgetown University Press, 1994.

Willimon, William. "The Preacher and the Virtue of Forgiveness." *Practice What You Preach*, pp. 157–169.

Wink, Walter. "Beyond Just War and Pacifism: Jesus' Nonviolent Way." *Review & Expositor* 89 (1992), pp. 197–214.

Chapter Seven

SIN AS FAILURE TO LOVE

I n movies and television programs, the word *sin* is rarely uttered. And when it is, it is often on the lips of fanatics or crazy persons. Even sincerely religious people today prefer to call someone "sick" rather than "a sinner." For many people today, sin is not an operative category.

As Harrington shows, however, the Bible is rich and comprehensive in its approach to sin and moral responsibility. The Bible recognizes the reality of sin and faces its consequences. In the history of Christian moral theology, as Keenan observes, there has been an unfortunate tendency to truncate the biblical doctrine of sin and to become preoccupied with categorizing sinful actions and delineating the areas in which real sins occur. With respect to sin, the Scriptures provide moral theology with a healthy corrective and a firm foundation. What emerges is the insight that at its root sin is a failure to love.

BIBLICAL PERSPECTIVES
D. J. Harrington

The Bible insists on sin as both a basic orientation and as evil actions, on individual responsibility and the social effects of "original sin," on the corporate and the individual dimensions of sin, and on punishment for sin in the present and in the future judgment.

WHAT DEFILES
(Mark 7:20–23)

20. And he [Jesus] said, "It is what comes out of a person that defiles. 21. For it is from within, from the human heart, that evil

intentions come: fornication, theft, murder, 22. adultery, avarice,
wickedness, deceit, licentiousness, envy, slander, pride, folly. 23.
All these things come from within, and they defile a person.

This list of vices appears at the end of the long discussion about ritual
purity and tradition in Mark 7:1–23. The passage criticizes the Pharisees
and scribes for presenting their traditions about handwashing as doctrines
from God (see 7:1–8), for allowing their teachings about offerings to God
(Corban—things offered to God) to override God's commandment about
honoring one's parents (see 7:9–13), and for placing ritual purity ahead of
moral purity (see 7:14–23). The point of Mark 7:20–23 is that moral purity
is more important than ritual purity. What comes out of a person is more
significant than what goes into a person's mouth and eventually goes out
into the sewer.

The short unit constituted by Mark 7:20–23 consists of a list of vices
(see 7:21–22) sandwiched between two general statements about the origin of sin (see 7:20, 23). The general statements echo what is regarded as
the key statement in Mark 7:1–23: "There is nothing outside a person that
by going in can defile, but the things that come out are what defile" (7:15).
From this statement Mark (and other early Christians) drew a radical conclusion: "Thus he [Jesus] declared all foods clean" (7:19). It is doubtful,
however, that Jesus himself went that far. Acts and Paul's letter to the
Galatians show that the topic of pure and impure foods was vigorously
debated among Christians long after Jesus' death.

The two general statements in the passage (see 7:20, 23) indicate that
moral evils come from within the person: "It is what comes out of a person
that defiles. . . . All these things come from within, and they defile a person."
Moreover, the list of vices is introduced by a statement that asserts: "For it
is from within, from the human heart, that evil intentions come" (7:21a). In
other words, sins proceed from a disordered inclination or disposition deep
within a person's heart. In the biblical concept of the human person, the
"heart" involves both understanding and emotion. It is analogous to our
use of "soul" to refer to the core or interior of the person.

While the disordered heart is the source of vices and sins within
humans, the list in Mark 7:21b–22 makes clear that there are evil actions
and dispositions that manifest the disordered heart. The list contains
twelve items. The first six items appear in the plural in Greek: "fornica-
tions, thefts, murders, adulteries, avarices, wickednesses." Some of these
items evoke the Ten Commandments, especially those that pertain to relations with other persons. The remaining six items appear in the singular:
"deceit, licentiousness, envy, slander, pride, folly." What is translated correctly as "envy" is literally "the evil eye," and what is rendered as "slander"

is literally "blasphemy." The list ends with "folly," which in the vocabulary of Jewish wisdom is the opposite of wisdom.

The list of vices in Mark 7:21b–22 establishes that evil actions and evil dispositions may proceed from and express an evil heart. At the same time, Mark 7:20–21a, 23 emphasizes that a person's heart or interior is the source of vices and sins, just as a good heart or interior is the source of virtues and good actions.

THE NATURE OF SIN

Mark 7:20–23 captures nicely the biblical dynamic of sin. In the Bible sin means abandoning the godly life for an evil way of life. It is a failure to love God, the neighbor, and the self. Conversely, repentance involves turning back to God and to a virtuous way of life under the guidance of the Holy Spirit. Individual sinful actions are symptomatic of a more general sinful orientation. In biblical language, a sinner misses the mark, transgresses, errs, wanders, rebels, refuses, profanes, and/or acts treacherously. A sinner is bad, worthless, twisted, and/or guilty.

Sin is failure to acknowledge and obey God as the only true Lord. Moreover, just as God's people Israel can violate its collective relationship with God, so individuals within God's people can do the same. Sin violates the relationship of the person or the community with God. This relationship is described in terms taken over from the covenant (see Exodus 19:4–6), the family (father and son, see Deuteronomy 8:5–6), and marriage (see Hosea 2:14–15). For Paul and John, "sin" may refer to a state of being in revolt against God and to an evil way of life. In Romans 5–7 Paul personifies Sin as a mythological power standing with Death and the Law over against Christ. One must decide whether one's lord will be Christ or Sin (along with Death and the Law).

At the same time, certain actions or tendencies are singled out as evils or vices in the New Testament. The epistles contain several lists of vices that are much like Mark 7:21b–22; Romans 1:29–31; 1 Corinthians 6:9–10; Galatians 5:19–21; 1 Timothy 1:9–10; and 2 Timothy 3:2–4. For example, in Galatians 5:19, Paul calls the vices "the works of the flesh"—what those who are under the power of Sin and so in "the flesh" do, as opposed to the virtuous behavior of those who are under the Holy Spirit (see Galatians 5:22–23). According to Galatians 5:19–21, "the works of the flesh" include "fornication, impurity, licentiousness, idolatry, sorcery, enmities, strife, jealousy, anger, quarrels, dissensions, factions, envy, drunkenness, carousing, and things like these."

There are similar lists of vices in the works of Greco-Roman moralists, Jewish writings contemporary with the New Testament (see Wisdom

14:25–26; 4 Maccabees 1:2–4; 1 Enoch 91:6–7; Jubilees 23:14), and the Dead Sea Scrolls. For example, the Qumran *Rule of the Community* 4:9–12 lists "the ways of the spirit of falsehood" as follows: "greed, and slackness in the search for righteousness, wickedness and lies, haughtiness and pride, falseness and deceit, cruelty and abundant evil, ill-temper and much folly and brazen insolence, abominable deeds (committed) in a spirit of lust, and ways of lewdness in the service of uncleanness, a blaspheming tongue, blindness of eye and dullness of ear, stiffness of neck and heaviness of heart."[1]

In the Old Testament, remedies for sin(s) are sought in returning to God and in God's mercy, as well as observing the Torah as the revelation of God's will. The system of sacrifices ("sin offerings") was concerned in large part with atoning or expiating for sins committed both consciously or unconsciously. According to the New Testament, the paschal mystery constituted by the life, death, and resurrection of Jesus is God's own effective remedy for sin(s). In Matthew 1:21, the name of Jesus is linked to his mission: "He will save his people from their sins." According to John 1:29, John the Baptist identifies Jesus as "the Lamb of God who takes away the sin of the world." And in Romans 8:3–4, Paul describes how, through Christ Jesus, God set humans free from the law of Sin and Death: "For God has done what the Law, weakened by the flesh, could not do: by sending his own Son in the likeness of sinful flesh, and to deal with sin, he condemned sin in the flesh, so that the just requirement of the Law might be fulfilled in us, who walk not according to the flesh but according to the Spirit."

THE ORIGIN OF SIN

Most biblical authors trace the origin of sin to something mysterious in the human heart (as in Mark 7:20–21a, 23). According to Genesis 6:5, "Every inclination of the thoughts of their [humankind's] hearts was only evil continually." This passage is the biblical basis for the concept of the "evil inclination" (*yeser hara*) that was very influential in Jewish rabbinic theology. The prophet Jeremiah observes that "the heart is devious above all else; it is perverse—who can understand it?" (Jeremiah 17:9). And Paul in his famous meditation on the human condition before and apart from Christ confesses: "I do not understand my own actions. For I do not do what I want, but I do the very thing I hate" (Romans 7:15).

The most famous and influential (at least in Christian circles) biblical effort at explaining the origin of sin is the story of the "fall" of Adam and Eve in Genesis 3—a brilliant depiction of the dynamics of sin and an explanation of how sin began and how people since Adam and Eve have suffered its effects. However, in the rest of the Old Testament there is surprisingly little mention about Adam's sin. Indeed some Jewish writings (see 1 Enoch 1–36) make the mating of "the sons of God" (understood as rebellious angels) with "the daughters of humans" in Genesis 6:1–4 the proper locus for original sin.

In Romans 5:12–19, Paul blames Adam for the entrance of sin into the world and works out an elaborate contrast between Adam's legacy of sin to all and Christ's offer of salvation to all. However, Paul attempts to balance the apparent determinism flowing from Adam's sin ("Therefore, just as sin came into the world through one man, and death came through sin, and so death spread to all," Romans 5:12a–c) with a stress on individual responsibility ("because all have sinned," 5:12d). The suggestion that all humans repeat the experience of Adam is a common theme in Jewish writings contemporary with the New Testament (see 4 Ezra 7:116–119; 2 Baruch 48:45–47; 54:15). Thus, the universal and individual dimensions of sin remain in some tension.

The "devil made me do it" explanation of sin as due to demonic forces (Satan, the devil, the tempter, the evil one) is not common in the Old Testament. The most dramatic example appears in Job 1–2 where Satan nevertheless is still a member of the heavenly court and acts as the "prosecuting attorney" under the divine permission. An interesting change occurs between a relatively early account and a later account of David's census. Whereas in 2 Samuel 24:1, "the anger of the Lord" incites David to count the people and so brings disaster upon Israel, according to 1 Chronicles 21:1, "Satan stood up against Israel, and incited David to count the people of Israel." Likewise, the New Testament, especially when compared with some contemporary Jewish writings with an apocalyptic bent, is rather slow to emphasize Satan or the devil as the origin of human sin (but see Mark 1:12–13 and parallels; John 8:44; 1 Peter 5:8; James 4:7).

SOCIAL SIN

In its early history, Israel was strongly influenced by a corporate notion of sin and guilt. Thus in Joshua 7, not only Achan but also his family and all his possessions are destroyed (see 7:24–26), because he had taken from the spoils of war dedicated to the Lord. The prophets proclaimed that the whole nation was a "people laden with iniquity" (Isaiah 1:4), not merely a few wicked individuals. Lamentations 5:7 explains the destruction of Jerusalem and the exile to Babylon as the result of the sins committed by past generations: "Our ancestors sinned; they are no more, and we bear their iniquities" (5:7). Indeed, the whole covenantal structure of ancient Israel's faith encourages individuals to view themselves as members of an elect people and to define their identities as parts of a collectivity.

Against such a communal understanding of sin and its deterministic assumption, the prophets Jeremiah (see Jeremiah 31:29–30) and Ezekiel (see Ezekiel 18; 33:10–20) contended that individuals are responsible for their own sins and not for the sins of others: "All shall die for their own sins" (Jeremiah 31:30). These two prophets of Israel's exile in the early sixth century B.C. emphasized that even though God's people would experience great calamities, individuals and the people as a whole could find hope in repenting and returning to God. This strand of prophetic thinking is prominent in Jesus' call to "sinners" to repent in the face of the coming kingdom of God (see Mark 1:14–15; Luke 15:1–32) and in the early church's willingness to accept "sinners" and Gentiles.

EFFECTS OF SIN

Sin initiates a series of evil consequences. Adam's sin not only issues in death for himself and all humans (see Genesis 3:19) but it also sets off a chain of other sins: Cain's murder of Abel (see 4:1–16), general human wickedness leading to the great flood (see 6:1–7:24), and the arrogance displayed in building the Tower of Babel (see 11:1–9). Only God's call to Abraham (see 12:1–3) to form a new people interrupts the cycle of sin and punishment. Likewise in Romans 1:18–32, Paul traces the degradation of the Gentile world back to its initial failure to recognize and acknowledge God in creation. The result is a world filled with vices: "wickedness, evil, covetousness, malice . . . envy, murder, strife" (Romans 1:29–31). Only the manifestation of God's righteousness in Christ can allow humans to make a new beginning in right relationship with God (see Romans 1:16–17; 3:21–26).

Sin may be punished in this life and/or in the final judgment. The Torah decrees capital punishment for heinous crimes, and the ultimate penalty for all human sins is death (see Genesis 3:19). God can use Israel's enemies as instruments for punishing the people's sins (see Isaiah 10:5–11). The last judgment represents God's final reckoning in vindicating the righteous and punishing the wicked (see Isaiah 24:21–23; Daniel 12:1–3; Matthew 25:31–46). Some biblical texts (see Job 15:17–35; John 5:14) assume a direct connection between sin and suffering, while others explicitly reject such a link (see Job as a whole; Luke 13:2–4; John 9:3). According to Paul, before and apart from Christ "all, both Jews and Greeks, are under the power of sin" (Romans 3:9). The great exception is Jesus (see 2 Corinthians 5:21; Hebrews 4:15; 7:26; 1 Peter 1:19; 2:22; 1 John 3:5).

MORAL THEOLOGICAL REFLECTIONS
J. F. Keenan

In his important work, *The Making of Moral Theology*, John Mahoney, a Jesuit moral theologian in Scotland, contends that the roots of moral theology are found in the penitential and confessional manuals from the sixth to the sixteenth century.[2] These manuals were designed to help priests in hearing penitents' confessions of sin. These manuals, then, were what most Christians understood moral theology to be. Later, in the seventeenth century, more complex moral manuals were established and, as we saw in the first chapter, these too were exclusively concerned with sin and "moral pathology."

BEING OBSESSED BUT IGNORANT ABOUT SIN

Mahoney argues that with such a focus on sin, moral theology became obsessed with sin. He adds that even though moral theology often reflected exclusively on what we should avoid as opposed to what we should pursue, nevertheless the theology of sin that we find implicitly within these manuals was extraordinarily poor.

Mahoney is especially concerned about the tradition's attempts to categorize our sinfulness into neat groupings of discreet individual actions. Our tradition has helped us to "manage" sin, to "isolate" it or "streamline" it into disposable descriptions that we can rattle off in a confessional. Mahoney rightly notes that these methods only indicate to what degree the tradition trivialized and domesticated sin.

Thomas Tentler, a church historian, describes the roots of our need to categorize neatly the state of our sinfulness.[3] Since Roman Catholicism insisted that we could not know with certitude that we were saved and since it was presumed that most people were damned (the damned masses or *massa damnata* was a common medieval and modern assumption), the only way Christians could find some comfort about the next life was by making an adequate confession that at least removed the reasons for their possible damnation. Facing judgment day, many Christians were left terribly anxious and, inasmuch as they could not know whether they were actually among the saved, at least they could regularly make good confessions so as to avoid grounds for damnation. A thorough confession was, then, an extraordinarily purgative experience. It not only allowed Christians the ability to fully examine themselves but also provided a tangible sense of relief from the ever-pressing anxiety that Christians felt about their eternal lives.

Tentler notes how Martin Luther recognized the significance of the confessional. With the other Protestant Reformers, Luther sought to eradicate its powerful consoling function. Wanting Christians to rely primarily on Christ and the cross, Luther preached that by faith we could know of our salvation. Likewise, he believed that the confessional manuals only perpetuated this misguided search for consolation, and so he publicly burned one of the most tedious and influential manuals of his day.

In response to the Reformers, modern Catholicism perpetuated the legacy of the confessional manuals but strangely never developed an adequate theology of sin. Instead, the notion of sin that began in the sixth-century penitential handbooks remained the prevalent expression of sin: a simple list, according to the seven deadly sins, of certain actions that we should not perform.

Today we need to develop a more foundational understanding of sin, and we need to turn to Scripture to develop such an adequate theology. There we should acknowledge first that few figures in the New Testament ever recognize their sinfulness. As a matter of fact, few ever know whether they are bad or good. Consider, for instance, the judgment scene of Matthew 25:31–46. Both the goats and the sheep are surprised by the judgment upon them. There is no indication by anyone in that scene as to whether they will be among the elect or the damned: "But when did we see you . . ." (Matthew 25:37, 44). In the pericope about the rich man and Lazarus (see Luke 16:19–31), the rich man is stunned by his damnation and becomes convinced that Abraham must inform his brothers lest they too end up in Hades. Similarly, the guest without the wedding garment (see Matthew 22:11-14) is completely surprised by his sudden removal from the wedding hall. Likewise, Jesus' observation about the Pharisee in the Temple thanking God for his not being like the tax collector (see Luke 18:10–14) is another ironic reminder that we really are quite ignorant of what God thinks of us. No less than the over-inflated self-understanding of Peter (see Mark 14:29–31) can serve as a legitimate icon to the Gospel's repeated depiction of humanity's drastic lack of knowledge of its own moral state. Only Jesus recognizes our profound ignorance as he utters his dying words, "Forgive them for they know not what they do" (Luke 23:34).

The Pervasiveness of Sin

When the veil of ignorance is removed, we can see the breadth, depth, and pervasiveness of sin in our lives. Sin cannot be contained in neat, simple, disposable categories that the manuals provided because sin is too deeply rooted and too widespread in each of us. But we have an added difficulty in seeing this today because so much of contemporary thinking on sin is a backlash to the profoundly negative attitude that the tradition held in the presumption of the *massa damnata*. Since for centuries it was presumed that the masses were damned, now with equal conviction we overthrow that presumption by believing that everyone is saved. To diminish the anxiety about damnation and to convince ourselves that we are saved, we first discount the seriousness of sin in our lives. Thus, while our predecessors sought to eliminate our sinfulness through preestablished categories, more recently some have sought to eliminate sin by insisting on our profound goodness. In the mainline churches, at least, Cotton Mather's warnings against falling into the hands of an angry God, and James Joyce's parody of the Jesuit "hell-fire and damnation" sermon in his *Portrait of an Artist as a Young Man,* have largely yielded to preachers' confident assertions about universal salvation and funeral orators who seem to assume that practically everyone has been taken up into heaven at the moment of death.

Despite the extraordinary difference between the two contradictory beliefs that most are damned or that most are saved, three important similarities exist between them. First, there are no convincing warrants in Scripture for either presumption. Who is to know where most people's destiny is? Only God.

Second, and more importantly, both approaches radically underemphasize the mercy of Jesus' redemptive passion, death, and resurrection. Those who hold that most are damned believe that Jesus, the merciful redeemer, is really the severe judge. Others, by diminishing any recognition of the seriousness of sin in our lives, eliminate the need for Jesus' mercy, whether in our redemption or in our condemnation.

We can only recognize our own sinfulness, however, if we first allow the mercy of Jesus to enter our lives. In order to fathom the depth of our sinfulness, we can only do so in the comforting light of the one who is merciful to us while we are still sinners. We know, for instance, that holy Christians, like Dorothy Day, repeatedly acknowledged that the closer they got to the Lord, the more they were able to acknowledge their sinfulness. Jesus never abandons us in our sinfulness. Rather, he repeatedly embraces us in his mercy and lets us see our sinfulness.

When we see our own sinfulness, we find more easily the grounds for being reconciled with others. As Jesus protected the woman caught in adultery by reminding her potential attackers that they could only cast stones at her if they were without sin themselves (see John 7:53–8:11), Jesus always warns us against presuming that our righteousness is self-made (see Luke 18:9). A righteousness won by Jesus' mercy provides a smooth path toward realizing the road to reconciliation with others. For as Paul writes: "All this is from God, who through Christ reconciled us to himself and gave us the ministry of reconciliation; that is, in Christ God was reconciling the world to himself, not counting their trespasses against them, and entrusting to us the ministry of reconciliation" (2 Corinthians 5:18–19).

The third point of similarity between each assumption is that neither approach promotes the virtue of hope. Here we can recall that because virtue is the mean between extremes, then for every virtue there are two vices, with each vice being a virtue's extremes. The despair that characterized many souls in the medieval and modern church was as extensive as the presumption that dominates many people today. Thus, in a merciless understanding of the pervasiveness of sin, many earlier preachers and theologians left us with little hope and great despairing anxiety. Conversely, dismissing our sinfulness and ignoring the gift of Jesus' mercy, today's preachers insist on our goodness, leaving us with the vice of presumption instead of the virtue of hope. Many of us today stand convinced like the Pharisee that we are not sinners like the tax collector (see Luke 18:10–14).

THE FAILURE TO BOTHER TO LOVE

Here we can recall the fourth chapter where we saw the comments of both Dietrich Bonhoeffer, who warned us against ignoring the costliness of grace, and Klaus Demmer, who called us to see the tangible effects that the mercy of Christ has produced in the face of sin and death. But we can also think of the insight of the late German moral theologian and the former president of the University of Bonn, Franz Böckle, who noted that we naturally block any recognition of our sinfulness.[4] He recognized that the act of confessing one's sinfulness is itself an effective action. That is, when we are at odds with another, for instance, we rarely consider ourselves as the cause. Before we move toward reconciliation, we usually dwell on the offenses of the other. But if we move even slightly toward reconciliation, we usually begin to see the possibility that our own conduct might have contributed to the strife we have with another. Our willingness to be reconciled, then, provides a new insight into the history of our strife with another: By reconciliation we *begin* to sense that we too could be at fault. When we let down our defenses and consider the possibility of our own moral fallibility—when that minor admission is made—then we begin to glimpse our own faults. Furthermore, the more we are willing to subject ourselves to a self-examination, the more we can see that we are subject to the various ways in which sin inhibits our ability to love. In fact, we begin to realize that our sinfulness is not solely constituted by our actually committing wrong actions. Our sinfulness is rooted first in our failure to bother to love.

Not bothering to love is precisely the scriptural concept of sin. For instance, Jesus tells us that the love commandment is the sum of the law (see Matthew 22:40). When someone asks him to clarify his teaching, Jesus tells the parable of the Good Samaritan (see Luke 10:25–37). When we hear the story we recognize on the one hand that the one who showed mercy is the Samaritan, but on the other hand, that those who failed to love, that is, the priest and Levite, are sinners. Surprisingly we may notice that while Jesus has indicted (implicitly) the priest and the Levite, he does not leave the listener to consider the wrongdoing of those who attacked the poor man on the road to Jericho.

In fact, throughout the Gospels, sin is often attributed not to obvious wrongdoers, but rather to those who do not bother to love. We can revisit the texts that we mentioned at the beginning of this section. The parable of the rich man and Lazarus is about a man who never bothered to notice his brother at the gate and so he is punished with hellfire. The guest who fails to bother with the proper wedding garment is cast outside to gnash his teeth. The Matthean last judgment scene separates as saved those who bothered to feed the hungry, clothe the naked, and visit the imprisoned, from those who did not bother and so are condemned. Sin in the Gospels is about not bothering to love.

When pushed, most people are able to recognize their wrongdoing. We know that whenever we cause harm by lying, misrepresenting, stealing, and so on, we can recognize it. Similarly we can easily name and often confess these activities. But we do not so easily recognize our failures to love. This then explains why in Scripture the one who sins is usually blind to the sinning. The rich man does not know that he has sinned. The "goats" ask where and when they sinned. And even the pious Pharisee who stands in the Temple with the breast-beating tax collector is clueless to his own sinfulness.

Certainly one reason why we are blind to our sinfulness is that for centuries we have had an overly simplistic view of sin: anything wrong that we did, we called sin. But we never looked at the root of sin, which inevitably harkens back to the failure to bother to love.

According to American Catholic Old Testament scholar Bruce Vawter, the reason for the sin of ancient Israel was always eventually found in their hearts that were not fervent, in their gratitude that dramatically diminished, and in their memory of the works of God they eventually forgot.[5] Our failure to love is always the cause of any subsequent sin.

Josef Fuchs, a German Jesuit moral theologian who taught in Rome for many years, distinguishes here between regret and repentance.[6] When people love and err, they regret. For instance, friends, parents, or lovers who cause harm by accident, by misguided intentions, or by some other fault, usually regret their errors more than anyone who was affected by the harm. Loving people regret the harm that their shortcomings cause.

Repentance is much different. Unlike regret that comes from within the loving person, repentance usually comes as a summons from without. Repentance challenges us to see where we did not bother to strive, to grow, to love. Unlike regret, which usually is about those areas of our lives where we are weak, repentance addresses those areas where we are strong, specifically, where we could have bothered, where we were able. In those strong areas of our lives the call to repentance asks, Could we have tried more or better?

Too easily we associate sin with weakness, with those weaknesses in ourselves that lead to wrong, harmful, and easily specifiable actions. But in Scripture, sin resides not so much in our weaknesses but in our strengths. The rich man could have shared his riches; the priest and the Levite could have taken care of the wounded man; and the "goats" could have responded to the neighbor in need. Indeed, most people address their faults or weaknesses, and struggle with them. But there is often little moral effort where we are strong. The story of sin, like the call to repentance, concerns those areas of our lives where we could have tried harder, precisely because we were so able. Christ judges not the weak heart that struggles, but rather the strong heart that does not bother. As we develop a theology of sin, we see that we sin out of strength, not weakness.

The difficulty we have with this notion of strength is that precisely where we are strong is precisely where we think we have no need for God's mercy, and, likewise, this is precisely where we do not bother to see whether there is anything lacking. What is lacking, of course, is our willingness to bother to love. And just as the Pharisee, priest and Levite, "goats," wedding guest, and rich man could not arrive at that insight, neither have we nor has our tradition. Sin blinds us to our sinfulness, for that is its nature. Only when we are willing to recognize the presumption of our age, can we begin to glimpse the profound deception of sin, the need we have for God's mercy, and the power of the hope that saves.

Finally, when we recognize the profound deception of sin, we can understand why so many Christians in the industrialized world resist the notion of social sin. Social sin claims that those who are wealthy participants in the structures of power are ultimately morally accountable for both the unjust distribution of the world's assets and the suffering that results from that inequity. Social sin insists that the wealthy fail to love the poor as subjects and that they sin socially precisely from their strength: they could have made the world more fair and just for others. Throughout the industrialized world, however, social sin is frequently rejected because like the rest of humanity, wealthy Christians prefer to think of their sin in terms of neat, specifiable actions that they perform, that they can easily recognize, and that they believe are rooted in personal weaknesses. Social sin stands then as a healthy theological challenge to the profoundly wicked nature of our contemporary presumptuousness.

Questions for Reflection and Discussion

1. What implications might a more biblically based theology of sin have for the sacrament of reconciliation?

2. What are some of the ironies about a theology of sin that categorizes sins according to neat pre-established categories?

3. If sin is the failure to bother to love, how can we best teach that insight?

Notes

1. *Rule of the Community*, trans. Geza Vermes, *The Complete Dead Sea Scrolls in English* (London: Penguin, 1997), p. 102.

2. John Mahoney, *The Making of Moral Theology: A Study of the Roman Catholic Tradition* (Oxford: Clarendon Press, 1987), pp. 1–36.

3. Thomas N. Tentler, *Sin and Confession on the Eve of the Reformation* (Princeton: Princeton University Press, 1977).

4. Franz Böckle, *Fundamental Moral Theology* (Dublin: Gill and Macmillan, 1980).

5. Bruce Vawter, "Missing the Mark," in *Introduction to Christian Ethics: A Reader*, Ronald Hamel and Kenneth Himes eds. (New York: Paulist Press, 1989), pp. 199–205.

6. Josef Fuchs, "The 'Sin of the World' and Normative Morality," in *Personal Responsibility and Christian Morality* (Washington, D.C.: Georgetown University Press, 1983), pp. 153–157.

Select Bibliography

Böckle, Franz. *Fundamental Moral Theology.* Dublin: Gill and Macmillan, 1980.

Buckley, Thomas W. *Seventy Times Seven: Sin, Judgment, and Forgiveness in Matthew's Gospel.* Collegeville: Liturgical Press, 1991.

Fuchs, Josef. "The 'Sin of the World' and Normative Morality." In *Personal Responsibility and Christian Morality*. Washington, D.C.: Georgetown University Press, 1983, pp. 153–175.

Gelin, Albert and Albert Descamps. *Sin in the Bible*. New York: Descleé, 1965.

Lyonnet, Stanislaus and Leopold Sabourin. *Sin, Redemption, and Sacrifice*. Rome: Biblical Institute Press, 1970.

Mahoney, John. *The Making of Moral Theology: A Study of the Roman Catholic Tradition*. Oxford: Clarendon Press, 1987, pp. 1–36.

Maly, Eugene. *Sin: Biblical Perspectives*. Dayton: Pflaum, 1973.

Miller, Patrick D. *Sin and Judgment in the Prophets*. Chico, CA: Scholars Press, 1982.

Tentler, Thomas. *Sin and Confession on the Eve of the Reformation*. Princeton: Princeton University Press, 1977.

Vawter, Bruce. "Missing the Mark." In Ronald P. Hamel and Kenneth R. Himes (eds.), *Introduction to Christian Ethics: A Reader*. New York: Paulist Press, 1989, pp. 199–205.

Chapter Eight

POLITICS FROM A
MARGINAL PERSPECTIVE

When most Americans hear the term *politics*, they think of Democrats and Republicans. But *politics* derives from the Greek word for "city" (*polis*) and refers to the whole of human existence in relation to other persons outside one's own household. Keenan contrasts the liberal and liberationist approaches to politics today, and reflects on the need to balance the common good and the claims of individuals. Then Harrington notes that, whereas in ancient Greek society citizens of the *polis* were free persons of social and economic substance (elites), the Scriptures and recent developments in theology have taught us that poor and socially marginal persons may sometimes see the real shape of political (community) life more clearly than the elites do. Many (but not all!) early Christians fit into those socioeconomic categories, and much of the New Testament's political wisdom comes from their "outsider" and powerless perspective. This historical fact means that we cannot expect from the New Testament a doctrine of church and state, a blueprint for a Christian political party, or even a "just war" theory. What we can expect is a cautious and marginal perspective on who really is "King of kings" and "Lord of lords."

MORAL THEOLOGICAL REFLECTIONS
J. F. Keenan

In his *Nicomachean Ethics*, Aristotle argues that politics is the greatest practical science.[1] He makes this claim because politics is the study of how the "polis" or the city should pursue the end that is the good for the human community. What good could be more important? he asks.

In a manner of speaking, for Aristotle all ethics is political because all ethics is for the betterment or full flourishing of the community. This understanding of ethics helps us see that ethics is always strategic in two important ways: it always determines the end where the good of the community is found, and it always considers the most appropriately effective way for attaining or realizing that end. For Aristotle, then, ethics needs to have practical effectiveness. It is never enough to *know* the right; one has to *do* it, and do it rightly. Similarly, to be virtuous, one needs not only to desire the end of a virtue like justice, but one must also prudently determine the right means for growing in the virtue. Getting to the realization of the end—that is, becoming the better community—is the end of political science which is also the end of ethics.

Aristotle associates prudence with political science.[2] Prudence is always concerned with reality. It needs to know the end as real, and it needs to know the real, concrete way for attaining or realizing the end. Prudence and political science therefore keep one another and all of ethics in the real world. When we speak of ethics, then, we are inevitably faced with its practical impact or significance. Ethics is never simply the study of ends, goals, or ideals; it is actually the practical knowledge toward attaining or realizing those goals.

When we turn to the subject of this book, we need to ask, Is the New Testament ethical in this way? Does the New Testament tell us not only that the end is the kingdom of God but also how we can move as persons and as community into the realization of the kingdom? This is an important question. If the New Testament does not, then, help us in this regard, the Bible is utopian, giving us ideals but no real guidance. It tells us the end, but offers no practical insights into how we are to find the way. If we answer this question negatively, then we might as well abandon the project of this book as well as the project of living the Christian life.

In asking this question about whether the New Testament is practical, another important question about history arises. We saw this question earlier when we noted Klaus Demmer's comments on the effective history of the Christ event. Demmer asks, Does the Christ event have any practical, historical impact on our lives? Does the way we live in the face of death change by the fact that Christ has conquered death? Is the way we live in a world trapped by the effective history of sin and death at all changed by the fact that Christ has freed us from sin and death?

Demmer insists on the historical significance of the Christ event. We cannot answer "no" to his questions, for to do so would be to deny Christ. The Christ event must have historical significance or else we are truly the greatest of fools, as Paul reminds us (see 1 Corinthians 15:17–19).

LIBERAL THEOLOGY VERSUS
LIBERATION THEOLOGY

The question of the historical significance of the New Testament witness is the topic of a ringing critique of liberal theology by Dorothee Soelle, a German Protestant theologian teaching in the United States. She argues that a certain unexamined but often assumed presupposition is operative in liberal theology[3] (which claims to be progressive and is more attuned to the modern world than to the theological tradition) in general and in the exegetical assumptions of Rudolf Bultmann in particular. That presupposition is to read Scripture free of the historical. For the liberal theologians like Bultmann, the claims of revelation are found by transcending the historical limitations of texts.

This presupposition can be heard, for instance, when certain Scripture scholars or biblical theologians respond to the question whether the Bible can practically guide us in the moral life, by saying "It's not that kind of book."

Liberal theology attempts to take the transcendental truth out of its historical context. It uses the historical-critical method (intended to uncover the historical setting of an ancient text) not to get to history, but to get some insight out of or away from its history. We can think here for instance about the teachings on divorce or on homosexuality. Liberal theology relativizes the scriptural claims of these teachings by saying that we need to see the historical context. Of course, examining the historical context is a necessity. But liberal theologians tend to look to the historical context so as to repudiate the significance of the historical. If these teachings are only historical teachings, then the transcendental claims that they have on us are not evident.

By critiquing the liberals, Soelle is not advocating a new fundamentalism that simply repeats the words of Scripture. Rather, she argues that liberal theology's response of simply eliminating anything that has a hint of historicity begs the real hermeneutical question. What liberal theologians look for is the eternal, the transcendent; unfortunately they associate that with the ahistorical, or even the pre-historical. If we follow their lead, we do not need to worry about Scripture much. Eventually we get to the *kerygma* (the proclamation of Jesus), and this is basically all that liberal theologians claim as revelation.

Liberation theology thinks of revelation as in history, as inseparable from it. Revelation is not something inserted into Scripture. We do not need tools, therefore, to free revelation from its historical context; rather revelation is so incarnated in Scripture that the historical is now completely assumed into revelation. As noted by Ignacio Ellacuria, a Jesuit theologian killed in El Salvador: "Christian eternity is inexorably linked to temporality ever since the Word became history." [4]

In a particular way, our understanding of the kingdom of God is affected by this difference of paradigms, or basic approaches; our understanding of the kingdom, through the master lenses of community, cross, and creation, could be overly spiritualized if we read it through liberal theology. From the perspective of liberation theology, however, the kingdom is not something to be removed from history. The kingdom as revealed emerges through history.

To exemplify the difference between liberal and liberation theologians, Soelle uses a helpful topic: the virgin birth of Jesus. Liberal theologians see Jesus' virgin birth as a typical device to highlight divinity and, as such, it can be dismissed as a *typos* or a myth. The liberals' presupposition about history leads them to downplay the significance of Jesus' virginal conception.

For liberation theologians, however, the conception of Jesus to a single, young, poor unmarried woman is the suitable point of departure for the revelation narrative. With them, we enter into the historical context, not to separate it from revelation but to receive better what is being revealed.

Soelle's endorsement of liberation theology because of its appreciation of the nexus, or link, between history and transcendence, leads us to a second set of concerns. Liberation theologians like Gilberto da Silva Gorgulho, a Dominican theologian in Brazil, remind us that historians and exegetes must consider their social location. [5] Following the Aristotelian insight that things appear to us as we are, we are eventually led to Karl Mannheim, a German social philosopher (1893–1947), who taught about the importance and uniqueness of one's perspective. [6] If we must be sensitive to history, not to free revelation from it but rather to recognize history as the place where revelation occurs, then we need interpreters who are themselves sensitive to history.

Inevitably, at this point liberation theologians turn to the privileged perspective of marginal people and the preferential option for the poor (the biblical theme that God is on the side of the poor and hears their cries). The poor are the ones whose memories can guide us in understanding what has been revealed. Liberation theologians attribute this privileged perspective to the poor because God has been revealing God's self in history on the margins of society. It is in the memory of those on the margins where the texts originate. A privileged perspective gets us closer to the truth of reality. For liberation theologians, the poor have the critical eye, ear, heart, and mind for this type of perception. The texts of Scripture validate this claim as well.

Here then we see implicitly our earlier criticism of Richard Hays and his failure to emphasize the social location of the exegete. Unless the exegete has a self-understanding of the importance of the privileged perspective of the poor, the exegete will not fully appreciate the significance of the virgin birth. For this reason Jon Sobrino, a Jesuit theologian in El Salvador, insists that the first task of theology, from those who do exegesis to those who apply it in theological reflection, is to locate their work in the context of the suffering of the world.[7]

In theology, this appreciation of perspective is not primarily an anthropocentric (human-centered) move; it is a theocentric (God-centered) move. We are going to where God is found—in the experience and the memory of the poor. The poor are not necessarily morally better or worse than others, but they are the ones preferred by God. And, here, Gustavo Gutièrrez, known as one of the founders of liberation theology in Latin America, takes very seriously the antithetical presentations about the reign of God, particularly about the despised (and not the righteous) being the first to enter into God's kingdom (see Matthew 11:16–19; Luke 15:1–32).[8]

COMMUNITY, INDIVIDUAL PERSONS, AND EQUALITY

In turning toward a liberation paradigm, there are two important concerns that we need to keep in mind. First, liberation theology, like Aristotelian ethics, privileges the community over the individual. In the Aristotelian *polis* or in the Latino community today, the individual's claims are at best "assumed," and at worst they are ignored or denied. Inevitably, if an individual's claims conflict with the common good, the common good trumps the individual's claims.

In light of their experience of World War II, many European ethicists became very suspicious of collective and social systems that do not adequately safeguard the rights of the individual. Their experience helped them to see the potential intolerance of the "herd" mentality. They are concerned when the community, by becoming intolerant of its own diversity, represses the dissenting individuals and devolve themselves into the collective.

Their defense of individual rights ought not be viewed as a wholesale endorsement of the Enlightenment. As Brian Tierney, a historian of the late-medieval church, has pointed out, concern for personal rights first manifested itself within church circles, particularly among late medieval canonists who explored the notion of natural law.[9] Tierney argues that while the Stoics (a school of philosophers in the Greco-Roman world) and Cicero (the Roman philosopher and orator) claimed that *ius naturale* was the universal, objective, natural law recognizable by humans, twelfth-century church canonists defined it as a subjective force, faculty, or power inherent in individual human persons. Concerned to protect individuals, these early canonists developed the first expressions of natural rights from an anthropological vision of the person as rational, self-aware, and morally responsible.

In like manner, contemporary moral theologians discuss the importance of an autonomous moral theology, not because they are endorsing a Kantian view of the moral universe, but rather because they recognize personal conscience as the source of moral norm-making. An autonomous morality in the context of Christian faith inevitably means a morality that defends the conscience as the place where the human person listens and morally responds to God. If the personal conscience is not protected, where would morality learn the difference between right and wrong?

Still, these European theologians recognize how much they are indebted to liberation theologians' call to community, and for that reason most have modified their earlier anthropology by insisting that the autonomous person is always constitutively relational.

A second concern is raised by feminists. Catholic theologian Maria Pilar Aquino, for instance, endorses bringing feminist methods into liberation theology in order to develop a politics of political strategy.[10] She sees three processes as particularly important for all theologians, from the exegete to the practical theologian: 1) to discover and interpret the saving historical value of reality; 2) to unmask and dismantle theological formulations that support and perpetuate the interpretation of humanity in patriarchal terms; and 3) to recognize and describe women's history. She brings a feminist suspicion as a theoretical category to biblical interpretation.

Evidently her first concern overlaps with Soelle's concern. But her second and third concerns are particularly indebted to the work of Elisabeth Schüssler Fiorenza who calls for a subversive remembering.[11] Schüssler Fiorenza does not assume the liberal apolitical character of the Bible. Rather, she looks, for instance, at the household codes (see Colossians 3:18–4:1; Ephesians 5:22–6:9; 1 Peter 2:18–3:7) and shows how they replaced the ideal of the coequality of all disciples in the early Jesus movement with an Aristotelian ethics that privileged men over women. Thus she brings the historical relevance of revelation to the task of critiquing history, and to discovering where we can see the good news transforming history and where it is not transforming history. In a word, she not only wants to concern herself with history but she also wants to evaluate it.

Although there were emancipatory societal tendencies in the first century, especially in what Schüssler Fiorenza calls the co-equal discipleship model, the hierarchizing tendency of the household codes that accepted Aristotelian gender differences also appeared. She wants to know how the household codes developed, and why and whether their legitimating arguments are indeed legitimating today—if ever they were. She wants to arrive at the lived historical ethos of early Christians that developed in interaction with its patriarchal cultural contexts and to evaluate critically its continuing structures of alienation and liberation. She brings our first concern about individuals into our second concern regarding equality and women in general. She asserts that unless women are liberated, the concern for each person is overlooked, and that history, while good, is in need of constant redemption. For this reason, the political understanding of the texts of Scriptures is now as urgent as ever.

BIBLICAL PERSPECTIVES
D. J. Harrington

The New Testament provides no uniform doctrine of "church and state." When the texts were being passed on and written down, the church was too small, and the state (the Roman Empire) was too large. The New Testament does, however, offer three perspectives or attitudes toward the Roman Empire: caution (see Mark 12:13–17), cooperation (see Romans 13:1–7), and resistance (see Revelation). All three attitudes need to be kept alive as part of a Christian ethical stance today.

PAYING BACK TO THE EMPEROR AND TO GOD
(Mark 12:13–17)

13. Then they sent to him some Pharisees and some Herodians to trap him in what he said. 14. And they came and said to him, "Teacher, we know that you are sincere, and show deference to no one; for you do not regard people with partiality, but teach the way of God in accordance with truth. Is it lawful to pay taxes to the emperor, or not? 15. Should we pay them, or should we not?" But knowing their hypocrisy, he said to them, "Why are you putting me to the test? Bring me a denarius, and let me see it" 16. And they brought one. Then he said to them, "Whose head is this, and whose title?" They answered, "The emperor's." 17. Jesus said to them, "Give to the emperor the things that are the emperor's, and to God the things that are God's." And they were utterly amazed at him.

This famous passage must be read against the background of Jewish history. When in the mid-second century B.C. the Maccabees, a Jewish priestly family, succeeded in gaining independence and national identity for Judea, they entered into an alliance with the Romans (see 1 Maccabees 8) that led to ever greater Roman intrusion into Jewish affairs. A dispute over the Jewish high priesthood led to the Roman general Pompey's intervention in 63 B.C. and to the eventual establishment of Herod the Great (37–4 B.C.) as a client king. In Jesus' time Galilee was ruled by Herod Antipas, and Judea with Jerusalem as its capital was directly administered by the Roman prefect Pontius Pilate (A.D. 26–36).

According to the Gospels, Jesus was executed as the "King of the Jews." The punishment of crucifixion was generally reserved for slaves and political agitators. From Pilate's perspective Jesus looked like another in a long series of Jewish fanatics who used the traditional religion to gain popular support in their efforts at establishing the kingdom of God or a theocracy. When Jesus gathered crowds and proclaimed God as king, it seemed to the Romans and their Jewish collaborators to be more than a harmless religious revival.

Jesus' debate about paying taxes in Mark 12:13–17 (see Matthew 22:15–22; Luke 20:20–26) appears as part of the series of his controversies with various opponents in Jerusalem shortly before his passion and death. The opponents in this case are "some Pharisees" and "some Herodians." The Herodians are by their title presumed to be supporters of the Herod family and so also of their Roman patrons. Throughout their history, the Pharisees rose and fell in political influence, but here they seem to represent those religious Jews who were critical of the Romans and their local collaborators.

The opponents' strategy is to trap Jesus into saying something that will get him into trouble. They preface their question with flattery designed to elicit a clear response. Their question is, "Is it lawful to pay taxes to the emperor, or not?" The tax was a sign of submission to Roman authority. If Jesus responds positively, he loses favor with those Jews who were opposed to Roman rule. If he responds negatively, he reveals himself to be a rebel against Rome.

Instead of answering their question directly, Jesus calls for a Roman coin (note that he makes the opponents supply the coin) and asks them whose image and whose inscription it bears. The image on the Roman denarius would have been that of the emperor Tiberius (A.D. 14–37), and the inscription would have included titles that suggested the emperor's divinity. Thus Jesus forces his opponents to admit that they are using coins that bear the emperor's image and inscription (and to that extent belong to the emperor). Finally, Jesus issues his own pronouncement: "Give to the emperor the things that are the emperor's, and to God the things that are God's" (12:17). The passage ends with the narrator's comment: "And they were utterly amazed at him."

Why were they amazed? On the surface Jesus suggests that since the Pharisees and the Herodians were using the emperor's coins, they were already part of the Roman imperial system and so should pay the emperor's taxes: "Give to the emperor the things that are the emperor's." Thus the Herodians are silenced. On a deeper level, Jesus is challenging Jewish religious persons to be as observant (and more so) in fulfilling their obligations to God as they are to the Roman officials: " . . . and to God the things that are God's." Moreover, some could interpret the second part of Jesus' statement as a challenge to the authority of the Roman emperor. In this way the Pharisees and others who resented the Roman imperial order are silenced.

The opponents are amazed mainly because Jesus has eluded their trap. He has shown up his opponents as already participating in the Roman imperial order. But his answer is sufficiently ambiguous so as to leave both sides wondering whether Jesus was for or against them. And he leaves us with our own ambivalence about the rights and powers of government when viewed from a biblical perspective.

OLD TESTAMENT BACKGROUND

The Old Testament tells the story of God's people Israel in the various forms of its political existence. After liberation from slavery in Egypt and entrance into the promised land, Israel takes shape as a political entity in a confederation of twelve tribes responding to charismatic leaders (Judges). While some in Israel seek a king like other nations, others view human kings as a threat to Israel's fundamental belief in God as its king.

The monarchy begins around 1000 B.C. with Saul, David, and Solomon. It soon splits into two kingdoms, one in the north (Israel) and the other in the south (Judah). Both kingdoms become involved with a series of stronger neighbors, and are eventually destroyed in the eighth (Israel) and sixth (Judah) centuries. With the return from exile in 537 B.C. Judah becomes part of a Persian province, with its own governor and high priest as leaders. As a result of Alexander the Great's conquest, however, Judea is a segment first of the Ptolemaic/Egyptian kingdom (300–200 B.C.) and then of the Seleucid/Syrian kingdom (200–165 B.C.)—two of the parts into which Alexander's empire was divided.

The Maccabean uprising resulted in political independence for Judea. But Judea gradually got absorbed into the Roman Empire to the point that in Jesus' time the "state" was the Roman Empire. Throughout its history, ancient Israel had many forms of government and saw many outside political masters. The one persistent theme was that the God of Israel is its true king: "The Lord is king" (Psalms 97:1; 99:1).

COOPERATION

For early Christians in the Holy Land and in the Diaspora (Jewish settlements outside Palestine), the Roman Empire constituted the "state." The ambivalence displayed in Mark 12:13–17 captures nicely the "outsider" or "minority" approach that a religious Jew or Christian might take. There are, however, several texts in the New Testament epistles that counsel submission to and cooperation with the Roman government as positive values. The most famous and influential passage is Romans 13:1–7. But similar sentiments appear in 1 Peter 2:13–17 and Titus 3:1.

Paul's advice occurs as part of the paraenetic or hortatory section of his letter to the Romans, where he spells out some practical implications of his theology. The passage begins with a call to the Roman Christians to accept the authority of the Roman government officials: "Let every person be subject to the governing authorities; for there is no authority except from God, and those authorities that exist have been instituted by God" (13:1). This absolute statement is confirmed by the considerations that those who do what is right have nothing to fear from government officials, and that obedience to them is a way of escaping God's wrath at the final judgment and is also a matter of conscience in the present. Paul concludes his advice with a directive to the Roman Christians to pay their taxes: "Pay to all what is due them—taxes to whom taxes are due" (13:7).

On the surface, Paul's advice to the Christians at Rome echoes the first part of Jesus' teaching in Mark 12:17: "Give to the emperor the things that are the emperor's." It counsels that Christians should be good citizens of the Roman Empire. This teaching is often proposed as the Christian doctrine of church and state. And totalitarian governments have used it as a way of controlling sincere Christians and discouraging them from protesting or rising up against tyrannical rulers.

If we look beneath the surface of Romans 13:1–7, however, things are not so simple. Under the emperor Claudius (A.D. 41–54), the Jews of Rome (including Jewish Christians) were expelled from the city. When Paul wrote to the Roman Christians in A.D. 56–57, the Jewish members had only recently been allowed to return. If we take seriously this historical situation, it is possible that Romans 13:1–7 was intended as concrete pragmatic advice addressed to a specific crisis ("Don't make trouble now") and not as an expression of the Christian doctrine of church and state.

Moreover, a few verses later (see Romans 13:11–14), Paul suggests that the fullness of God's kingdom is imminent: "the night is far gone, the day is near." In that context Paul and other early Christians would be assuming the demise of the Roman Empire very soon and the universal recognition of God as king. Thus Paul's advice in Romans 13:1–7 would be a call for patient cooperation with Roman officials in the short term with an eye toward the imminent manifestation of God's eternal kingdom.

RESISTANCE

While the surface reading of Romans 13:1–7 assumes the Roman Empire acting at its best, Revelation presents it as acting at its worst. Written in the late first century (A.D. 95–96), Revelation gives a glimpse of a situation in western Asia Minor (present-day Turkey) in which Christians were apparently being forced to participate in civic religious rites honoring the Roman emperor as a god and the goddess Roma as the personification of the empire. The emperor Domitian (A.D. 81–96) is said to have enjoyed being addressed as "Lord and God," and a local official in western Asia Minor seems to have promoted these cults with enthusiasm and vigor.

The cults of the Roman emperor and of Roma presented Christians with a crisis of conscience. How could they worship the emperor as "Lord and God" when they believed that only the risen Jesus deserved these titles? Although some Christian teachers apparently allowed participation in these civic religious rituals, John was strongly opposed to any such accommodation. His book of Revelation is mainly concerned with the question, Who really is Lord and God? John wrote the book in large part to encourage Christians to remain faithful in their nonviolent resistance.

John's stance echoes the second part of Jesus' maxim in Mark 12:17: "Give . . . to God the things that are God's." In Revelation 12–13 John constructs an "unholy trinity" consisting of Satan, the emperor (the beast from the sea), and the local official (the beast from the land). And in Revelation 17, he portrays the emperor as "a scarlet beast that was full of blasphemous names" (17:3)—a clear reference to calling the emperor "Lord and God." In the same scene the goddess Roma is described as "the great whore who is seated on many waters" (17:1)—a reference to Rome's power over the Mediterranean Sea and its commercial activities (see 18:1–20).

Lest there be any doubt about the referent of these images, John identifies the seven heads on the beast as the "seven mountains on which the woman is seated" (17:9)—an allusion to the seven hills of Rome. Likewise, John ends his description of the beast and the prostitute by noting that "the woman you saw is the great city that rules over the kings of the earth" (17:18).

In the face of Roman persecution even to the point of martyrdom (see 2:13), John counsels nonparticipation and nonviolent resistance. He does so out of the conviction that the faithful righteous ones will overcome (see 2:7, 11, 17, etc.). This conviction is based on the belief that by his death and resurrection Jesus has already overcome the unholy trinity. Compared with the New Jerusalem that will come down from heaven (see chapters 21–22), the Roman Empire has little power or importance.

SIGNIFICANCE

Throughout the first century A.D. Christianity was a small movement that to most observers looked like a Jewish sect. According to one estimate,[12] there were probably about 1500 Christians in the world when Paul wrote his letter to the Romans and about 7500 when John wrote the Book of Revelation. The majority of these Christians were not from the social class that could have exerted political influence or directly affected social change in the Roman Empire.

There is no uniform teaching about "church and state" in the New Testament. The few passages that treat the topic approach it from perspectives that are related to their specific situations: caution and wariness in the face of the Roman occupation of Palestine (see Mark 12:13–17); dutiful cooperation with a legitimate Roman government acting justly and in accord with God's will (see Romans 13:1–7); and nonviolent resistance when Roman government officials overstep their authority and try to force Christians to go against their consciences (see Revelation). The problem for twenty-first-century Christians, of course, is to discern which of these situations is closest to their own, and which approach—caution, cooperation, or resistance—will best promote the common good and the worship of God.

Questions for Reflection and Discussion

1. In what sense can the political perspective of the poor be regarded as a privileged one?

2. Why and how can Christian ethics respect both the community and the individual?

3. What can Christians today learn from the different New Testament approaches to the Roman Empire: caution, cooperation, and resistance?

Notes

1. Aristotle, *Nicomachean Ethics*, 1094a.26ff.

2. Ibid., 1141a.19ff.

3. Dorothee Soelle, "The Use of the Bible: From the Liberal Paradigm to the Paradigm of Liberation Theology," in *Thinking about God: An Introduction to Theology* (Philadelphia: Trinity, 1990), pp. 32–41.

4. Ignacio Ellacuria, "Utopia and Prophecy in Latin America," in *Mysterium Liberationis: Fundamental Concepts of Liberation Theology* (Maryknoll, NY: Orbis, 1993), p. 289.

5. Gilberto da Silva Gorgulho, "Biblical Hermeneutics," in *Mysterium Liberationis: Fundamental Concepts of Liberation Theology* (Maryknoll, NY: Orbis, 1993), pp. 123–149.

6. Karl Mannheim, *Ideology and Utopia* (London: Routledge and Kegan Paul, 1936).

7. Jon Sobrino, "Theology in a Suffering World," in *Mysterium Liberationis: Fundamental Concepts of Liberation Theology* (Maryknoll, NY: Orbis, 1993), pp. 27–46.

8. Gustavo Gutiérrez, "Option for the Poor," in *Mysterium Liberationis: Fundamental Concepts of Liberation Theology* (Maryknoll, NY: Orbis, 1993), pp. 235–250.

9. Brian Tierney, *The Idea of Natural Rights: Studies on Natural Rights, Natural Law, and Church Law* (Atlanta: Scholars Press, 1997).

10. Maria Pilar Aquino, "Women's Contribution to Theology in Liberation," in Charles Curran, Margaret Farley, and Richard McCormick, eds., *Readings in Moral Theology No. 9: Feminist Ethics and the Catholic Moral Tradition* (Mahwah, NJ: Paulist Press, 1996), pp. 90–119.

11. Elisabeth Schüssler Fiorenza, *In Memory of Her: A Feminist Theological Reconstruction of Christian Origins* (New York: Crossroads, 1983).

12. See Rodney Stark, *The Rise of Christianity: A Sociologist Reconsiders History* (Princeton: Princeton University Press, 1996), p. 7.

Select Bibliography

Aquino, Maria Pilar. "Women's Contribution to Theology in Liberation." In Charles Curran, Margaret Farley, and Richard McCormick (eds.), *Readings in Moral Theology No. 9: Feminist Ethics and the Catholic Moral Tradition*. Mahwah, NJ: Paulist Press, 1996, pp. 90–119.

Cassidy, Richard J. *Christians and Roman Rule in the New Testament*. New York: Crossroad, 2001.

Cullmann, Oscar. *The State in the New Testament*. New York: Scribners, 1966.

Ellacuria, Ignacio. "Utopia and Prophecy in Latin America." In *Mysterium Liberationis: Fundamental Concepts of Liberation Theology*. Maryknoll, NY: Orbis, 1993, pp. 289–328.

Gorgulho, Gilberto da Silva. "Biblical Hermeneutics." *Mysterium Liberationis: Fundamental Concepts of Liberation Theology*. Maryknoll, NY: Orbis, 1993, pp. 123–149.

Gustafson, James M. *Can Ethics Be Christian?* Chicago: University of Chicago Press, 1975.

Gutiérrez, Gustavo. "Option for the Poor." *Mysterium Liberationis: Fundamental Concepts of Liberation Theology*. Maryknoll, NY: Orbis, 1993, pp. 235–250.

Hengel, Martin. *Christ and Power*. Philadelphia: Fortress, 1977.

Mannheim, Karl. *Ideology and Utopia*. London: Routledge and Kegan Paul, 1936.

Pilgrim, Walter E. *Uneasy Neighbors: Church and State in the New Testament*. Minneapolis: Fortress, 1999, pp. 181–212.

Schüssler Fiorenza, Elisabeth. "Discipleship and Patriarchy." In *Readings in Moral Theology No. 9*, pp. 33–65.

_____. In *Memory of Her: A Feminist Theological Reconstruction of Christian Origins*. New York: Crossroads, 1983.

Sobrino, Jon. "Theology in a Suffering World." *Mysterium Liberationis: Fundamental Concepts of Liberation Theology*. Maryknoll, NY: Orbis, 1993, pp. 27–46.

Soelle, Dorothee. "The Use of the Bible: From the Liberal Paradigm to the Paradigm of Liberation Theology." In *Thinking about God: An Introduction to Theology*. Philadelphia: Trinity, 1990, pp. 32–41.

Sweet, J. P. M. "The Zealots and Jesus." In Ernst Bammel and C. D. Moule (eds.), *Jesus and the Politics of His Day*. Cambridge, UK: Cambridge University Press, 1984, pp. 1–9.

Tierney, Brian. *The Idea of Natural Rights: Studies on Natural Rights, Natural Law, and Church Law*. Atlanta: Scholars Press, 1997.

Wood, John A. *Perspectives on War in the Bible*. Macon, GA: Mercer University Press, 1998.

Wright, N.T. "The New Testament and the 'State.'" *Themelios* 16 (1990), pp. 11–17.

Chapter Nine

JUSTICE AND SOCIAL JUSTICE

"Let justice roll down like waters, and righteousness like an ever-flowing stream" (Amos 5:24). This great biblical prayer reminds us that justice/righteousness has its origin in God, and that the well-ordered society is one in which its members treat one another as they wish that God might treat them. In the human sphere, the virtue of justice refers to how we relate to one another.

In this chapter Keenan explores the place of justice among the classical cardinal virtues, and proposes a new constellation of justice, fidelity, self-care, and prudence. Harrington highlights the Bible's special interest in social justice. The Old Testament contains many laws and prophecies about fairness in the ways in which humans deal with one another. It insists that special care be given to the most vulnerable members of society (widows and orphans). Since social justice frequently pertains to material possessions in general and money in particular, it is not surprising that the New Testament should give particular attention to attitudes toward the use of material goods.

MORAL THEOLOGICAL REFLECTIONS
J. F. Keenan

The call to realize the kingdom as Jesus' disciples is the call to love. Love in the concrete is the call to seek the "right." But what the right is, we have yet to determine.

IS JUSTICE ENOUGH?

We saw in the last chapter that the right must be real, concrete, and appropriate; and it must promote the common good with a particular attentiveness to the poor and the marginalized as well as to women, since we recognize that throughout history, and even in Scripture, the message of equality has been compromised by existing patriarchal social structures. Moreover, we have seen that to talk about understanding the human being, that is, to have an appropriate anthropology, we ought to at least recognize the human person as constitutively relational.

How do these insights come together? The tradition has commonly defined the "right" that love seeks as being justice. Thomas Aquinas, for instance, did. Justice is the virtue that "perfects" or orders the will and is about giving to each and every person his or her due.

Aquinas privileged the virtue of justice. Among the four acquired cardinal virtues, justice was the virtue that the other three virtues served. Temperance and fortitude "perfected" or ordered the passions so as to help the virtuous person to be just, while prudence, which "perfected" or ordered the practical intellect, tried to determine in the here and now what the just course of action should be. In this way, Aquinas could always be recognized as having a profoundly relational ethics. The end of virtue was really to be the just person, and justice was the virtue for having ordered relations with others.

Two questions about the appropriateness of Aquinas's model immediately arise: Does virtue "perfect" a person's power? Does justice alone adequately define the right?

Before responding to these questions, we first recognize that our answers must be tentative. This is because the virtues are traditional heuristic guides that collectively aim for the right realization of human identity. They are heuristic because, in their nature, they are about the end, and as teleological, they need to be continually realized and redefined; their final definition always remains outstanding. Their nature is, then, historically dynamic; being in themselves goal oriented, they resist classicist constructions and require us continually to understand, acquire, develop, and reformulate them.

The interplay of the virtues with a relational and a historically emerging anthropology prompts us now to answer the two questions about Aquinas's foundational premises in virtue ethics. First, we need to think of the virtues not in the classicist expression as perfecting individual powers within an individual person but rather as rightly realizing the ways that we are related. The virtues perfect or order or rightly realize the relationships we have with one another. Second, these virtues could be in competition with one another. On this latter point, Catholic moral theologian William Spohn contends that contemporary virtue ethicists generally agree that virtues conflict.[1] Those who write on the virtues share with other ethicists the presupposition that conflict among key directing guidelines is inherent to all methods of moral reasoning. Moreover, inevitably, because justice has always been considered the primary virtue or principle, the notion of conflict arises precisely because ethicists are no longer convinced that justice alone adequately covers "the right."

For instance, in his landmark work, *Ethics*, philosopher William Frankena first argues for the principle of beneficence to supplement the principle of justice (fairness).[2] Then he raises "the problem of possible conflict" between the two principles and writes: "I see no way out of this. It does seem to me that the two principles may come into conflict, both at the level of individual action and at that of social policy, and I know of no formula that will always tell us how to solve such conflicts."[3]

Likewise, in their enormously influential work, *The Principles of Biomedical Ethics*, Christian ethicists Tom Beauchamp and James Childress promote justice as well as beneficence, autonomy, and nonmaleficence.[4] Then they add that "there is no premier and overriding authority in either the patient or the physician and no preeminent principle in biomedical ethics—not even the admonition to act in the patient's best interest."[5]

A NEW APPROACH
TO THE CARDINAL VIRTUES

In light of these issues regarding the sufficiency of justice, the probability of conflict among the virtues, and the notion that virtues perfect ways that we are related, I have developed elsewhere a tentative but contemporary "Proposing Cardinal Virtues," *Theological Studies* 56 (1995): 709–29. Here I can only express it briefly.

Our identity is relational in three ways: generally, specifically, and uniquely. Each of these relational ways of being demands a cardinal virtue: as relational beings *in general*, we are called to justice; as relational beings *specifically*, we are called to fidelity; and as relational beings *uniquely*, we are called to self-care. These three virtues are cardinal. Unlike the classic foursome, justice is not ethically prior to the others; rather, all three have equally urgent claims and should be pursued as ends in themselves. We are not called to be faithful and self-caring in order to be just, nor are we called to be self-caring and just in order to be faithful. None is auxiliary to the others. They are distinctive virtues with none being a subset or subcategory of the other. They are cardinal (in the sense of being a "hinge"). The fourth cardinal virtue is prudence, which determines what constitutes the just, faithful, and self-caring way of life.

Our relationality is generally directed by an ordered appreciation for the common good in which we treat all people equally. As members of the human race, we are expected to respond to all members equally and impartially. We are to treat every human being, regardless of any other way of relating to those human beings (that is, as friends or enemies), with a sense of fairness and impartiality, simply because they are human beings.

If justice urges us to treat all people with impartiality, then fidelity (calling us to uphold specific, existing relationships) calls us to partiality and makes distinctively different claims. Here, with Paul Ricoeur, we recognize that ethical claims about impartiality and partiality are found in all cultures and in all major texts.[6] Thus Philip Wogaman, a Protestant pastor and preacher, notes that in Scripture we can find the endorsement of universal salvation as well the specific call of God's chosen people.[7] We can see Jesus breaking down social boundaries and extending himself with equal regard to all, whether Jew, Samaritan, Syrophoenician, or Roman. And yet we see his partiality toward John, Mary, Martha, Lazarus, Peter, and others. Fidelity provides, therefore, a specific counterbalance to justice's call to impartiality. Fidelity is the virtue that nurtures and sustains the bonds of those special relationships that humans enjoy whether by blood, marriage, love, citizenship, or sacrament. If justice rests on impartiality and universality, then fidelity rests on partiality and particularity.

Neither of these virtues, however, addresses the unique relationship that each person has with oneself. Care for the self is found deep within our tradition, particularly in the command to love God and one's neighbor as oneself. Thomas Aquinas developed this into a specific disposition in his writings on the order of charity.

Finally, prudence has the task of integrating the three other virtues (justice, fidelity, and self-care) into the narrative of our lives. This is not easy. If, as in other ethical methods, the virtues conflict with one another, then the function of the virtue of prudence greatly expands. In the more harmonious classical list of virtues, prudence's primary task was to determine justice when dealing with our actions. It also determined the concrete expressions of the auxiliary virtues of temperance, when dealing with our desires, and of fortitude, when dealing with our struggles. But with this contemporary understanding, prudence has to name not only the claim of each particular virtue but also the priority that the claim enjoys.

Prudence is, moreover, always vigilant—looking to the future—trying not only to realize the claims of justice, fidelity, and self-care in the here and now but also to call us to anticipate occasions when each of these virtues can be more fully acquired. In this way, prudence is clearly a virtue that pursues ends and effectively establishes the moral agenda for the person growing in these virtues. But these ends are not in opposition to or in isolation from one another. Rather, prudence helps each virtue to shape its end as more inclusive of the other two; that is, the conflict among the virtuous claims is to be eventually integrated.

Prudence, however, does not work alone. Aristotle departed from Socrates's belief that prudence is sufficient for self-realization and self-determination. Prudence, Aristotle warned us, depends upon the other virtues, and those virtues are dialectally dependent upon prudence.[8]

Prudence grows, then, in the narrative of the lives we live. Stanley Hauerwas reminds us that we have the task of sorting out "conflicting loyalties" throughout our lives.[9] That sorting out means that we must incorporate the variety of relational claims being made on us. We do this through the narrative of the lives we live. The virtues are related, then, to one another but not in some inherent way as they seem to be in the classical list of the cardinal virtues. That is to say, the virtues do not perfect individual powers—as if these powers ever actually existed beyond metaphysics! Nor do the virtues *per se* complement one another. Rather, they become integrated in the life of the prudent person who lives them. The unity of the virtues is found not in the theoretical positing of the cardinal virtues, but rather in the final living out of lives shaped by prudence anticipating and responding to virtuous claims.

The task of developing an integrative narrative has been the task for the disciple of Christ since the beginning of Christianity. We can recall, for instance, how Gedaliahu Stroumsa noted that integrating the divinity and humanity of Christ was the major theological task and accomplishment of the early church: "The unity of Christ, possessor of two natures but remaining nonetheless one single persona, is, of course, in a nutshell, the main achievement of centuries of Christological and Trinitarian pugnacious investigations."[10] This achievement took a historical, practical significance in the ascetical imitation of Christ that called disciples of Christ to seek a unified self like that of Christ: as Christ brought divinity and humanity into one, Christians are called to bring body and soul together. Integration became a key task for all early Christians.

In summary, it is hard to imagine any culture that would not minimally recognize the claims of partiality and impartiality as well as some sense of self-regard. Thus, I claim that all persons in every culture are constituted by these three ways of being related. Moreover, by naming these virtues as cardinal, I propose a device for talking cross-culturally. This device is based, however, on modest claims. The cardinal virtues do not purport to offer a complete picture of the ideal person or to exhaust the entire domain of virtue. Rather than being the last word on virtue, they are among the first words, providing the bare essentials for right human living and specific action. The cardinal virtues provide, then, a skeleton of both what human persons should basically be and at what human action should basically aim. All other issues of virtue hang on the skeletal structures of both rightly integrated dispositions and right moral action.

I only claim that we can find a basic concern for these three ways of being related—generally, specifically and uniquely—in every culture. As we saw earlier in chapter five, however, each culture has a way of thickening the virtues. For instance, autonomy considerably dominates the culture in the United States. Autonomy thickens justice inasmuch as we would not give "the due" to any persons without their consent. Our health care, for instance, so powerfully protects the rights of the individual that we could not imagine justice in a health care system that did not privilege informed consent. Similarly, any number of contemporary essays that advise us on our particular relationships routinely urge us not to set agendas without an understanding of the wishes of the other. In North American culture, autonomy thickens our understanding of the contemporary cardinal virtues.

I claimed earlier that mercy is a defining mark of Christianity. In Christian cultures, mercy "thickens" our understanding of justice, fidelity, and self-care. Inasmuch as mercy is the willingness to enter into the chaos of another so as to respond to the other, we could not imagine a Christian justice that did not take into account the chaos of the most marginalized. Nor could we imagine the Christian fidelity, for instance, of a marriage that was not thickened by the yeast of mercy in which spouses enter the other's chaos seventy times seven times. Nor in our own self-caring could we imagine a Christian self-care that did not urge the self to enter into the deep chaos of our distinctively complicated lives. In the quest to grow as integrated and constitutively relational persons, these cardinal virtues are constantly being defined in history through the virtue of mercy.

BIBLICAL PERSPECTIVES
D. J. Harrington

In the Bible, justice is not simply fair and honest dealings between humans. Rather, justice is first of all a divine attribute. The God of the Bible lays down the laws that should govern human justice and at the same time manifests a special care for the poor and weak. With regard to money and material possessions the Synoptic Gospels present sharing by the rich as a way of combating economic poverty, wealth as a possible obstacle to discipleship, and material poverty as possibly a help toward greater dependence upon God.

SHARE YOUR GOODS NOW!
(Luke 16:19–31)

19. There was a rich man who was dressed in purple and fine linen and who feasted sumptuously every day. 20. And at his gate lay a poor man named Lazarus, covered with sores, 21. who longed to satisfy his hunger with what fell from the rich man's table; even the dogs would come and lick his sores. 22. The poor man died and was carried away by the angels to be with Abraham. The rich man also died and was buried. 23. In Hades, where he was being tormented, he looked up and saw Abraham far away with Lazarus by his side.

24. He called out, "Father Abraham, have mercy on me, and send Lazarus to dip the tip of his finger in water and cool my tongue; for I am in agony in these flames." 25. But Abraham said, "Child, remember that during your lifetime you received your good things, and Lazarus in like manner evil things; but now he is comforted here, and you are in agony. 26. Besides all this, between you and us a great chasm has been fixed, so that those who might want to pass from here to you cannot do so, and no one can cross from there to us." 27. He said, "Then, father, I beg you to send him to my father's house 28.—for I have five brothers—that he may warn them, so that they will not also come into this place of torment." 29. Abraham replied, "They have Moses and the prophets; they should listen to them." 30. He said, "No, father Abraham; but if someone goes to them from the dead, they will repent." 31. He said to him, "If they do not listen to Moses and the prophets, neither will they be convinced even if someone rises from the dead."

The story of the rich man and Lazarus appears as part of Luke's Journey Narrative in 9:51–19:44. It presents economic poverty as an evil to be combated now by the wealthy sharing their material possessions with the poor. In Luke's two-volume work, this theme is more prominent in the Acts of the Apostles than it is in his Gospel. The sharing of goods is an important element in Luke's idealized picture of the early Christian community at Jerusalem: "All who believed were together and had all things in common; they would sell their possessions and goods and distribute the proceeds to all, as any had need" (Acts 2:44–45; see 4:31–5:11).

In Luke's Gospel most of chapter 16 is devoted to the topic of money. The parable of the dishonest steward in 16:1–8a illustrates how a shrewd man of the world averts economic and social ruin by taking prudent actions in a crisis. The moral of the story is presented in 16:8b: "The children of this age are more shrewd in dealing with their own generation than are the children of light." This is followed by various instructions about the use of money: use money wisely now to make friends who might welcome you into God's kingdom (see 16:9); fidelity and honesty in the use of money are signs of one's general character and responsibility (see 16:10–12); and no one can serve two masters—in this case God and wealth/Mammon (see 16:13). Then a critique of the Pharisees and their teachings in 16:14–18 is introduced by the comment that the Pharisees were "lovers of money" (16:14).

The story of the rich man and Lazarus in Luke 16:19–31 consists of a narrative (see 16:19–23) and a dialogue (16:24–31). The narrative first contrasts the two characters during their lifetimes (see 16:19–21). The rich man dresses in "purple and fine linen" and feasts daily, while at the rich man's gate Lazarus is covered with sores and would gladly eat the scraps from the rich man's table. When both die, however, there is a reversal so that Lazarus is in "Abraham's bosom" and the rich man is in hell (see 16:22–23). Their respective fates mirror the first beatitude ("Blessed are you who are poor, for yours is the kingdom of God," Luke 6:20) and the first woe ("But woe to you who are rich, for you have received your consolation," Luke 6:24) in the Sermon on the Plain.

The dialogue between the rich man and Abraham in 16:24–31 proceeds in three steps. First, in 16:24–26, we learn that there is a judgment after death and the result is irreversible: "Between you and us a great chasm is fixed." Then in 16:27–29, we are told that the rich man and his brothers should know enough to share their goods with poor people from the social teachings in the Old Testament: "They have Moses and the prophets." And finally, in 16:30–31, we are reminded that if the rich will not listen to the social teachings of the Old Testament, they also will not listen to someone who came back from the dead.

Luke 16:19–31 is designed to scare the wealthy. Its basic message is this: Share your material possessions in the present time before it is too late. During your lives on earth, you rich people can help the poor. After death it will be too late. Therefore do it now!

The story also continues the Lukan theme of the great reversal: the exaltation of the lowly and the humbling of the wealthy in God's kingdom. This theme is most prominent in Mary's *Magnificat* (see Luke 1:46–55) and in the Blessings and Woes (see 6:20–26). It thus provides a warning to those who hold the view that earthly riches are a sign of God's approval. The point is that earthly riches are no guarantee of happiness and no criterion of moral value now or in the future life. The passage is also a plea to rich people to recognize the existence and personhood of the poor. The rich man seems to be unaware that Lazarus was right outside his gate and that he did anything wrong in ignoring him (see Matthew 25:31–46). And the story is also an endorsement of the perduring value of social teachings found in the Old Testament ("Moses and the prophets").

BIBLICAL JUSTICE

There is a long-standing division among Bible translators about whether Hebrew *sedeqah* and Greek *dikaiosynē* (and related terms) should be rendered as "righteousness" or "justice." There is no dispute, however, about the centrality of the theme in both testaments. In the Bible justice is first of all an attribute of God, who is faithful to his covenant and to his people. Justice for humans is fidelity to their covenant relationships involving God and other people. Concern for marginal persons is based on the biblical concept of God as defender of the oppressed.

That justice is an attribute of God is illustrated by Psalms 99:4: "Mighty King, lover of justice, you have established equity; you have executed justice and righteousness in Jacob." The laws that are set down in the Torah are presented as divine revelation, as the means by which God's people can live in harmony with God, with one another, and with the land.

That the God of the Bible has a special concern for marginal people is a major theme in God's revelation to Moses in Exodus 3. Indeed, that revelation is a response to Israel's oppression in Egypt: "I have observed the misery of my people . . . I know their sufferings" (3:7). God's care for the poor and the defenseless is an important part of God's justice according to Deuteronomy 10:17–18: "the great God, mighty and awesome, who is not partial and takes no bribe, who executes justice for the orphan and the widow, and who loves the strangers, providing them food and clothing."

The call for justice on the part of God's people is one of the great themes of the Old Testament prophets: "What does the Lord require of you but to do justice, and to love kindness, and to walk humbly with your God?" (Micah 6:8). Often called the prophet of social justice, Amos accuses Israel of sins against justice: "they who trample the head of the poor into the dust of the earth, and push the afflicted out of the way" (2:7). What Amos hopes for is that God's people might practice justice: "But let justice roll down like waters, and righteousness like an ever-flowing stream" (5:24). Likewise, the post-exilic prophet in Isaiah 56–66 urges the people of Jerusalem "to loose the bonds of injustice . . . to let the oppressed go free . . . to share your bread with the hungry and bring the homeless poor into your house" (58:6–7).

The apocalyptic vision of the kingdom of God is closely related to the biblical theme of justice. At the last judgment the God of justice will vindicate the just and punish the wicked, and from then on perfect justice will prevail (see Daniel 12:1–3; Wisdom 1–5). The fullness of the kingdom is a display of the justice or righteousness of God. The mission of Jesus is to make possible again our right relationship with God (justification), and his coming among us (and especially his death and resurrection) is described by Paul as the revelation or manifestation of the justice of God (see Romans 1:17). What emerges from the Bible is the concept of redemptive or restorative justice, which moves beyond retribution and seeks for healing and reconciliation with God and the community.

WEALTH, PROPERTY, AND MATERIAL GOODS

In the Old Testament, the right to possess property is taken for granted. But it is also assumed that God owns the land and the people are tenants on his property. There are many regulations to protect the land (for example, sabbatical and jubilee years) and to care for the weak and poor among God's people. The prophets frequently criticize greed and avarice, and indicate that the rights and privileges of the rich are subordinate to the needs of the weaker members of society.

In the Synoptic Gospels it is possible to discern three different attitudes regarding wealth, property, and material goods. One such strand has already been treated in the exposition of the story of the rich man and Lazarus in Luke 16:19–31. That story illustrates the idea that economic poverty is an evil to be combated in the present time by the rich sharing their goods with the needy poor.

A second attitude views riches and possessions as possible obstacles to the life of discipleship and to entering God's kingdom. When Jesus challenges a rich man to move beyond keeping the commandments and to "sell what you own, and give the money to the poor ... then come, follow me" (Mark 10:21), the man is shocked and goes away sad. He is shocked because he and most of his contemporaries (including Jesus' disciples) regarded wealth and material possessions as signs of God's favor upon righteous people (see Deuteronomy 28:1–14). In word and deed, however, Jesus challenges this assumption. He goes so far as to declare: "How hard it will be for those who have wealth to enter the kingdom of God!" (Mark 10:23). The lifestyle that Jesus and his first followers adopt is one of itinerant radicalism—going from place to place, spreading the gospel, and relying upon the kindness of strangers along the way. This way of discipleship is rooted in absolute dependence on God. And it has the effect of protecting against making money or material possessions into divine entities: "You cannot serve God and wealth" (Luke 16:13).

The third perspective comes from the Old Testament emphasis on God's special care for the poor. The idea is that the poor are in a position of unique openness to God and that their prayers are heard. In other words,

God has a preferential option for the poor. This attitude is expressed in the first Lukan beatitude: "Blessed are you who are poor, for yours is the kingdom of God" (6:20). Matthew in 5:3 "spiritualizes" the beatitude when he has Jesus declare "Blessed are the poor in spirit." Nevertheless, the economic element remains in the sense that the poor are those who live in total dependence on God.

SOME OTHER PERSPECTIVES

The New Testament paradoxically promises great rewards to those who accept Jesus' challenge to follow him in total dependence upon God. To those who constitute his new family, Jesus offers "a hundredfold now in this age—houses, brothers and sisters, mothers and children, and fields with persecutions—and in the age to come eternal life" (Mark 10:30). The phrase *with persecutions* is generally regarded as Mark's addition to introduce the realism of the cross into an otherwise rosy picture. And Mary's *Magnificat* describes a great social reversal: "He has brought down the powerful from their thrones, and lifted up the lowly; he has filled the hungry with good things, and sent the rich away empty" (Luke 1:52–53).

The letter of James contains a vigorous attack against rich people who defraud their workers and live in luxury. With prophetic vigor James, the most eloquent New Testament advocate for social justice, warns: "Come now, you rich people, weep and wail for the miseries that are coming to you" (James 5:1). The Pastoral Epistles propose an ideal of "godliness combined with contentment" and warn against the love of money as "a root of all kinds of evil" (1 Timothy 6:6, 10).

Questions for Reflection and Discussion

1. What is the virtue of justice? How does justice relate to fidelity, self-care, and prudence?

2. Which translation do you prefer—"justice" or "righteousness"? Why?

3. How do you fit together the following three biblical attitudes: economic poverty as an evil to be combated, riches and possessions as possible obstacles to discipleship, and God's special care for the poor?

Notes

1. William C. Spohn, "Scripture, Use of in Catholic Social Ethics," in Judith Dwyer, ed., *The New Dictionary of Catholic Social Thought* (Collegeville, MN: Liturgical Press, 1994), pp. 861–874.

2. William Frankena, *Ethics* (2nd ed.; Englewood Cliffs, NJ: Prentice-Hall, 1973).

3. Ibid., p. 52.

4. Tom Beauchamp and James Childress, *Principles of Biomedical Ethics* (New York: Oxford University Press, 1989).

5. Ibid., p. 211.

6. Paul Ricoeur, "Love and Justice," in Werner G. Jeanrond and Jennifer L. Rike, eds., *Radical Pluralism and Truth: David Tracy and the Hermeneutics of Religion* (New York: Crossroad, 1991), pp. 187–202.

7. Philip J. Wogaman, "The Biblical Legacy of Ethics," in *Christian Ethics: A Historical Introduction* (Louisville: John Knox, 1993), pp. 2–15.

8. Aristotle, *Nichomachean Ethics*, 1144b.10–1145a.11.

9. Stanley Hauerwas, "Casuistry as Narrative Art," *Interpretation* 37 (1993), pp. 377–88.

10. Gedaliahu Stroumsa, *"Caro salutis cardo:* Shaping the Person in Early Christian Thought," in *History of Religions* 30 (1990), pp. 25–50.

Select Bibliography

Beauchamp, Tom and James Childress, *Principles of Biomedical Ethics*. New York: Oxford University Press, 1989.

Blomberg, Craig L. *Neither Poverty Nor Riches: A Biblical Theology of Material Possessions*. Grand Rapids: Eerdmans, 1999.

Curran, Charles E. *Catholic Social Teaching 1891–Present: A Historical, Theological, and Ethical Analysis*. Washington, D.C.: Georgetown University Press, 2002.

Donahue, John R. "Biblical Perspectives on Justice." In *The Faith That Does Justice*, ed. J. Haughey. New York: Paulist, 1977, pp. 68–112.

Frankena, William. *Ethics*. 2nd ed. Englewood Cliffs, NJ: Prentice-Hall, 1973.

Hauerwas, Stanley. *A Community of Character: Toward a Constructive Christian Social Ethic*. Notre Dame: University of Notre Dame Press, 1981.

Hengel, Martin. *Property and Riches in the Early Church*. Philadelphia: Fortress, 1974.

Hoppe, Leslie. *Being Poor: A Biblical Study*. Wilmington, DE: Glazier, 1987.

Johnson, Luke T. *Sharing Possessions: Mandate and Symbol of Faith*. Philadelphia: Fortress, 1981.

Keenan, James F. "Virtue and Identity." In *Creating Identity: Biographical, Moral, Religious*. Hermann Häring, Maureen Junker-Kenny, and Dietmar Mieth (eds.), *Concilium* 2000/2 (London: SCM Press, 2000), pp. 69–77.

Langan, John. "The Unity of the Virtues." *Harvard Theological Review* 72–73 (1979), pp. 81–95.

Lauritzen, Paul. "The Self and Its Discontents." *Journal of Religious Ethics* 22 (1994), pp. 189–210.

Longenecker, Richard N. *New Testament Social Ethics for Today*. Grand Rapids: Eerdmans, 1984.

Marshall, Christopher D. *Beyond Retribution: A New Testament Vision for Justice, Crime, and Punishment*. Grand Rapids: Eerdmans, 2001.

Mieth, Dietmar. "Moral Identity—How is it Narrated?" *Creating Identity*, pp. 11–22.

Mott, Steven. *Biblical Ethics and Social Change*. New York–Oxford: Oxford University Press, 1982.

Nelson, Daniel Mark. *The Priority of Prudence: Virtue and the Natural Law in Thomas Aquinas and the Implications for Modern Ethics*. University Park, PA: Pennsylvania State University Press, 1992.

Pope, Stephen (ed.). *The Aquinas Reader*. Washington, D.C.: Georgetown University Press, 2002.

Ricoeur, Paul. "Love and Justice." In Werner G. Jeanrond and Jennifer L. Rike (eds.), *Radical Pluralism and Truth: David Tracy and the Hermeneutics of Religion*. New York: Crossroad, 1991, pp. 187–202.

Spohn, William C. "Scripture, Use of in Catholic Social Ethics." In Judith Dwyer (ed.), *The New Dictionary of Catholic Social Thought*. Collegeville: Liturgical Press, 1994, pp. 861–874.

Wheeler, Sondra E. *Wealth as Peril and Obligation*. Grand Rapids: Eerdmans, 1995.

Wogaman, J. Philip. "The Biblical Legacy of Ethics." In *Christian Ethics: A Historical Introduction*. Louisville: John Knox, 1993, pp. 2–15.

Chapter Ten

EMBODIMENT AND COMMUNITY AS THE CONTEXT FOR SEXUAL ETHICS

Through the centuries Christians have often been accused of despising or denigrating the body and material things. This charge, however, is not well founded in the Christian Scriptures or in Christian practice. Indeed, Christianity proclaims that "the Word became flesh" (John 1:14). In its view of the human condition (anthropology) it insists that the human person is a body (*sōma*) and does not merely have a body. One of its most powerful images for the Church is the Body of Christ. Another powerful image of the Church is the new family of Jesus made up of persons dedicated to doing the will of God.

In this chapter Keenan explores how early Christians understood their existence as "embodied," while Harrington shows how they regarded their movement as the new family of Jesus and gave prominence to women. The twin emphasis on embodied existence and the new family of Jesus provides the context for our treatment of various aspects of sexual ethics in the next three chapters.

MORAL THEOLOGICAL REFLECTIONS
J. F. Keenan

The call to recognize the effective history of Scripture has always been essential for Christianity. Earlier we saw from Klaus Demmer that our understanding of sin and death is dramatically affected by our redemption through Jesus Christ. Another manifestation of that effective history is seen through the way in which Christians understand themselves as embodied. We saw, for instance, in the first chapter that the integration of the person as corporeally and spiritually one was the moral challenge for the followers of the Redeemer, who himself was integrated fully as human and divine. Thus, as an innovation, Christian women developed the practice of perpetual virginity whereby they literally embodied the spirit of their generosity.

The longstanding importance of the Christian's self-understanding as embodied is caught by famous German Catholic theologian and now Cardinal Walter Kasper, when he writes:

> The body is God's creation and it always describes the whole of the human and not just a part. But this whole person is not conceived as a figure enclosed in itself, as in classical Greece, nor as a fleshy substance, as in materialism, nor as a person and personality, as in idealism. The body is the whole human in relationship to God and humanity. It is the human's place of meeting with God and humanity. The body is the possibility and the reality of communication.[1]

SCRIPTURE SCHOLARSHIP
AND THE BODY

Recent attention by Scripture scholars and others brings us to a heightened awareness of the human body in Scripture. For instance, reflecting on the Greek word for body, *sōma*, German Protestant New Testament theologian Rudolf Bultmann argued that for Paul "*sōma* belongs inseparably, constitutively, to human existence . . . The only human existence there is— even in the sphere of the Spirit—is somatic existence."[2] Thus Bultmann notes that Paul never uses *sōma* to describe a corpse. Moreover, the body is so integrated into human existence that, as Bultmann claims, the human does not *have* a *sōma* but rather *is sōma*.

Echoing Bultmann, American Protestant biblical scholar Robert Jewett begins his work with the remark that "for Paul theology is anthropology."[3] Investigating anthropological terms in Scripture, Jewett finds, on the one hand, that the word *sarx* ("flesh") generally describes those negative desires for righteousness that keep us from God. On the other hand, the word *sōma* is used to combat gnostic individualism and provides the basis for both the metaphysical unity of the person and for the possibility of relationship between persons.

Other writers consider the notion of relationality that develops from the scriptural understanding of the body. While granting that the Greek concept *sōma* conveys a "circumscribed totality" serving as the basis of personal unity, Antoine Vergote, a Catholic philosopher in Belgium, notes that the Semitic notion of body is expressed through organs, like the heart, kidneys, and lungs, that metaphorically represent "the ensemble of rapports" that we enjoy with the world and God. For the Semite, then, the human "is not an individualized entity but an ensemble of diversely qualified relations."[4]

Still, both the Greek and Semitic traditions would hold, Vergote contends, that the human "is not someone who has a body but whose existence is corporal." In this light, the scriptural understanding of "the resurrection event does not imply the thesis of an immortal soul; on the contrary, it suggests the idea that the body is the whole man."[5] In short, the ability of the human body to explain human existence, personality, and relatedness provides the sufficient stuff for resurrection. Through corporeality, the believer is related and, thus, can be caught up in Christ, who transforms that corporeality. Wayne Meeks, a biblical scholar at Yale University, expresses a similar insight when he echoes Paul: "Christ will be magnified *in my body*, either by life or by death" (emphasis added; Philippians 1:20).[6]

Scripture reveals, then, not only who we are in Christ but also who we will be. If our corporeality encompasses our existence and is the basis for our relationality, then the resurrection of our bodies means that we will never be at war within our bodies again.

Does that promise of glorious integration have any bearing on the moral task for a Christian? Catholic moral theologian Patricia Jung pursues this question. She proposes a "sanctification of bodily needs" that helps assimilate a vision of our bodies as transformable and that seeks forms of moral action to foster our self-understanding as fully corporeal persons.[7]

Several biblical scholars take similar positions. They interpret the promise of the resurrection of our bodies as a call to the moral task to treat our bodies today as fully incorporated subjects. In sum, both Scripture scholars and theologians point out that the body as basis for unity and relationality is the end we should seek both as eschatological promise and as contemporary moral challenge.

Another Scripture scholar, Jerome Neyrey, a Jesuit teaching at Notre Dame, looks at Paul's anthropology in a different way. Taking British anthropologist Mary Douglas's model of the correlation between the physical human body and the body of society, Neyrey finds in the corporeal language of 1 Corinthians the self-understanding of the Corinthian church in terms of the Body of Christ.[8] Examining its different members, Neyrey argues: "The body of Christ, then, is a structured and differentiated body." Neyrey develops Jewett's thesis that Paul's theology is anthropological by adding that his ecclesiology is anthropological as well. In reading the Gospel of Mark, Neyrey again uses Douglas's thesis and engages the more visceral dimensions of that gospel. According to Douglas, purity laws not only protect the physical body but also provide norms for members within a particular social body.[9] Thus, purity laws set both hygienic and social boundaries. Neyrey finds that Jesus, through his own practices, reformed the purity laws and thus provided a new hermeneutics for determining membership in the community (see especially Mark 7:1–23).

Similarly, Majella Franzmann, a biblical scholar in Australia, sees in the eating practices of Jesus another way of understanding how Jesus set normative standards for the believing community.[10] The invitation to approach the table and eat the body of Christ is rooted in the eating practices of Jesus himself. Thus, the human body revealed in the body of Christ emerges as central not only for the self-understanding of the individual Christian but also for the entire believing community. As the basis for personal and social integration, the human body finds in the body of Christ the call to and the expression of human fulfillment.

Christians understand that by being embodied and by being redeemed, they are called to a dynamic personal integration as well as to a full incorporation into the community. These insights from Scripture were well received by early Christians.

EARLY CHRISTIAN SELF-UNDERSTANDING AND THE HUMAN BODY

Human fulfillment as embodied in the risen Christ is central for understanding the hopes and moral responsibilities of early Christians. Brian Daley, a Jesuit patristics scholar at Notre Dame, captures the importance of the early church's hope in resurrection and immortality in establishing the Christian task to seek integration.[11] He claims that early Christians believed the integrated morality of body and spirit was an anthropological necessity: only the immortality of the whole person could make the present struggle to integrate the body and spirit meaningful. Like the Scripture scholars, Daley finds in human destiny as defined in the risen Christ the opportunity and the demand for all people to find in their own bodies the fullness of the spirit of Christ.

Integration of body and soul was not an aim for the pagan contemporaries of the early Christians. Meeks and Vergote both insist that in Greek thought the self was distinct from the body. Gedaliahu Stroumsa comments that for Plato "to know oneself . . . meant to attend to one's soul, at the exclusion of the body."[12] Thus when Christianity, on the belief that the human is in God's image, made integrating the body and soul both a theological expression of humanity's integrity *and* a normative task, it proposed to the Western world a new claim on the human body. Stroumsa calls the proposal of the person as a unified composite of soul and body "a Christian discovery."[13]

Peter Brown, the great scholar of Late Antiquity, argues likewise and points to the historical effects that our embodied, redemptive self-understanding had on sexuality. Although sometimes we may think that the Christian traditional understanding of sexuality was a flight from the body, Brown claims that "the doctrine of sexuality as a privileged symptom of personal transformation was the most consequential rendering ever achieved of the ancient and Christian yearning for a single heart."[14]

Brown investigates how Christian doctrine freed citizens from Roman control over their bodies. That control exercised itself in two ways. The nobility were to conduct themselves publicly as images of the state's own dignity, and all citizens were to reproduce so as to give the state control over the chain of generative life. Thus the Roman state was assured of both its pride and the children it needed and, in return, gave to its citizens freedom to do whatever they wanted with their bodies so long as they did it with proper discipline. In this exchange, Brown claims that the state vested the human body with a dignity derived from the state's needs and not from the body's own integrity.

Christians and Jews resisted this licentious exchange and charged that the state or polis bestowed the human body with a false indeterminacy. For them, the body was created in God's image. Recouping that determinacy meant a rejection of a great deal of sexual liberties. But in doing so the Church liberated the human body from the city's control. As Brown writes:

> Christian attitudes to sexuality delivered the death-blow to the ancient notion of the city as the arbiter of the body. Christian preachers endowed the body with intrinsic, inalienable qualities. It was no longer a neutral indeterminate outcrop of the natural world, whose use and very right to exist was subject to predominantly civic considerations of status and utility.[15]

Particularly noteworthy is Brown's claim that chastity played a decisive role in liberating women from the claims of the city. Women benefactresses, in either their widowed or virginal states, freed themselves from the claims of the city to reproduce and became, instead, models of generosity in the life of the Church. Thus Ambrose wrote about the paradox of the closed womb as a sign of a woman's openness to Scripture, Christ, and the poor. These chaste women became, then, models of and for the Church.

Early church historian Joyce Salisbury is, however, less enthusiastic about the closed womb.[16] For her, this theme was not a sign of freedom, but another exercise of control. As the woman was to absent herself from all sexual activity, likewise she was to remove herself from all other worldly commerce. In particular, for the true virgin and good Christian woman, the closed mouth became a necessary corollary for the closed womb. Thus, the Christian community raised such a woman to a privileged position on account of her chastity, but the same community paradoxically silenced her in return for the privilege.

Scholars of the early church demonstrate, then, that religion and the state wrestled through a kind of dialectic for the social construction of the body. The struggle between the two appears most striking in those arenas where Christians were martyred. As Catholic patristics specialist Francine Cardman notes, their deaths were "the most intimate of bodily choices."[17] Surprising though it may seem, the shock of early Christian martyrdom did not come from the brutality of the spectacles. Athletic events and gladiatorial combats in particular had conditioned Roman audiences to slaughter. Rather, the introduction of women into the arena stunned Romans in general and Christians in particular. The claims on women's bodies again became the focal point of the struggle between the two. In fact, during their torments, women became victims of sexual abuse. Their chastity—praised by the Christian community—became the target that their persecutors most sought to destroy. Too much weighed upon the persecutors' attempts to wrestle that chastity from these women martyrs. As Cardman remarks: "The dissolution of the social body is mirrored in the destruction of the martyrs' own bodies."[18] The battle continued after their death. While the state made these women's bodies objects of attack and derision, the Church depicted them as gloriously triumphant.

The beauty of the martyrs' bodies became a key motif in Christian hagiography. David Morris (an essayist who has written on medical culture) notes that, among all the martyrs' bodies, Sebastian's body emerged as a paradigm.[19] Unlike others who were martyred, Sebastian's body remained intact. Pain and beauty could be captured at once in his body. Morris translates the depictions of Sebastian as a "visionary pain" that "employs the body in order to free us from the body."[20] Morris's interpretation of the experience of being freed of the body is, however, more Platonist than Christian. He misses what the historians, theologians, and Scripture scholars continuously stress. As Cardman reminds us, in martyrdom the Christian finds freedom, not from the body but from death. The martyr's body triumphs. Like Salisbury, however, Cardman is not entirely sanguine about the cost of this victory: "For women especially, the making of a martyr meant the unmaking of the body—her own as well as her world's."[21]

The Christian effective history of our redemption plays itself out particularly in terms of our need to imitate Christ—who was completely one as human and divine—by a personal integration of body and soul and by a thorough incorporation of the community of the Church into the one Body of Christ. This double task led in turn to a move to liberate the body from the state by making claims that Christians as embodied understood themselves indebted to God but believed in that indebtedness that as embodied they would one day experience their embodied glorification.

BIBLICAL PERSPECTIVES
D. J. Harrington

Recognition of the Christian emphasis on embodiment is one important element in developing a more biblically based approach to sexual ethics. A second important element is supplied by the New Testament emphasis on the true family of Jesus. Membership in that family is based not on blood ties but rather by a commitment to do the will of God. Belonging to such a community should influence how we approach and resolve our ethical dilemmas. Here some feminist ethicists have grasped the point well and can teach others an important lesson. That point has been nicely expressed by Lisa Sowle Cahill, professor of Christian ethics at Boston College:

> A Christian feminist biblical perspective on sex would give a central place to the values of community, solidarity, inclusiveness, and compassion as exhibited, symbolized, and realized through concrete social relationships and the behavior expected of "disciples."[22]

THE TRUE FAMILY OF JESUS
(Mark 3:31–35)

31. Then his mother and his brothers came; and standing outside, they sent to him and called him. 32. A crowd was sitting around him; and they said to him, "Your mother and your brothers and sisters are outside, asking for you." 33. And he replied, "Who are my mother and my brothers?" 34. And looking at those who sat around him, he said, "Here are my mother and my brothers! 35. Whoever does the will of God is my brother and sister and mother."

The Greco-Roman world in Jesus' time was a patriarchal, hierarchical, and class-conscious society. The emperor, government officials, and almost all the important people were men. The *paterfamilias* or head male in the family had the final say in matters pertaining to the household. Women married, produced children, and oversaw daily affairs in the household. Many women died young, due mainly to complications in childbirth. Slave women were regarded as property, and lower-class women might work outside the household. The social structure has been compared to a pyramid, with the noble/wealthy few at the top and the vast majority at the bottom. Knowing one's place in society was important, and it is was difficult to move from one class to another. It was not enough to have a lot of money.

As part of the Roman Empire, the Jews of Palestine adopted many social values from the wider Greco-Roman world. And the patriarchal family and household had already been prominent values in ancient Near Eastern and Israelite societies. In this context, Jesus' teaching about his true family in Mark 3:31–35 was radical and challenging. The passage is the second part in an intercalation or "sandwich" that begins in Mark 3:20–21 with a notice about Jesus' blood family being disturbed at the public attention that he was getting. Some people were saying that Jesus "has gone out of his mind" (3:21). And so his family sought to restrain him. The reason was that he was becoming an embarrassment to them and was bringing shame on the whole family. In this kind of society, what others thought of you and your family was very important, and bringing shame on your family was a serious offense.

After Jesus' debate with the scribes from Jerusalem (see Mark 3:22–30) about the source of his powers (Is it Satan or the Holy Spirit?), Jesus is informed in 3:31–32 that his mother and his brothers and sisters are outside asking for him. Rather than acceding to them and going away quietly, Jesus asks his audience inside a question that challenges the very concept of family dominant in his society: "Who are my mother and my brothers?" (3:33). The point is that the true family of Jesus is inside the house, not outside. The true family of Jesus consists of those who are dedicated to serving God and one another in the spirit of Jesus. And so he says: "Here are my mother and my brothers! Whoever does the will of God is my brother and sister and mother" (3:34b–35).

Jesus' declaration about his true family is an example of what is called *fictive kinship*. The people who make up Jesus' true family are not blood relatives of him or of one another, and so in the strict sense they are not "kin." What makes them into a family and into kin is their commitment to do the will of God. Their kinship is based on the "fiction" that shared spiritual values rather than blood ties make them into the family of Jesus.

Although this kinship may be fictive on the biological level, it is nonetheless real. In fact, in the context of the New Testament and the early church, what binds together members of Jesus' true family—dedication to doing God's will—is far more important than blood ties and biological family.

In the family of Jesus, God is the father. In Jesus' definition of his true family in Mark 3:35, there is no mention of a father. Likewise, in Jesus' promise of rewards for those who have left everything to follow him, there is mention of "houses, brothers and sisters, mothers and children, and fields" (Mark 10:30). But there is no mention of fathers. The fatherhood of God trumps or overrides all human patriarchy. Where God is acknowledged as the true father, the social values of patriarchy, hierarchy, and class-consciousness are made relative at best.

The concept of the true family of Jesus as those who are committed to doing God's will is a powerful image of the Church. Indeed, this is exactly what the Church is: the community of those who take Jesus as the authoritative revealer and revelation of God's will. In this system of fictive kinship, water (spiritual kinship in baptism) is stronger than blood (biological kinship). And this image may have radical social implications, as expressed in the early baptismal slogan preserved in Galatians 3:28: "There is no longer Jew or Greek, there is no longer slave or free, there is no longer male and female; for all of you are one in Christ Jesus."

WOMEN IN THE JESUS MOVEMENT

The true family of Jesus offered a challenge to the patriarchal, hierarchical, and class-conscious society in which it arose. The unanimous testimony of the Gospels is that women were prominent in the early Jesus movement. This fact can be explained on historical and sociological grounds, since new religious movements tend to be fluid in their structures and less observant of social hierarchies. More importantly, it can also be explained theologically as a corollary of the Jesus movement's identity as the new family of Jesus (see Mark 3:31–35). Whether this phenomenon can be described as the "discipleship of equals" (as Elisabeth Schüssler Fiorenza notes[23]) and whether women followers should be called "apostles" or "disciples" in a technical sense are matters of dispute. But it is clear that women were an integral part of the movement begun by Jesus.

According to Mark's Gospel, women were recipients of Jesus' healing power (see 1:29–31; 5:21–43), and a Gentile women even talks Jesus into healing her daughter (see 7:24–30). In anointing Jesus at Bethany, an unnamed woman provides the interpretive key for the entire passion narrative (see 14:3–9). Only at Jesus' death, however, does Mark inform us that Jesus had many women followers all through his ministry: "These used to follow him and provided for him when he was in Galilee; and there were many other women who had come up with him to Jerusalem" (15:41).

The women followers are the witnesses to Jesus' death and resurrection: They saw him die, saw where he was buried, and found his tomb empty on Easter Sunday morning (see 15:40–16:8).

Luke provides information about Jesus' women followers relatively early, during his account of Jesus' ministry in Galilee (see 8:1–3). The key figure is Mary Magdalene who (with the other women) accompanies Jesus throughout his public ministry and at Easter serves as "the apostle to the apostles" in that she tells the male disciples that Jesus' tomb is empty and that he has been raised from the dead (see 24:10). Moreover, in his infancy narrative (see chapters 1–2), Luke portrays several women—Elizabeth, Mary, and Anna—as models of biblical piety. Indeed, Luke describes Mary the mother of Jesus in such a way that she incarnates the ideal of discipleship as hearing the word of God and acting upon it (see 8:21; 11:28). Luke also presents parables about women (see 15:8–10; 18:1–8) and tells the story of Mary and Martha (see 10:38–42) in which Mary's desire to hear the teaching of Jesus is encouraged as superior ("the better part") to the household tasks ordinarily carried out by women like Martha.

In his presentation of women, Matthew generally follows Mark. But his inclusion of five women in the genealogy of Jesus (see 1:1–17) is striking. And John presents a long dialogue between Jesus and the Samaritan woman (see 4:1–42) that issues in her becoming a missionary: "Many Samaritans from that city believed in him because of the woman's testimony" (4:39).

The part of the baptismal slogan that says "there is no longer male and female" (Galatians 3:28) seems to have been taken with some seriousness in the early Pauline mission. The personal greeting contained in Romans 16 features the names of many women (Phoebe, Prisca, Mary, and so on) and attaches to them titles that suggest their active roles in early Christian movement: deacon, co-worker, and even apostle (in the case of Junia). In Paul's description of the Christian assembly at Corinth, it is assumed that women pray and prophesy (see 1 Corinthians 11:5). The rule that women should be silent in church (see 14:34–35) seems to be the position of Paul's opponents that Paul then vehemently rejects (see 14:36).

In the later Pauline writings, the reversion to the general cultural standards of the Greco-Roman world regarding the place of women is noticeable. The household codes (see Colossians 3:18–4:1; Ephesians 5:22–6:9; 1 Peter 2:18–3:7) accept the subordination of women to their husbands in the household. They do insist, however, on mutual respect and the recognition that all social relations are now "in the Lord." The ideal of social respectability that is encouraged especially in the Pastoral Epistles became part of the Church's missionary strategy of good example. However, there is no reason to exalt this post-Pauline development into the norm for the

Church in all times and places. Indeed, the theme of the true family of Jesus seems to offer an older and better approach today.

THEOLOGICAL SIGNIFICANCE

The New Testament is not a book about sex or sexual ethics; its explicit teachings on these topics are few and far between. But its relative silence does not necessarily indicate indifference to these matters. It does suggest that its teachings about sexual ethics and other ethical issues are part of the larger story of the paschal mystery: Jesus' life, death, and resurrection, and their significance for us as embodied persons.

The New Testament directives about sexual ethics need to be interpreted in the wider context of Jesus' double love commandment and the recognition of the dignity and value of human persons promoted by the Sermon of the Mount. And they should be placed in the communal context of the true family of Jesus. As Lisa Cahill states: "Sexual sins, not a major focus of the New Testament, were defined in relation to the unity of the community and to equal consideration of all its members."[24]

Questions for Reflection and Discussion

1. What is the difference between being a body and having a body?

2. Why and how did early Christians interpret social entities such as a city, community, or church as a body?

3. What difference might it make to place Christian sexual ethics in the communal context of the true family of Jesus?

Notes

1. Walter Kasper, *Jesus the Christ* (New York: Paulist, 1976), p. 150.

2. Rudolf Bultmann, *Theology of the New Testament* (London: SCM, 1952), p. 192.

3. Robert Jewett, *Paul's Anthropological Terms* (Leiden: Brill, 1971), p. 1.

4. Antoine Vergote, "The Body as Understood in Contemporary Thought and Biblical Categories," in *Philosophy Today* 35 (1991), pp. 35–105.

5. Ibid., p. 95.

6. Wayne A. Meeks, *The Origins of Christian Morality* (New Haven, CT: Yale University Press, 1993).

7. Patricia Beattie Jung, "Sanctification: An Interpretation in Light of Embodiment," in *Journal of Religious Ethics* 11 (1983), pp. 75–95.

8. Jerome H. Neyrey, "Body Language in 1 Corinthians," in *Semeia* 35 (1986), pp. 129–170.

9. Mary Douglas, *Purity and Danger: An Analysis of Concepts of Pollution and Taboo* (London: Routledge and Kegan Paul, 1966).

10. Majella Franzmann, "Of Food, Bodies, and the Boundless Reign of God in the Synoptic Gospels," in *Pacifica* 5 (1992), pp. 17–31.

11. Brian Daley, *The Hope of the Early Church: A Handbook of Patristic Eschatology* (New York: Cambridge University Press, 1991).

12. Gedaliahu Stroumsa, "*Caro salutis cardo:* Shaping the Person in Early Christian Thought," in *History of Religions* 30 (1990), p. 33.

13. Ibid., p. 44.

14. Peter Brown, "Late Antiquity," in P. Veyne, ed., *A History of Private Life*, vol. 1, *From Pagan Rome to Byzantium* (Cambridge, MA-London: Harvard University Press, 1987), p. 300.

15. Peter Brown, *The Body and Society: Men, Women, and Sexual Renunciation in Early Christianity* (New York: Columbia University Press, 1988), p. 437.

16. Joyce Salisbury, *Church Fathers, Independent Virgins* (London: Verso, 1991).

17. Francine Cardman, "Acts of the Women Martyrs," in *Anglican Theological Review* 70 (1989), p. 147.

18. Ibid., 148.

19. David Morris, *The Culture of Pain* (Berkeley: University of California Press, 1991).

20. Ibid., p. 135.

21. Cardman, op. cit., p. 150.

22. Lisa Sowle Cahill, "Sexual Ethics: A Feminist Biblical Perspective," in *Interpretation* 49 (1995), p. 10.

23. Elisabeth Schüssler Fiorenza, *In Memory of Her* (New York: Crossroad, 1983), pp. 97–159.

24. Cahill, op. cit., p. 12.

Select Bibliography

Brown, Peter. *The Body and Society: Men, Women, and Sexual Renunciation in Early Christianity*. New York: Columbia University Press, 1988.

_____. "Late Antiquity." In P. Veyne (ed.), *A History of Private Life*. Vol. 1, *From Pagan Rome to Byzantium*. Cambridge, MA–London: Harvard University Press, 1987, pp. 237–311.

Bultmann, Rudolf. *Theology of the New Testament*. London: SCM, 1952, pp. 1:192–203.

Cahill, Lisa S. *Family. A Christian Social Perspective*. Minneapolis: Fortress, 2000.

_____. "Sexual Ethics. A Feminist Biblical Perspective." In *Interpretation* 49 (1995), pp. 5–16.

Cardman, Francine. "Acts of the Women Martyrs." In *Anglican Theological Review* 70 (1989), pp. 144–150.

Collins, Raymond F. *Sexual Ethics and the New Testament: Behavior and Belief*. New York: Crossroad, 2000.

Daley, Brian. *The Hope of the Early Church: A Handbook of Patristic Eschatology*. New York: Cambridge University Press, 1991.

Douglas, Mary. *Purity and Danger: An Analysis of Concepts of Pollution and Taboo*. London: Routledge and Kegan Paul, 1966.

Franzmann, Majella. "Of Food, Bodies, and the Boundless Reign of God in the Synoptic Gospels." In *Pacifica* 5 (1992), pp. 17–31.

Garrison, Roman. "Paul's Use of the Athlete Metaphor in 1 Cor. 9." In *Studies in Religion* 22 (1993), pp. 209–218.

Jewett, Robert. *Paul's Anthropological Terms*. Leiden: Brill, 1971.

Jung, Patricia Beattie. "Sanctification: An Interpretation in Light of Embodiment." In *Journal of Religious Ethics* 11 (1983), pp. 75–95.

Kasper, Walter. *Jesus the Christ*. New York: Paulist, 1976.

Keenan, James F. "Christian Perspectives on the Human Body." In *Theological Studies* 55 (1994), pp. 330–346.

Meeks, Wayne A. *The Origins of Christian Morality*. New Haven: Yale University Press, 1993.

Morris, David. *The Culture of Pain.* Berkeley: University of California Press, 1991.

Neyrey, Jerome H. "Body Language in 1 Corinthians." In *Semeia* 35 (1986), pp. 129–170.

_____. "The Idea of Purity in Mark's Gospel." In *Semeia* 35 (1986), pp. 91–128.

Osiek, Carolyn and David Balch. *Families in the New Testament World.* Louisville: Westminster, 1997.

Rahner, Karl. "The Resurrection of the Body." In *Theological Investigations* II. K. Kruger (trans.). Baltimore: Helicon, 1963, pp. 203–216.

_____. "The Body in the Order of Salvation." In *Theological Investigations* XVII. Margaret Kohl (trans.). New York: Crossroad, 1981, pp. 71–89.

Salisbury, Joyce. *Church Fathers, Independent Virgins.* London: Verso, 1991.

Schüssler Fiorenza, Elisabeth. *In Memory of Her: A Feminist Theological Reconstruction of Christian Origins.* New York: Crossroad, 1983.

Vergote, Antoine. "The Body as Understood in Contemporary Thought and Biblical Categories." In *Philosophy Today* 35 (1991), pp. 93–105.

Witherington, Ben. *Women in the Ministry of Jesus.* Cambridge, UK: Cambridge University Press, 1984.

Wordelman, Amy L. "Everyday Life—Women in the Period of the New Testament." In Carol Newsom and Sharon Ringe (eds.), *The Women's Bible Commentary.* Louisville: Westminster/Knox, 1992, pp. 390–396.

Chapter Eleven

MARRIAGE AND DIVORCE

For most Christian preachers, one of the most difficult and uncomfortable gospel texts in the Sunday lectionary comes on the Twenty-seventh Sunday in Ordinary Time of the Year B. It is Mark 10:2–12, which contains Jesus' absolute prohibition of divorce and remarriage: "Whoever divorces his wife and marries another commits adultery against her; and if she divorces her husband and marries another, she commits adultery" (10:11–12).

Today divorce is a reality in every Christian community and almost every family (including those of most preachers). Every Catholic congregation contains some members who think that the Church is too hard on divorced persons and others who think that it is too easy. But our obsession with the legal question of divorce can obscure the very positive biblical ideal of Christian marriage as fidelity in community: "So they are no longer two, but one flesh. Therefore what God has joined together, let no one separate" (Mark 10:8–9). Emphasis on this positive dimension might, in turn, help to make divorce less frequent and less painful. In this chapter Harrington surveys the New Testament texts that treat marriage and divorce, while Keenan highlights the early Christian emphasis on fidelity in community and applies it to the marriage relationship.

BIBLICAL PERSPECTIVES
D. J. Harrington

Jesus (and the New Testament writers) taught lifelong fidelity as the ideal in marriage. However, Matthew and Paul seem to have allowed for some exceptions. What do we look for when we turn to the New Testament on this matter? Is it a divinely revealed law? Or is it a process of understanding and adaptation?

NO DIVORCE
(Luke 16:18)

Anyone who divorces his wife and marries another commits adultery, and whoever marries a woman divorced from her husband commits adultery.

The shortest and most likely the earliest form of Jesus' teaching about marriage and divorce appears in the context of Luke's travel narrative in Luke 9:51–19:44. Taking over the idea of the final journey of Jesus and his disciples up to Jerusalem from Mark 8:22–10:52, Luke greatly expanded the amount of teaching along the way and made the journey into an even more powerful vehicle for instruction about who Jesus is (Christology) and what it means to follow him (discipleship).

Jesus' teaching about marriage and divorce appears at the center of Luke 16. Thus it is flanked by the parable of the dishonest steward and related teachings about the use of money (see 16:1–13) and the story about the rich man and Lazarus (see 16:19–31). Luke 16:18 is the last part of a unit introduced by a criticism of the Pharisees as "lovers of money." It sits somewhat awkwardly beside a claim about the enduring value of the Torah in 16:17, since divorce is clearly permitted by the Old Testament Law (see Deuteronomy 24:1–4). The juxtaposition suggests that what endures for Christians is the Torah as interpreted and adapted by Jesus as the authoritative teacher.

Luke 16:18 defines divorce and remarriage as adultery, an act clearly forbidden in both versions of the Ten Commandments (see Exodus 20:14; Deuteronomy 5:18). The result is an absolute prohibition of divorce and remarriage. In the first case, a man who divorces his wife and marries another woman is accused of adultery. In the second case, a man who marries a divorced woman is accused of adultery. This teaching is presented without any rationale and without exceptions. Its radical content sets Jesus apart from other Jewish teachers who developed elaborate procedures surrounding divorce and even from the Torah which took divorce for granted and never equated it with adultery.

There is a close parallel to Luke 16:18 in Matthew 5:32 (apart from the parenthetical clause): "Anyone who divorces his wife, except on the ground of unchastity, causes her to commit adultery; and whoever marries a divorced woman commits adultery." See also Mark 10:11 and 1 Corinthians 7:10–11 for very similar teachings. According to the widely accepted explanation of the relationships among the Synoptic Gospels, both Luke and Matthew independently took over this teaching from the Sayings Source Q (which is customarily dated to around A.D. 50). Since Luke is generally the more conservative editor of Q, Luke 16:18 is very likely the earliest form of Jesus' teaching to which we have access.

That Jesus himself taught something like what now appears in Luke 16:18 is indicated by its attestation in several different sources (Q, Paul, Mark, Matthew) and by the lack of parallels in Judaism. And its content fits well with the radical ethical stance that Jesus proposes in the face of the coming kingdom of God.

The ideal put forward by Jesus is that marriage is a lifelong union between man and woman. While presented as a prohibition, Jesus' radical teaching about marriage and divorce has the positive effect of encouraging married persons to work at lifelong fidelity and to do everything possible to contribute to their mutual flourishing within marriage. When there is no easy exit, spouses must work through their problems and challenges—at least that is the theory. Moreover, the absolute prohibition of divorce protected women in a patriarchal society from being summarily dismissed by their husbands. In the arrangement envisioned by Luke 16:18, the husband is obliged to stay with and care for his wife as long as they both shall live.

OLD TESTAMENT AND JEWISH BACKGROUND

In Judaism in Jesus' time (and in most of the Greco-Roman world), marriages were arranged between the bride's father and the groom (and/or his father). Between the engagement and the wedding (about a year), the couple might meet under supervision and get to know each other. Once the marriage contract with its stipulations about the bride's dowry was signed, the bride would be brought to the household of the groom (see Matthew 25:1–13).

The Old Testament takes divorce for granted and speaks about it only indirectly in Deuteronomy 24:1–4, in connection with the case of whether a man may remarry a wife whom he had divorced once and who was then divorced from another man. The answer is no. In passing, we learn that to divorce a wife, the husband had only to write a certificate of divorce, hand it to his wife, and send her out of his household (see 24:1). Josephus, a Jewish contemporary of Jesus, states: "For it is only the man who is permitted by us to do this, and not even a divorced woman may marry again on her own initiative unless her former husband consents."[1] Under Roman law women could initiate divorce proceedings. And even Josephus gives some contrary examples in which a Jewish woman seems to take the initiative. In both contexts, divorce was a matter between husband and wife, not a public legal action.

The Dead Sea Scrolls have provided some valuable documentation regarding marriage and divorce among Jews in New Testament times. A marriage contract from Murabba'at gives the date (in the early second century A.D. by our reckoning), the names of the parties, stipulations about property and dowry, provisions regarding divorce and death, and the names of the witnesses. In a divorce decree from the same site, Joseph the son of Naqsan states: "I divorce and repudiate of my own free will today . . . my wife Miriam." He goes on to promise to pay back the dowry and to replace the divorce decree if necessary.

Two passages among the Qumran scrolls have sometimes been interpreted as forbidding divorce. The *Damascus Document* 4–5 rules against "taking a second wife while the first is still alive." Likewise, the *Temple Scroll* 57 states that the king "shall not take another wife in addition to her [his first wife], for she alone shall be with him all the time of her life." But most scholars today regard these texts as forbidding polygamy rather than divorce and remarriage.

The most controversial issue among Jews in Jesus' time was the reason or grounds for the divorce. According to Deuteronomy 24:1, a man could divorce his wife if he found "something objectionable about her." The Hebrew phrase *'erwat dabar* ("shamefulness of a matter") is vague, and so its precise meaning became a topic of debate among Jewish teachers in Jesus' time. The usually conservative Jewish teacher Shammai reversed the order of the Hebrew words to yield *debar 'erwah* ("something of shame") and so seems to restrict the meaning to acts of unchastity on the wife's part. The more liberal Hillel gave the husband greater latitude: "Even if she spoiled a dish for him." And the second-century A.D. teacher Aqiba allowed divorce "even if he found another more beautiful than she is."[2] Thus Hillel and Aqiba gave the husband almost absolute freedom in initiating a divorce and sending his wife away.

THEOLOGICAL RATIONALE

As noted above in the exposition of Luke 16:18, there is widespread agreement among New Testament sources that Jesus prohibited divorce (see Matthew 16:18; Mark 10:11; Luke 16:18; 1 Corinthians 7:10–11), although there is some variation in the wording of the cases. A biblical-theological rationale for this teaching appears in Mark 10:2–9 (and in Matthew 19:3–9, but in a different order). The Pharisees ask Jesus: "Is it lawful for a man to divorce his wife?" (Mark 10:2). Their question is labeled as a "test," and one gets the impression that the opponents already knew Jesus' position and wanted to expose him publicly as being in contradiction to the Torah and Jewish customs.

In response, Jesus dismisses Deuteronomy 24:1 as merely God's concession to the hardness of human hearts. Instead, Jesus directs his opponents to two biblical quotations: Genesis 1:27 ("God made them male and female") and 2:24 ("For this reason a man shall leave his father and mother and be joined to his wife, and the two shall become one flesh"). These quotations are put forward as expressing the original will of God for humans before Adam's sin (see Genesis 3). The kingdom of God breaking in through Jesus' ministry represents a return to the order of creation as God planned it. The end-time is the primeval time again (in German *Endzeit ist Urzeit*). The ideal of marriage as set forth by Jesus is that "they are no longer two, but one flesh" (Mark 10:8; Matthew 19:6). The consequence is that no man (husband) has the right to separate from his wife and dissolve the marriage bond.

EXCEPTIONS

While Matthew and Paul transmit Jesus' prohibition of divorce, they both add statements that seem to modify its absolute character. In two places, Matthew makes an exception for *porneia* (see 5:32; 19:9). While not the technical Greek term for "adultery" (*moicheia*), most scholars today regard *porneia* here as a reference to sexual misconduct on the wife's part, although some take it as referring to an illicit marriage within the degrees of kinship forbidden in the Torah and elsewhere in the New Testament (see Leviticus 18:6–18; Acts 15:20, 29). By rephrasing the Pharisees' question ("Is it lawful for a man to divorce his wife *for any cause?*" emphasis added) in 19:3 and by adjusting Jesus' absolute teaching in 19:9 (see 5:32) to exclude the case of *porneia*, Matthew brings Jesus into the contemporary Jewish debate about the grounds for divorce and in line with the position of Shammai (who allowed divorce in case of "something shameful" on the woman's part).

In 1 Corinthians 7, Paul moves from restating Jesus' prohibition of divorce in 7:10–11 to take up in 7:12–16 cases regarding "mixed marriages" between Christian and non-Christian spouses. Such marriages resulted at Corinth, especially when one spouse became a Christian and the other did not. Paul's advice ("I and not the Lord," 7:12) is that if both agree to continue the marriage, there is no objection (and perhaps the other spouse and the children may thus be "made holy"). But if the non-Christian spouse wishes to separate, then Paul says: "Let it be so; in such a case the brother or sister is not bound. It is to peace that God has called you" (7:15). The expression "not bound" suggests that the Christian is then free to marry someone else.

SIGNIFICANCE

There is little doubt that Jesus taught lifelong fidelity within marriage, and that this teaching was as radical then as it is now. At the same time, it appears that the evangelist Matthew and the apostle Paul modified Jesus' teaching to leave room for exceptions in light of the circumstances of the Christians to whom they ministered. The problem is, How are we to understand Jesus' teaching on marriage and divorce? As law, example, or ideal? And how can we best put it into practice (while protecting against spousal abuse)? And what significance are we to attribute to the willingness of Matthew and Paul to adapt the teaching of Jesus?

MORAL THEOLOGICAL REFLECTIONS
J. F. Keenan

Fidelity is the virtue for specific relationships. If justice is the virtue by which to cultivate an ordered, fair, and impartial disposition toward all people, then fidelity is about nurturing and sustaining those relationships about which we are naturally very partial: family, friends, neighbors, and so on.

This counterbalance between virtues is nothing new. God is certainly impartial in Scripture, willing the best for all of humanity. But God is also partial toward people like Israel in general, or persons like David in the Old Testament or Mary in the New Testament.

Thus while the Judeo-Christian tradition has always proposed justice to its members, it has equally promoted fidelity. Fidelity is what Israel experienced through Yahweh's frequently reiterated covenantal pledge, even in the face of Israel's inconstancy. The Old Testament is a narrative of God training the chosen people into becoming a faithful nation, a covenantal partner.

FIDELITY IN COMMUNITY

In the New Testament, we find in Jesus Christ the one who is faithful to God and to us, and who pledges in the new covenant to be the inauguration of the kingdom itself. Like Israel, then, the Christian community is called by Christ into being faithful to the God who calls and to the community into which we are invited. Baptism, then, is the sacramental initiation into the life of Christian fidelity with God and the Church.

The early church defined itself by mercy and fidelity. Both were extraordinarily normative for all Christians, for in practice they afforded Christians a way to imitate the example of God and of Christ—an *imitatio Dei* and an *imitatio Christi*. God and Christ were revealed as merciful and faithful. Christians were to be and do likewise.

In *The Rise of Christianity*, sociologist Rodney Stark argues that "Christianity was an urban movement, and the New Testament was set down by urbanites."[3] Those urban areas were dreadful. Stark describes the conditions in those areas as "social chaos and chronic urban misery." This chaos resulted in part from population density. At the end of the first century, Antioch's population was 150,000 within the city walls or 117 persons per acre. Today, New York City has a density of 37 persons per acre, and Manhattan, with its high rise apartments, has 100 persons per acre. Moreover, contrary to common assumptions, Greco-Roman cities were not settled places whose inhabitants descended from previous generations. With high infant mortality and short life expectancy, these cities required "a constant and substantial stream of newcomers" in order to maintain their population levels. As a result, the cities were largely comprised of strangers. These strangers were well treated by early Christians, many of whom, again contrary to assumptions, were anything but poor. Through a variety of ways of caring for newcomers, financially secure Christians welcomed the newly arrived immigrants.

Moreover, their religion was new. Certain demands were imposed by the gods of the pagan religions. But these demands were ritual in substance; they were not neighbor-directed. And while pagan Romans knew generosity, that generosity did not stem from any divine command. A nurse who cared for a victim of an epidemic knew that her life might be lost. If she were a pagan, there was no expectation of divine reward for her generosity; if she were a Christian, however, she believed that she would be rewarded in the next life for having done what God commanded in this life.

The Christian religion was new to the Roman Empire, therefore, because the Christian God required mercy and fidelity to be practiced toward all who called upon the name of the Lord. Christianity required the recognition of the stranger in need as neighbor and, inevitably, as sibling. Christianity commanded the Christian to embrace faithfully the one in need of mercy. Stark writes:

> This was the moral climate in which Christianity taught that mercy is one of the primary virtues—that a merciful God requires humans to be merciful. Moreover, the corollary that *because* God loves humanity, Christians may not please God unless they *love one another* was entirely new. Perhaps even more revolutionary was the principle that Christian love and charity must

extend beyond the boundaries of family and tribe, that it must extend to "all those who in every place call on the name of our Lord Jesus Christ" (1 Corinthians 1:2). This was revolutionary stuff. Indeed, it was the cultural basis for the revitalization of a Roman world groaning under a host of miseries.[4]

Incorporating newcomers into the community of faith meant that these newly baptized persons were now constituted by a new fellowship, one by which they were brothers and sisters with one another in the Lord. They were aliens no longer. Stark summarizes:

> Christianity revitalized life in Greco-Roman cities by providing new norms and new kinds of social relationships able to cope with many urgent urban problems. To cities filled with the homeless and impoverished, Christianity offered charity as well as hope. To cities filled with newcomers and strangers, Christianity offered an immediate basis for attachments. To cities filled with orphans and widows, Christianity provided a new and expanded sense of family.[5]

Like Stark, Lisa Sowle Cahill in her writings on New Testament ethics reminds us of what church historian Jaroslav Pelikan pointed out years ago, that the early church was defined by a new social solidarity.[6] This solidarity with those in need of mercy remains from the first century a consistent call for all Christians.

Thus, the early church welcomed people into the community and established strong bonds of fidelity through baptism and the Eucharist. We see this concern for one another worked out continuously. Christians are called to be responsible for one another whether in avoiding scandal over idol meat (see 1 Corinthians 8–10) or in the call to holiness (see 1 Thessalonians 4–5). We are called to be faithful to all Christians, for Christ has been faithful to us.

Merciful fidelity to the stranger in need is made possible only by the cross, as the sign of reconciliation, and by hope, as the sign of the new creation. By the cross and by the promise, Christ has trained us, disciplined us into his fidelity, and made us capable of imitating him.

We know that the great sin in the early church concerned failure in fidelity. Apostasy was the sin of abandonment or denial of the faith. It was the sin by which Christians *de facto* removed themselves from the community of faith. The struggles with denial and abandonment are also the subjects of stories told in the gospel narratives themselves. We know, too, the extraordinary stories of the Twelve during Jesus' passion. Their betrayal, denial, and abandonment are tales of infidelity (see Mark 14:26–72).

Yet, those stories of flight are interfaced with those of faithfulness (see Mark 14:1–11), and this is a key for understanding how in the early church women grew into enhanced roles in the church. Throughout the Gospels we find women being faithful—by staying at the foot of the cross, attending to the body of Jesus in the tomb, and witnessing the empty tomb. These stories of merciful fidelity, however, are not limited to the passion accounts. We can think easily, for instance, of the benefactresses mentioned in Luke 8:1–3, a report that heralds the prominence of the virgins that we saw in previous chapters.

The stories of women being faithful to Jesus are accompanied also by stories of women being accorded privileged positions in the early church. Here an obvious example is the presence of Mary at the Pentecost (see Acts 1:14). Early texts (see Romans 16) show that women were, as Cahill and others argue, clearly accorded greater leadership roles. This original recognition was accomplished within the communities where women faithfully supported the community members in a variety of ways.

Did the Church sustain this early insight? This is in effect the question raised by Elisabeth Schüssler Fiorenza.[7] The original insight into the fundamental equality of all men and women as sisters and brothers in Christ (that is, as co-equal disciples) was not a remotely asserted cognitive claim. Rather, it was an experienced reality among early Christians who continually supported one another in the ministries of the Church (see Romans 16). In a shared ministry, the communities of faith recognized more and more that women were their sisters in the Lord, able, merciful, and faithful witnesses, disciples, and community members.

The recognition of women as equals was experienced through a greater and greater sharing in the life of Christ. Although virginity is, as we have seen, a distinctively Christian innovation, Christian marriage is no less a distinctively Christian achievement. It is to be marked always by fidelity, so much so that it becomes a paradigmatic symbol of Christ's fidelity to the Church (see Ephesians 5:21-33).

FIDELITY, MARRIAGE, AND DIVORCE

Privileging Christian marriage in this way helps us to understand, in part, the acute issue of divorce. Just as Christ could not be separated from the Church (see Ephesians 5:21–33), so spouses should not separate. It is really only through a hermeneutics of fidelity, therefore, that we can understand 1 Corinthians 7:10–16. Paul's first directive to the newly baptized who are married to unbelieving spouses is to remain in their marriage, since by their faithful relationship they may consecrate their spouses and children. But if the unbelieving spouse wants no part of life with the new initiate, then the new brother or sister is no longer bound to the marriage. Ultimately, for Christians, the main concern is to remain faithful to the community as brothers and sisters of the Lord.

While the symbiotic congruency between both Christ and his Church and between spouses in Christian marriages provides one reason for the strong stance against divorce in the New Testament, another reason derives from the very notion of the co-equal discipleship of men and women. The call to fidelity in marriage was a call to support women who, in other dispensations, could have been abandoned unilaterally by their husbands. Prohibiting divorce, therefore, prohibited men from treating their wives as objects to be disposed at will. By affirming the marital bond, the Christian community gave witness to its own confident insistence on fidelity and therefore equality.

Thus the Church must ask itself today how well it fosters among its members a sense of fidelity whereby they view one another as equals, in solidarity with one another, and as more and more inclined to removing constructed barriers of division and bias. Is the Church's leadership fostering a fidelity among equals?

Similarly, understanding the divorce prohibition as pro-women is important for understanding today how the Church needs to proceed, for instance, in the face of abusive marriages in those places where women have no significant social, political, or economic support and where a woman cannot leave such a situation because divorce is outlawed.

Jesuit biblical scholar George MacRae (1928–1985) helps us with this question as he proposes a differentiation between a once and for all absolute, divinely revealed law on the one hand and a process for articulating the teaching of Jesus and implementing it in the present reality on the other hand.[8] His notion of the contemporary present reality is that the teaching of Jesus was not given once for all time and then simply received and repeated by Paul or Matthew. Rather, the teaching of Jesus must be received today as it was in the time of Paul and Matthew. MacRae, then, does not dismiss Jesus' teaching against divorce as ideal or unimportant, nor does he reduce it to an unattainable goal. Rather, like Klaus Demmer, he situates Jesus' teaching in history and invites us to emulate Paul and Matthew as they historically received and interpreted the teaching of Jesus. Our concern for the abused is no less valid than Paul's concern for the newly baptized.

Margaret Farley offers us help, too, in understanding how fidelity is not simply a task for those who have marital vows.[9] The complexity of our specific relationships must always be moderated by that sense of fidelity that makes us Christians; that is, the cross of Christ and the effective hope that it brings. Inescapably, Christians are called to realize that their call to be faithful extends to all their relationships and that the exercises of reconciliation that the Church provides for its members are exercises to be appropriated in turn by its members.

ABUSED SPOUSES

When faced with an evidently abused spouse, those in ministry should ask themselves how they are being faithful to serving the needs of such persons. Some ministers wrongly believe that their primary responsibility is to uphold the indissolubility of marriage in all instances, including these. But they should reflect on how Jesus might act in fidelity with such abused spouses.

Similarly, those who are in abusive relationships often believe that they must remain faithful to their abusive spouse. But we have seen that the love command has always been a call to love one's neighbor and one's self, and that therefore self-care should be considered a cardinal virtue. In these instances, abused spouses must prudently reflect on the tension between the call to fidelity in marriage and the call to self-care. In doing this prudential reflection, they should appeal to Jesus and ask whether Jesus would really want them to return to or remain in a marriage that endangers them. That is to say, would Jesus recognize this marriage as a Christian one? Or would Jesus offer some sort of bridge to safety, to a more faithful and just community of faith? Indeed, these were the very same type of questions that Matthew and Paul wrestled with as they considered the call to fidelity in marriage and the call of the community to be faithful to individual community members in need.

Questions for Reflection and Discussion

1. How might Jesus' prohibition of divorce and remarriage have improved the life of women in the first century?

2. How do you put together Jesus' absolute prohibition of divorce and the apparent exceptions introduced by Matthew and Paul?

3. How might a greater emphasis on fidelity in community help people to appreciate better the New Testament passages about marriage and divorce?

Notes

1. Joseph, *Antiquities*, 15:259.

2. *Mishnah Gittin*, 9:10.

3. Rodney Stark, *The Rise of Christianity: A Sociologist Reconsiders History* (Princeton: Princeton University Press, 1996), p. 147.

4. Ibid., p. 212.

5. Ibid., p. 161.

6. Lisa Sowle Cahill, "Sexual Ethics: A Feminist Biblical Perspective," in *Interpretation* 49 (1995), pp. 5–16.

7. Elisabeth Schüssler Fiorenza, *In Memory of Her* (New York: Crossroad, 1983).

8. George W. MacRae, "New Testament Perspectives on Marriage and Divorce," in *Studies in the New Testament and Gnosticism* (Wilmington: Glazier, 1987), pp. 115–129.

9. Margaret Farley, *Personal Commitments: Beginning, Keeping, Changing* (San Francisco: Harper and Row, 1990).

Select Bibliography

Cahill, Lisa Sowle. "Sexual Ethics: A Feminist Biblical Perspective." In *Interpretation* 49 (1995), pp. 5–16.

Collins, Raymond F. *Divorce in the New Testament*. Collegeville: Liturgical Press, 1992.

Farley, Margaret. *Personal Commitments: Beginning, Keeping, Changing*. San Francisco: Harper and Row, 1990.

Fitzmyer, Joseph A. "The Matthean Divorce Texts and Some Palestinian Evidence." In *Theological Studies* 37 (1976), pp. 197–226.

Instone Brewer, David. *Divorce and Remarriage in the Bible: The Social and Literary Context*. Grand Rapids: Erdmans, 2002.

MacRae, George W. "New Testament Perspectives on Marriage and Divorce." In *Studies in the New Testament and Gnosticism*. Wilmington: Glazier, 1987, pp. 115–129.

Pelikan, Jaroslav. *The Excellent Empire: The Fall of Rome and the Triumph of the Church*. San Francisco: Harper and Row, 1987.

Stark, Rodney. *The Rise of Christianity: A Sociologist Reconsiders History*. Princeton: Princeton University Press, 1996.

Chapter Twelve

CELIBACY, HOMOSEXUALITY, AND ABORTION

T he topics treated in this chapter are certainly controversial. One might hear a radio talk show in which celibacy is treated without any religious context and ridiculed as a new and bizarre idea for tired "singles." Or you might go for a walk and be confronted (depending on one's neighborhood) by bumper stickers that proclaim "Keep Abortion Safe and Legal" or "God Made Adam and Eve, not Adam and Steve."

In a recent survey of middle class moral attitudes in the United States, the sociologist Alan Wolfe found a surprising convergence on many topics but much disagreement about homosexuality and abortion.[1] This chapter will not repeat the usual arguments on either side of these controversial issues. Rather, Harrington presents the biblical and other evidence that pertains to celibacy, homosexuality, and abortion. Keenan then offers some suggestions about how Christians committed to fidelity in community might approach them today in a constructive and positive way.

BIBLICAL PERSPECTIVES
D. J. Harrington

Chapter 10 developed the biblical themes of embodiment and the true family of Jesus as basic for developing a more biblically based Christian sexual ethics. And throughout our work, we have highlighted the importance of the double love commandment (involving God and neighbor) and the cultivation of the Christian virtues. When the controversial issues of celibacy, homosexuality, and abortion are treated in this framework, they may look a little different from how they have appeared in all the debates swirling around us. Again, Lisa Sowle Cahill, writing from a feminist perspective, makes our point very well:

163

A feminist biblical sexual ethic does not "dilute" or "reject" the normative force of the biblical witness. However, it does shift the focus of the Bible's interpretation from specific action-guiding norms, especially exclusionary norms, to a positive vision and communal practice that is compassionate and egalitarian.[2]

PURITY OF HEART
(Matthew 5:8)

Blessed are the pure in heart,
for they will see God.

The historical background to the beatitude about the pure in heart is Psalm 24. That psalm was originally associated with pilgrimages to Jerusalem and entering the temple complex there to pray and offer sacrifices. The question is raised in Psalm 24:3: "Who shall ascend the hill of the Lord? And who shall stand in his holy place?" The response is given in 24:4: "those who have clean hands and pure hearts, who do not lift up their souls to what is false, and do not swear deceitfully." In other words, only people of integrity may enter the Jerusalem temple complex. Such persons are promised "blessing from the Lord" (24:5) and are said to "seek the face of the God of Jacob" (24:6). By coming to the Temple they hope to experience Yahweh the God of Jacob and thus to receive a blessing from this God.

The Matthean beatitude in 5:8 has no parallel in Luke 6:20–23. It may have been taken over from tradition or composed directly by the Evangelist. For the literary context of this beatitude in the Sermon on the Mount and in Matthew's gospel as a whole, see the treatment in the "Biblical Perspectives" section in chapter 5 on "The Sermon on the Mount and Christian Virtue Ethics."

In three respects, Matthew 5:8 reflects the influence of Psalm 24:4–6: the theme of God's blessing, the reference to the pure in heart, and the promise that such persons will see God. In the Matthean context, however, the place in which they will see God is not the Jerusalem Temple but rather the kingdom of God (as in the whole of Matthew 5:3–12). The expression "pure in heart" refers to people of integrity, as in Psalm 24:4. In the Bible, the heart is the seat of not only the emotions but also the intellect; it is the core of the person, the true or real self. The pure in heart are those who desire to please God and to do God's will above everything else, and so they work toward a perfect correspondence between their inner thoughts and desires and their external actions (see Matthew 7:13–27). These single-hearted persons are focused entirely on doing God's will and so qualify as members of the true family of Jesus (see Mark 3:35).

Matthew 5:8 is not primarily or directly concerned with sexual purity or chastity. But the wider sense of the "pure in heart" as persons of integrity provides a good basis for an integral chastity. People of integrity after the pattern of Psalm 24:4 and Matthew 5:8 live virtuous and faithful lives that are marked by authentic piety ("who do not lift up their souls to what is false") and justice ("and do not swear deceitfully"). They are people of "peace" (*shalom*) in its root sense of wholeness. The positive ideal of purity in heart makes it possible for disciples of Jesus to face up to the radical challenges that he places before them regarding matters of sexuality.

With the biblical concept of purity in heart providing the framework, we can move to the biblical perspectives on three very controversial issues: celibacy, homosexuality, and abortion. None of these topics is treated extensively in the Bible. But the few relevant texts have exercised enormous influence. It is important to know what the Bible says and does not say about these topics.

CELIBACY

In ancient Judaism, the practice of lifelong celibacy was not common. Indeed, one rabbi said: "Any Jew who does not have a wife is not a man."[3] Marriage with children was the usual pattern for Jews in accord with what was regarded as the first commandment in the Torah: "Be fruitful and multiply" (Genesis 1:28). There were, however, exceptions to the usual pattern. Some Essenes and the Therapeutae, members of Jewish religious sects who lived a communal life analogous to that of later Christian monks, were celibate. And there is no positive indication from the New Testament or any other ancient sources that John the Baptist, Jesus, and Paul married.

The only mention of celibacy in the Gospels comes attached to Jesus' teaching about marriage and divorce in Matthew 19:10–12. When his disciples express amazement at his radical teaching, they conclude that "it is better not to marry." Jesus, however, recommends celibacy for "only those to whom it is given." He goes on to speak of people "who have made themselves eunuchs for the sake of the kingdom of God" (19:12). Likewise, Paul, in 1 Corinthians 7, recommends celibacy ("He who refrains from marriage will do better," 7:39) when it is undertaken in the context of expectations about God's coming kingdom. Both Jesus and Paul associate celibacy with witness to the kingdom of God and insist on its voluntary character in response to God's gift.

In the early centuries of the Christian movement, many women embraced celibacy as a way of life, either after being widowed or before any marriage at all. The latter phenomenon of young women proclaiming their celibacy and refusing to marry at all had the effect of disrupting the patriarchal system whereby fathers arranged the marriages of their daughters and stood to gain socially and financially from them. The practice of celibacy ensured for some Christian women a measure of freedom and independence, and contributed to the reputation that the Christian movement gained for being dangerous to Roman society. Men also took up celibacy as an aspect of the monastic spirituality of "singleness of heart," and admiration for this practice among Christians contributed to the choice of celibate males as church leaders in the fourth and fifth centuries. In both cases the eschatological context of celibacy so prominent in the New Testament texts became somewhat blurred.

HOMOSEXUALITY

Homosexuality also is not a major topic in the Bible. The Old Testament narratives about the men of Sodom in Genesis 19 and the Levite's concubine in Judges 19 are more concerned with egregious failures in hospitality and gang rape than with homosexuality *per se.* The relationship between David and Jonathan in 1 Samuel 18–20 is best regarded as an example of male-male friendship, although the language is unusually strong: "The soul of Jonathan was bound to the soul of David, and Jonathan loved him as his own soul" (18:1). The only passage in the Gospels that might be relevant to the topic is Jesus' teaching about marriage as the union of man and woman in "one flesh" (Mark 10:8; Matthew 19:6), which can be construed as an argument for heterosexual marriage only as God's will and so an argument against homosexual unions.

The two explicit Old Testament prohibitions of homosexual behavior appear in the Holiness Code of Leviticus. Both occur in the context of such "abominations" as sexual relations with close relatives, child sacrifice, and bestiality. Leviticus 18:22 decrees: "You shall not lie with a male as with a woman; it is an abomination." Leviticus 20:13 also forbids homosexual activity: "If a man lies with a male as with a woman, both of them have committed an abomination." It goes on to specify the punishment as death: "They shall be put to death; their blood is upon them." These laws reflect the concern for the "natural order" and ritual purity that is characteristic of Leviticus. There is, however, no evidence in the Bible that anyone in ancient Israel was actually put to death for homosexual activity.

The language of Leviticus ("those who sleep with males") gets picked up in the lists of vices that appear in 1 Corinthians 6:9 (*arsenokoitai*) and 1 Timothy 1:10 (*arsenokoitai*). The Greek word *arsenokoites* is a compound of the words for "male" (*arsen*) and for "bed" (*koitē*). The argument is sometimes made that by using the language of Leviticus, the New Testament vice lists accept that book's condemnation of homosexual activity as an abomination. The precise meaning of the term, however, is disputed on the grounds that *arsenokoites* often appears in economic contexts and with reference to male prostitutes. Likewise, the related term in 1 Corinthians 6:9, *malakoi*, literally means "soft" or "effeminate," and so carries a wider sense than "homosexual."

The only extensive New Testament treatment of homosexual activity appears in Romans 1:26–27:

> 26. For this reason God gave them up to degrading passions. Their women exchanged natural intercourse for unnatural, 27. and in the same way also the men, giving up natural intercourse with women, were consumed with passion for one another. Men committed shameless acts with men and received in their own persons the due penalty for their error.

This passage is part of Paul's theological reflection on why non-Jews needed the revelation of God's righteousness in Christ (see Romans 1:18–32). They needed it because they had rejected the knowledge of God that they could have discerned from creation and so they trapped themselves into a downward spiral of ignorance and sin. Paul here takes up the Jewish tradition about idolatry as the sin that leads to all other sins (see Wisdom 13–14). Placed between a description of general sexual immorality (see Romans 1:24–25) and a list of vices (see 1:28–31), this passage gives special weight to the notions of "natural" and "unnatural" without defining them, and condemns homosexual actions as "unnatural."

The few biblical texts about homosexuality raise many questions today. Did people in antiquity have any concept of homosexuality as a personal orientation? What did these people understand by "natural" and "unnatural"? Did they view sexuality mainly in terms of male power or dominance over women? Was there any concept of faithful same-sex relationships based on personal equality? Was Paul's horror at homosexual activity in Romans 1:26–27 simply part of his Jewish heritage coming into conflict with Greco-Roman "immorality"? Were his condemnations aimed at more specific sexual abuses associated with homosexual behavior, such as pederasty, promiscuity, and prostitution, rather than homosexuality *per se*?

ABORTION

Neither the Hebrew Bible nor the New Testament contains an explicit treatment of abortion. The Greek version (Septuagint) of Exodus 21:22–23, however, does distinguish between an "imperfectly formed" and a "perfectly formed" fetus when dealing with penalties for a miscarriage caused by a fight between two men: "If it be perfectly formed, he shall give life for life." While not dealing directly with abortion, this text does regard the fully formed fetus as a human person created in God's image (see Genesis 1:26–27) and so its loss is a matter of "life for life," according to the Old Testament law of retaliation (see Exodus 21:23–25; Leviticus 24:19–21; Deuteronomy 19:21).

Aristotle allowed the abortion of a male fetus up to forty days of pregnancy and of a female fetus up to ninety days. Roman legislators and moralists condemned abortion mainly because it was being used to limit the size of noble families.

No one in the early Jewish or early Christian tradition defends abortion. The Alexandrian Jewish philosopher Philo contended that abortion poses a threat to the survival of the human race. And the early Christian treatise known as the *Didache* states: "Do not kill a fetus by abortion or commit infanticide."[4] The early evidence is slim. But the reason for the relative silence on the matter is not clear. Was abortion routinely practiced in some circles and not placed on the same level as other moral evils? Or was abortion regarded as so morally unthinkable (in view of their convictions about the sanctity of life) as to be beyond discussion in Jewish and Christian sources?

THEOLOGICAL SIGNIFICANCE

The explicit biblical teachings on these three controversial issues—celibacy, homosexuality, and abortion—are scant and not always clear. However, the pertinent texts can and do make constructive contributions if we listen carefully to them and place them in the wider framework of the double love commandment and virtue ethics.

According to the Bible, celibacy is a voluntary response to God's grace and a witness to the all-surpassing value of the kingdom of God. It is not simply asceticism or self-mastery. While some biblical texts may condemn homosexual behavior, the Bible as a whole promotes a social vision in which every person is to be treated with the dignity and respect that befit one made in the image and likeness of God. No one should be consigned to live in fear or in degradation. And the biblical vision of humanity and society, if taken seriously, would produce a social atmosphere ("a positive vision and communal practice that is compassionate and egalitarian")[5] in which abortion would be unnecessary.

Moral Theological Reflections
J. F. Keenan

We saw in the last chapter how questions of early Christian identity inevitably turned to questions about fidelity and mercy. Thus a hermeneutics of fidelity and mercy helps us to navigate our understanding of Christian marriage and divorce. With this in mind, we turn now to three other issues: celibacy, homosexuality, and abortion (approached from the perspective of the sanctity of life). We can invoke a similar hermeneutics as we begin analyzing each of these.

Celibacy

We have already seen that the perpetual virginity practiced by Christians was an innovation, in some cases basically an imitation by daughters of the decision for celibacy made by their widowed mothers. These widows refused to remarry because they did not want to surrender their financial assets to a new husband. Rather, they wanted to continue giving their religious, moral, and financial support to the early missionary church in its preaching the gospel and in practicing the corporal works of mercy. Their daughters, similarly, saw in marriage the loss of their particular ability to continue support for the churches. Thus, rather than being faithful to Roman standards that required women to be child-bearers, they developed a new state in life that would ensure their ability to carry forward and support faithfully the work of the churches.

Today many members of religious orders as well as diocesan priests understand their celibacy as a way of continuing the legacy of generosity and fidelity of the first widows and virgins. In fact, many insist that their celibate state can be understood only in the context of their particular apostolic mission.

However, questions are inevitably being raised, especially in light of the child abuse/pedophilia scandal in the Church, about whether celibacy for diocesan priests and chastity for vowed religious is still constitutive of their vocation. With greater attention to embodiment and with greater awareness of the married laity responding to the call to serve ministerially in the life of the Church, many like Christian ethicist Michael Hartwig ask whether fidelity, mercy, and generosity necessarily need to be coupled with chastity or celibacy in order to exercise ministry and even ordained ministry in the Church.[6]

HOMOSEXUALITY

Before we talk about homosexuals as "them," as so often is the case, we need to recognize that within our communities there are gays and straights, just as there are men and women, clergy and laity, and other differentiations. It is important to recognize the call to be faithful that is issued to all Christians, including those among us who are gay and lesbian, because that call to fidelity has not always been fully heeded.

Recently, the conference of American bishops, through their Committee on Marriage and Family, published "Always Our Children: A Pastoral Message to Parents of Homosexual Children and Suggestions for Pastoral Ministers." It speaks about the need to recognize the inherent dignity of the homosexual person, who, like all human beings, is in the image of God. Throughout the document, family members and pastors are urged to love, support, and be faithful to those who are homosexual Christians. Moreover, the letter acknowledges that gay and lesbian Christians are called to service and leadership in the Christian community. Not only are they persons who receive the gospel, but they are, like all others, called to promote the gospel. The document notes that "more than twenty years ago we bishops stated that 'homosexuals . . . should have an active role in the Christian community.'"[7]

The bishops insist, also, in their letter that "[R]espect for the God-given dignity of all persons means the recognition of human rights and responsibilities. The teachings of the Church make it clear that the fundamental human rights of homosexual persons must be defended and that all of us must strive to eliminate any forms of injustice, oppression, or violence against them."[8] This stance of solidarity extends not only to support for an outward advocacy for equal rights but also to an inward disposition of Christian fidelity. The letter continues, citing from the *Catechism of the Catholic Church*: "It is not sufficient only to avoid unjust discrimination. Homosexual persons must be accepted with respect, compassion and sensitivity."[9]

We cannot overlook the significance of this call, since some Christians not only have overlooked their call to be faithful to all who call upon the name of Jesus but also have promoted in the name of Jesus a message of harm and hatred against gay and lesbian persons. We can think, for instance, of the chilling photo of those Christians who stood outside the funeral for Matthew Shepard while holding placards that read "God hates fags." Here in this photo we see a group of Christians taunting another group of Christians precisely as they are mourning.

Over the centuries some Christians have persecuted fellow Christians, solely because of sexual orientation. [On the history of the Christian churches' treatment of homosexuals, see John Boswell's *Christianity, Social*

Tolerance, and Homosexuality: Gay People in Western Europe from the Beginning of the Christian Era to the Fourteenth Century (Chicago: University of Chicago Press, 1981).] These persecutions often led to exile, imprisonment, and death. Not only that, but in many instances, Christians have used Scripture texts precisely as warrants for their hatred and vitriol. Using the gospel of mercy as an instrument to promote hatred stands then as a significantly problematic issue in the study of the New Testament and Christian ethics.

In the light of this history, Christian leaders must inevitably acknowledge that some of their predecessors have encouraged their congregations to hate in the name of Jesus Christ. Just as these leaders (notably, Pope John Paul II) have apologized for other unjust actions in the past, they need to address adequately the particularly longstanding harm that some of their predecessors brought to gay and lesbian Christians, for such truth-telling is integral to the process of reconciliation.

After recognizing that our communities of faith are comprised of straight and gay persons and *after* our leaders have sought reconciliation, we can begin to understand the significance of what specifically Scripture says about homosexuality. Here we can already observe considerable debate that we saw outlined in the previous section.

When we review the discussion by Scripture scholars, we discover that generally speaking the focus of the debate revolves around Romans 1:26–27. Protestant New Testament scholar Marion Soards, for instance, argues that the Sodom and Gomorrah texts (see Genesis 19; Judges 19) are wrongly received as concerned with homosexuality, that the holiness code of Leviticus 17–26 is as filled with cultural accretions as it is filled with the revealed will of God, and that the appearance of the Greek words *malakos* and *arsenokoites* in 1 Corinthians and 1 Timothy is incidental to the theology of Paul. But Soards does maintain that the text in Romans 1:26–27 is integral to Paul's theology and forbids all homosexual activity.[10]

In the context of God working to create saving faith in an otherwise sinful humanity, Paul discusses the hopeless sinful condition of humanity. In Romans 1:18–32, he turns to the Gentiles' fundamental sin of idolatry and cites homosexual relations as an example of the effects of their idolatry. Thus, homosexual relations is viewed as a clear symptom and result of idolatry. Soards believes that this example is so involved in Paul's argument that to remove the homosexual condemnation would be to "threaten the collapse of the entire exposition. . . . We cannot fault Paul's appraisal of homosexual behavior without denying the theological vision that informs his understanding of God and humanity."[11]

While acknowledging that Romans 1:26–27 is a disputed text, both Michael Hartwig and Patricia Beattie Jung contend that Paul's argument is not well really founded on an ontological connection between homosexuality and idolatry; that is, there is no necessary, intrinsic connection between the two. Rather, Paul's example is based on what Paul considered as a self-evident presumption in his day that anyone who commits homosexual acts must worship a false God.

Hartwig and Jung's point is grasped by considering another earlier-held and purportedly self-evident presupposition that persons who were cremated contested the existence of God. There may well have been (and probably still are) some who see in cremation a way of rejecting God's sovereignty. In some cases in the past, cremation was carried out as an explicit rejection of belief in life after death and resurrection. But today we know many persons whose choice of cremation is not at all inconsistent with their love for God and their Christian faith, and is accepted by church teaching within certain limits. In other words, there is no *necessary* connection between cremation and atheism (or agnosticism).

Likewise, experience shows that many homosexuals worship the living God. Indeed, the phenomenon of Christians today who acknowledge their homosexual orientation and live a faithful Christian life is a striking challenge to the assumption of a *necessary* link between idolatry and homosexuality. While the case of cremation is only an analogy, it cautions us against rejecting too quickly the fidelity to God and to other persons that many Christian homosexuals today display.

How are we to arbitrate the extensive debate among Scripture scholars about whether homosexuality is in itself intrinsic to the Pauline argument about idolatry in Romans 1:18–32? It is doubtful that Paul recognized that some persons were constituted in their natures as homosexual. (We can add that inasmuch as sexual orientation is hardly a first-century conceptual category, Paul also did not think in terms of constitutive heterosexuality either.) Yet, this insight about Paul's lack of familiarity with constitutive homosexuality does not necessarily undermine Soards's argument. Where then should we turn for resolution?

In his essay, Hartwig turns to Pope John Paul II for some guidance. In commenting on the Galileo affair, the pope acknowledges that "the central error of theologians was the failure to distinguish the meaning of Scripture from the meaning given to it by interpreters. If there seems to be a contradiction between Scripture and the discoveries of 'clear and certain reasoning,' the interpreter of Scripture does not understand it correctly."[12]

Christian historian Mark Jordan corroborates the pope's distinction between meaning and interpretation, for instance, in his study of theological interpretations of the destruction of Sodom (see Genesis 19).[13] Other writers have turned to experience and reason in light of the natural law to see better what the correct meaning of the text could be. Moral theologian Jean Porter analyzes the case of homosexuality in her work on the natural law,[14] while moral theologian Stephen Pope looks not only at constitutive homosexuality but also at the notion of human flourishment.[15] He suggests that inasmuch as human flourishment validates the right realization of our right inclinations, then such experiences of gay and lesbian persons serve as indications of the fact that one can rightly realize one's homosexual orientation.

ABORTION AND SANCTITY OF LIFE

The Church has long defended the right of unborn humans. Both moral theologian John Connery[16] and legal historian John T. Noonan, Jr.,[17] provide ample evidence that with few and then very specific exceptions, church teaching has been faithful in its support of unborn life.

More recently two developments have occurred that are of considerable moment. The first development concerns the grounds for a sanctity of life argument. In 1908, Jesuit Catholic moralist Thomas Slater wrote the first English language manual of moral theology.[18] There, in treating the fifth commandment, he wrote this about suicide: "The reason why suicide is unlawful is because we have not the free disposal of our own lives. God is the author of life and death, and He has reserved the ownership of human life to Himself."[19] He raised the ownership of life issue again in considering "mutilation" of self: "As we have not the ownership of life, so neither are we the owners of our limbs."[20] Slater's stance was repeated throughout the twentieth century. For instance, at the beginning of his presentation on the fifth commandment, Henry Davis wrote forty years later about the duty to preserve life: "By Natural law, man enjoys the use not the dominion of his life. He neither gave it nor may he take it away. God only is the author of life."[21]

In *Casti Connubi*, Pope Pius XI declared: "The life of each is equally sacred and no one has the power, not even the public authority, to destroy it."[22] Commenting on this encyclical, the Australian moralist Augustine Regan added: "His successor Pius XII made many pronouncements and statements during his long pontificate.... He reiterates as a constant refrain that man is not the author, and consequently is never the master, of human life, which is entrusted to him as its administrator. Therefore, it is always wrong for him to dispose of it as though he were its owner. In particular it can never be justified to attack directly the life of any innocent human being."[23]

Catholic moralist Gerald Coleman sums up the tradition well: "Human persons, then, have only a right to the use of human life, not to dominion over human life. What makes killing forbidden is that it usurps a divine prerogative and violates divine rights."[24]

Moreover, since there were sanctioned instances of self-defense and, in the history of capital punishment, similar instances of execution, it is interesting that the prohibition only extended to protect innocent human life. To take innocent human life directly was to violate God's prerogatives and rights.

Grounding the prohibition against killing in divine injunction language is problematic. For instance, British Jesuit ethicist Gerald Hughes notes that if the Church were to meet the rising interests in death-dealing practices like abortion and euthanasia, then the decision to stand against that tide needed to be based on reasoned and not voluntaristic grounds.[25] Likewise, German moral theologian Bruno Schüller writes that the "traditional" opposition to direct killing is nothing more than reiterating what needs to be proven: Why God's will is against it.[26] In answer to these charges, Dominican moralist Benedict Ashley argues for a need to "bolster" the argument from God's dominion.[27]

Pope John Paul II has done just that. Early in "Celebrate Life," he quotes from his address in Poland: "The Church defends the right to life, not only in regard to the majesty of the Creator, who is the first giver of this life, but also in respect of the essential good of the human person."[28] Here we find that human life is sacred due to a quality that is essential or internal to the human being. This insight emerges more clearly as the years of his pontificate advanced. Often it appears in the new meaning that the pope gives to the language regarding sanctity of life.

In its original form, *sanctity of life* functions as a euphemism for God's dominion. Life is sacred because its owner, God, willed it so; like other objects that God owned and sanctified (the marital bond), life cannot be violated. The sacredness of human life rests not necessarily in anything intrinsic to it. Rather, human life, like Christian marriage, is God's property; what God has made and joined, humans cannot destroy. Their sacral quality is simply in the fact that they are divine possessions.

In 1987, in *Christifideles Laici*, Pope John Paul II spoke at length about the inviolable right to life: "The inviolability of the person, which is a reflection of the absolute inviolability of God, finds its primary and fundamental expression in the inviolability of human life."[29] Nowhere did the pope refer to God's dominion or prerogatives. Rather, the argument was simply that we are in God's image. As God's person is inviolable, so is God's image. In *Donum vitae*, we find:

> Human life is sacred because from its beginning it involves the "creative action of God" and it remains forever in a special relationship with the Creator, who is its sole end. God alone is Lord of life from its beginning until its end: no one can in any

circumstance, claim for himself the right directly to destroy an innocent human being.[30]

This section is repeated in *Evangelium vitae*[31]and becomes the sole text in the *Catechism of the Catholic Church*[32] to interpret the fifth commandment. In it we see some key elements: Human life is singular, in God's image, uniquely created by God for a special relationship that is, in turn, the human's destiny, and, as the source and end of human life, God is Lord of life. While not at all abandoning the "Lord of life" argument, this paragraph gives it new meaning not by emphasizing God's dominion or prerogatives but by highlighting the uniqueness of human life.

In *Evangelium vitae* we read: "God proclaims that he is absolute Lord of the life of man, who is formed in his image and likeness (cf. Genesis 1:26–28). Human life is thus given a sacred and inviolable character, which reflects the inviolability of God."[33] Elsewhere the pope writes: "Man's life comes from God; it is his gift, his image and imprint, a sharing in his breath of life. God therefore is the sole Lord of this life: Man cannot do with it as he wills"[34]; and "Life is indelibly marked by a truth of its own."[35] When the lengthy encyclical was published by the Vatican, a summary was provided that highlighted this point:

Precious and fragile, full of promises and threatened by suffering and death, man's life bears within itself that seed of immortal life planted by the Creator in the human heart. . . . At this point we come to the decisive question, Why is life a good? Why is it always a good? The answer is simple and clear: because it is a gift from the Creator, who breathed into man the divine breath, thus making the human person the image of God.[36]

The act by which God created the human person is that which invests each human life with its inviolable character that now lies within the human, the image of God. The human is not to be killed, therefore, because of who the human is. This image of God is hardly extrinsic. Speaking of the Yahwist account of creation (see Genesis 2:4–25), the pope writes that we have within us that divine breath that draws us naturally to God.[37]

In John Paul II's writings, something very distinctive about human life emerges: All people are invited to see within human life an indelible mark of its sacredness. The pope breathes life into the concept of sanctity of life. Here we have reasoned argumentation that places the "God's dominion" position into the context of creation and leaves us looking at the human as having *in se* the dignity to claim inviolability.

This intrinsic quality gives solid theological ground then to protect all human life, not only that which is innocent. This insight gives further urgency to the second development; that is, the consistency of life ethics that was first launched by Cardinal Joseph Bernardin. The call for a consistent life ethics meant that Christian teaching on abortion, capital punishment, war, euthanasia, and suicide, as well as the developmental issues of universal health care must be bound by a common stance of respecting human life. The pope's contribution complements the cardinal's consistent life ethics by urging not only that we have a consistent stance toward human life but that in this stance we recognize that in itself human life is sacred.

Questions for Reflection and Discussion

1. How might adoption of "a positive vision and communal practice that is compassionate and egalitarian" help you to explain the biblical teachings about celibacy, homosexuality, and abortion?

2. Do you find Paul's argument in Romans 1:18–32 to be a persuasive condemnation of homosexuality? Why?

3. How does an emphasis on the intrinsic sacredness of human life constitute an argument against abortion and for a consistent ethic of life?

Notes

1. Alan Wolfe, *One Nation, After All: What Americans Really Think about God, Country, Family, Racism, Welfare, Immigration, Homosexuality, Work, The Right, The Left, and Each Other* (New York: Penguin, 1999).

2. Lisa Sowle Cahill, "Sexual Ethics: A Feminist Biblical Perspective," in *Interpretation* 49 (1995), pp. 14–15.

3. *Babylonian Talmud Yebamot,* 63a

4. *Didache,* 2:2

5. Cahill, op. cit., p. 15.

6. Michael J. Hartwig, "Galileo, Gene Researchers, and the Ethics of Homosexuality," in *Theology and Sexuality* 1 (1994), pp. 106–111.

7. "Always Our Children: A Pastoral Message to Parents of Homosexual Children and Suggestions for Pastoral Ministers," *Origins* 27/17 (1997), pp. 285, 287–291, see p. 290.

8. Ibid., p. 290.

9. *Catechism of the Catholic Church*, #2358.

10. Marion L. Soards, *Scripture and Homosexuality: Biblical Authority and the Church Today* (Louisville: Westminster John Knox, 1995).

11. Ibid., pp. 25–26.

12. Hartwig, op. cit., p. 107.

13. Mark D. Jordan, *The Silence of Sodom: Homosexuality in Modern Catholicism* (Chicago: University of Chicago Press, 2000).

14. Jean Porter, *Natural and Divine Law: Reclaiming the Tradition for Christian Ethics* (Grand Rapids: Eerdmans, 1999).

15. Stephen J. Pope, "Scientific and Natural Law Analyses of Homosexuality: A Methodological Study," in *Journal of Religious Ethics* 25 (1997), pp. 89–126.

16. John Connery, *Abortion: The Development of the Roman Catholic Perspective* (Chicago: Loyola University Press, 1977).

17. John T. Noonan, Jr., ed., *The Morality of Abortion* (Cambridge: Harvard University Press, 1970).

18. Thomas Slater, *A Manual of Moral Theology I* (New York: Benziger Brothers, 1908).

19. Ibid., vol. 1, p. 302.

20. Ibid., vol. 1, p. 303.

21. Henry Davis, *Moral and Pastoral Theology II* (London: Sheed & Ward, 1945).

22. Pope Pius XI, *Casti Connubi* (*Encyclical Letter on Christian Marriage*) (Boston: St. Paul Editions, 1930), #32.

23. Augustine Regan, *Thou Shalt Not Kill* (Dublin: Mercier Press, 1977), p. 29.

24. Gerald Coleman, "Assisted Suicide: An Ethical Perspective," in Robert Baird and Stuart Rosenbaum, eds., *Euthanasia* (Buffalo: Prometheus Books, 1989), p. 108.

25. Gerald Hughes, "Killing and Letting Die," in *The Month* 236 (February 1975), pp. 42–45.

26. Bruno Schüller, "The Double Effect in Catholic Thought," in Richard McCormick and Paul Ramsey, eds., *Doing Evil to Achieve Good: Moral Choice in Conflict Situations* (Chicago: Loyola University Press, 1978), pp. 165–192.

27. Benedict Ashley, "Dominion or Stewardship? Theological Reflections," in Kevin Wildes, ed., *Birth, Suffering, and Death: Catholic Perspectives on the Edge of Life* (Dordrecht: Kluwer Academic Publishers, 1992), pp. 85–106.

28. Pope John Paul II, "Celebrate Life," in *The Pope Speaks*, 24/4 (1979), p. 372.

29. Pope John Paul II, *Christifideles Laici*, in *Origins* 18/35 (1989), #38.

30. *Donum vitae*, in *Origins* 16/40 (1987), #5.

31. Pope John Paul II, *Evangelium vitae* in *Origins* 24/42 (1995), #53.

32. *Catechism of the Catholic Church*, #2258.

33. Pope John Paul II, *Evangelium vitae*, #53.

34. Ibid., #39.

35. Ibid., #48.

36. Ibid., p. 729.

37. Ibid, #35.

Select Bibliography

Ashley, Benedict. "Dominion or Stewardship? Theological Reflections." In Kevin Wildes (ed.), *Birth, Suffering, and Death: Catholic Perspectives at the Edge of Life*. Dordrecht: Kluwer Academic Publishers, 1992, pp. 85–106.

Balch, David (ed.). *Homosexuality, Science, and the "Plain Sense" of Scripture*. Grand Rapids: Eerdmans, 2000.

Bayertz, Kurt (ed.), *Sanctity of Life and Human Dignity*. Dordrecht: Kluwer Academic Publishers, 1996.

Bernardin, Joseph. *Consistent Ethic of Life*. New York: Sheed & Ward, 1988.

Boswell, John. *Christianity, Social Tolerance, and Homosexuality*. Chicago: University of Chicago Press, 1980.

Brawley, Robert L. (ed.). *Biblical Ethics and Homosexuality.* Louisville: Westminster, 1996.

Brooten, Bernadette. *Love Between Women.* Chicago: University of Chicago Press, 1997.

Coleman, Gerald. "Assisted Suicide: An Ethical Perspective." In Robert Baird and Stuart Rosenbaum (eds.), *Euthanasia.* Buffalo: Prometheus Books, 1989.

Congregation for the Doctrine of the Faith. "Declaration on Euthanasia." In Austin Flannery (ed.), *Vatican Council II: More Post Conciliar Documents.* Northport, NY: Costello Publishing Co., 1982, pp. 510–517.

_____. *Instruction on the Respect for Human Life in its Origin and on the Dignity of Procreation (Donum vitae).* Origins 16/40 (1987), pp. 697, 699–703.

Connery, John. *Abortion: The Development of the Roman Catholic Perspective.* Chicago: Loyola University Press, 1977.

Davis, Henry. *Moral and Pastoral Theology* II. London: Sheed & Ward, 1945.

Gagnon, R. A. J. *The Bible and Homosexual Practice: Texts and Hermeneutics.* Nashville: Abingdon, 2001.

Gorman, Michael J. *Abortion and the Early Church: Christian, Jewish and Pagan Attitudes in the Greco-Roman World.* New York: Paulist, 1982.

Hartwig, Michael J. "Galileo, Gene Researchers and the Ethics of Homosexuality." In *Theology and Sexuality* 1 (1994), pp. 106–111.

_____. *The Poetics of Intimacy and the Problem of Sexual Abstinence.* New York: Peter Lang, 2000.

Hughes, Gerald. "Killing and Letting Die." In *The Month* 236 (February 1975), pp. 42–45.

Jordan, Mark D. *The Silence of Sodom: Homosexuality in Modern Catholicism.* Chicago: University of Chicago Press, 2000.

Jung, Patricia Beattie and Ralph Smith. *Heterosexism: An Ethical Challenge.* Albany: State University of New York Press, 1993.

Keenan, James F. "The Moral Argumentation of *Evangelium vitae.*" In Kevin Wildes (ed.), *Choosing Life: A Dialogue on* Evangelium vitae. Washington, D.C.: Georgetown University Press, 1997, pp. 46–62.

Lindemann, Andreas. "'Do not let a woman destroy the unborn babe in her belly': Abortion in Ancient Judaism and Christianity." In *Studia Theologica* 49 (1995), pp. 253–271.

Martin, Dale B. "*Arsenokoites* and *Malakos*: Meanings and Consequences." In Robert L. Brawley (ed.), *Biblical Ethics & Homosexuality*. Louisville: Westminster John Knox, 1996, pp. 117–136.

Mitchell, Alan. "The Use of Scripture in *Evangelium Vitae*." In *Choosing Life*, pp. 63–70.

Moore, Stephen D. *God's Beauty Parlor and Other Queer Spaces in and around the Bible*. Stanford, CA: Stanford University Press, 2001.

Noonan, Jr., John T. (ed.), *The Morality of Abortion*. Cambridge: Harvard University Press, 1970.

Pope Pius XI. *Encyclical Letter on Christian Marriage*. Boston: St. Paul Editions, 1930.

Pope John Paul II. "Celebrate Life." In *The Pope Speaks* 24/4 (1979), pp. 371–374.

_____. *Christifideles Laici*. In *Origins* 18/35 (1989), pp. 561, 563–589.

_____. *Evangelium vitae*. In *Origins* 24/42 (1995), pp. 689, 691–730.

Pope, Stephen J. "Scientific and Natural Law Analyses of Homosexuality: A Methodological Study." In *Journal of Religious Ethics* 25 (1997), pp. 89–126.

Porter, Jean. *Natural and Divine Law: Reclaiming the Tradition for Christian Ethics*. Grand Rapids: Eerdmans, 1999.

Regan, Augustine. *Thou Shalt Not Kill*. Dublin: Mercier Press, 1977.

Schüller, Bruno. "The Double Effect in Catholic Thought." In Richard McCormick and Paul Ramsey (eds.), *Doing Evil to Achieve Good: Moral Choice in Conflict Situations*. Chicago: Loyola University Press, 1978, pp. 165–192.

Slater, Thomas. *A Manual of Moral Theology I*. New York: Benziger Brothers, 1908.

Soards, Marion L. *Scripture and Homosexuality: Biblical Authority and the Church Today*. Louisville: Westminster John Knox, 1995.

"The Vatican's Summary of *Evangelium vitae*." In *Origins* 24/42 (1995), pp. 728–730.

Wold, Donald J. *Out of Order: Homosexuality in the Bible and the Ancient Near East*. Grand Rapids: Baker, 1998.

Wolfe, Alan. *One Nation, After All: What Americans Really Think about God, Country, Family, Racism, Welfare, Immigration, Homosexuality, Work, The Right, The Left, and Each Other.* New York: Penguin, 1999.

Chapter Thirteen

THE BIBLE AND NATURE: FRIENDS OR FOES?

T he twentieth century was a time of astounding scientific and tech-
nological progress. Life in the early twenty-first century differs
radically from life at the close of the nineteenth century. Yet, this
great "progress" has exacted a steep price in increased air pollution, loss of
forest and farm lands, and health problems (cancers, obesity, and so on) for
humans. Some people blame the Bible, with its talk about humankind having dominion over all the earth (see Genesis 1:26), for promoting insensitivity,
especially among the peoples of the industrialized West, to the magnitude
of our current environmental crisis.

Is the Bible friend or foe of the natural environment? On the one
hand, the Bible exalts humans as being made in God's image and warns
against worshiping the sun, the moon, or other created entities. On the
other hand, people in biblical times lived close to the cycle of nature,
because their lives depended on it more than ours do. As we will see, the
problem is not so much with the Bible as it is with what some people have
made of the Bible. In this chapter, Harrington discusses various biblical
perspectives on the relationships among God, humans, and nature. Keenan
then brings the concept of embodied existence to bear on our approach to
the natural environment today.

BIBLICAL PERSPECTIVES
D. J. Harrington

Ecology is the study of how changes in human ways affect nonhuman
nature. One explanation for our present environmental crisis traces it to an
overemphasis in the West on the biblical vision of humans as created in
God's image and as having been granted dominion over the rest of creation
(see Genesis 1:26, 28). While there is something to this charge from the

perspective of Western history, the Bible offers many resources for confronting the environmental crisis in constructive ways, especially the christocentric vision of creation proposed in Colossians 1:15–20.

GOD'S LOVING CARE
(Matthew 6:26, 28b–29)

26. Look at the birds of the air; they neither sow nor reap nor gather into barns, and yet your heavenly Father feeds them.... 28. Consider the lilies of the field, how they grow; they neither toil nor spin, 29. yet I tell you, even Solomon in all his glory was not clothed like one of these.

Many of Jesus' teachings in the Synoptic Gospels reflect the conditions of rural life in first-century Galilee. For example, when Jesus wants to illustrate the nature of the kingdom of God, he uses parables about seed growing by itself and a mustard seed (see Mark 4:26–32). And to explain the mixed reception accorded to his proclamation of God's kingdom, he tells the parable of the fates of good seeds sown in the different types of soils (see Mark 4:3–9).

The audience for much of Jesus' teaching consisted of farmers and fishermen, people who lived close to the cycles of nature. Those cycles in Palestine were quite regular and stable, and they provided the basic principle underlying the calendar with its succession of agricultural festivals (Passover, Pentecost, Tabernacles). When the cycle went awry, as in a drought, prayer became the people's major recourse.

As part of a diverse set of wisdom instructions in Matthew 6:19–7:12, Jesus warns his audience about the foolishness of anxiety: "Can any of you by worrying add a single hour to your span of life?" (6:27). In this advice, Jesus uses images that would have been especially effective in speaking about anxiety to people who were close to nature.

One such consideration concerns birds (see Matthew 6:26). Unlike humans, birds do not grow their own food. Nevertheless, God sees to their feeding and preservation. This image is not an invitation to laziness or to lack of planning on the part of farmers. Rather, it is a reminder to overanxious farmers that God is in charge of creation and God provides the care needed for all his creatures in remarkable ways.

The second consideration concerns wild flowers (see Matthew 6:28–29). Every spring in Galilee, beautiful flowers emerge mysteriously and spontaneously from the earth. Jesus alludes to the splendor of King Solomon's court (see 1 Kings 10:4–7) and observes that the natural beauty provided by the "lilies of the field" is far superior. This natural beauty is due to God, for the flowers "neither toil nor spin" (6:28).

These illustrations about birds and wild flowers appear in the context of wise advice about dealing with excessive and unproductive anxiety. They promote a wider perspective when looking at the world as God's world, and offer a reminder that God is in charge of the universe. The people in first-century Galilee were much more dependent on the cycles of nature than we are, and so could easily become anxious about it, since their livelihood and very existence were at stake. Indeed, much of "primitive" religion was closely tied to the cycle of nature.

It is sometimes charged that the Bible places human beings at the center of the world (anthropocentrism). This charge is often countered by affirming that God is at the center of the Bible's story (theocentrism). However, the advice given in Matthew 6:25–34 ("Strive first for the kingdom of God and his righteousness, and all these things will be given to you as well," 6:33) suggests that in the case of the natural environment, the stories of humankind and nature should be placed in the wider story of God's continuing care for creation that includes humankind and nature. The Bible thus blends anthropocentrism and theocentrism, and holds them in a fruitful tension. What is needed is the balanced perspective that humans are at best God's stewards in parts of creation, in the sense that humans act as God's servants in caring for the domains in which they can contribute most positively.

Old Testament Texts

The Priestly account of creation in Genesis 1:1–2:4 reaches its climax with the sixth day, when God creates humankind: "Let us make humankind in our image, according to our likeness" (1:26). In creating humans, God gives them "dominion over the fish of the sea, and over the birds of the air" (1:26, 28). The Hebrew verb *radah* can be taken in a strong sense as "subdue, rule over" or in a softer sense of "govern" as a steward or servant. In a famous essay published in 1967, Lynn White, a historian of science, traced the modern ecological crisis in large part to the "strong" interpretive tradition surrounding these texts according to which humans made in God's image transcend nature and creation is viewed as intended by God to serve human purposes.[1] However, it is also possible to read these texts in a softer way, as portraying humans as part of God's seven-day plan for creation and as serving God's purposes in overseeing nature. In either reading of the Priestly creation narrative, however, humans have a special place as the crown or pinnacle in God's work of creation.

God's speeches from the whirlwind in Job 38–41 approach creation from a different perspective—from God's perspective. After Job has lamented over his sufferings and his friends have tried to help him make sense out of these sufferings, God finally speaks and reminds Job that his vision is too self-centered and human-centered. Through these speeches, God gives a tour of the cosmos as seen from the divine perspective. The idea is to put Job (and all humans) in his proper place as one among many of God's creatures. God does so by describing God's effortless work of creation, the parts of the universe never seen by humans, and the animals and other creatures that are beyond human control. If Genesis 1 promotes an anthropocentric vision of creation, the Book of Job represents a theocentric approach.

Psalm 104 offers a good balance between the two perspectives. This psalm may well have originated as a prayer for rain—at least it contains a large amount of water imagery (see 104:10–13). It begins in vv. 1–9 by praising God for the work of creation: "O Lord my God, you are very great." It depicts God as the architect and builder of the universe: "You stretch out the heavens like a tent" (104:2). In vv. 10–18, it describes how God's gift of water makes the earth come alive and sustains all kinds of creatures, and vv. 19–26 depicts an orderly and harmonious world whose times are marked by the sun and the moon: "O Lord, how manifest are your works! In wisdom you have made them all" (104:24). In this framework, God governs and rules the universe. Humans recognize and acknowledge God's sovereignty over creation and approach God as suppliants who know their place: "These all look to you to give them their food in due season" (104:27). Neither the anthropocentrism of Genesis 1 nor the theocentrism of Job 38–41 represents the whole biblical vision concerning the natural environment. Psalm 104 reminds us humans that we are part of God's creation and that we depend upon God's loving care for our sustenance, while at the same time we approach God with praise and petition as stewards of God's creation.

Another psalm, Psalm 29, suggests that God can be experienced in nature, even in a fierce storm. Psalm 29 is regarded as one of the oldest psalms and may even be based on a Canaanite prototype. It is sometimes called the psalm of the "seven thunders," because it features seven occurrences of the phrase "the voice of the Lord" with reference to a thunderstorm: "The voice of the Lord is over the waters . . . is powerful . . . is full of majesty . . . breaks the cedars . . . flashes forth flames of fire . . . shakes the wilderness . . . causes the oaks to whirl and strips the forest bare." The storm is taken to be a manifestation of the power of God, and so a natural phenomenon serves as the occasion for humans to praise God: " . . . and in his temple all say, 'Glory'" (29:9).

NEW TESTAMENT TEXTS

Early Christianity outside of Palestine was primarily an urban movement. And unlike the Gospels that often reflect conditions in rural Galilee, the Epistles contain relatively few references to nature or the environment. However, there are some texts—for example, Colossians 1:15–20 and Romans 8:18–25—that situate the life, death, and resurrection of Jesus in a cosmic context, and so make important contributions to the Christian vision of the natural environment.

It is widely accepted that Colossians 1:15–20 is an early Christian hymn that celebrates Jesus as the wisdom of God in the order of creation (see 1:15–17) and in the order of redemption or reconciliation (see 1:18–20). In portraying Christ as the Wisdom of God present at creation, the hymn echoes a theme found in Proverbs 8:22–31 and developed in various ways in Sirach 24, Wisdom 7, and 1 Enoch 42:1-3. In this vision of creation, Christ as God's Wisdom and the new Adam ("the image of the invisible God") was present at creation and holds all things together: "All things have been created through him and for him" (1:16). The first part of the hymn places Christ as the center of creation and so offers a christocentric view of creation.

The hymn then places the risen Christ ("the firstborn from the dead") at the center of the order of redemption. In Christ "the fullness of God was pleased to dwell," and the reconciliation that Christ brought about embraces the whole of God's creation: " . . . and through him God was pleased to reconcile to himself all things, whether on earth or in heaven, by making peace through the blood of the cross" (1:20). The hymn contained in Colossians 1:15–20 presents a christocentric vision of God's created universe, with Christ as God's pre-existent wisdom engaged in the work of creation and with Christ's death and resurrection bringing about reconciliation on a cosmic scale.

Whereas the hymn in Colossians 1:15–20 stresses what God has already done in the cosmos through the person of Jesus Christ, Paul's meditation on life in the Spirit in Romans 8:18–25 looks forward to the fullness of God's kingdom and what the world must go through before that time. According to Paul, the fullness of God's reign will involve not only humans but also all of God's creation. There is a kind of sympathetic relationship between humans and the cosmos as they await "the revealing of the children of God" (8:19).

At present, creation is "subjected to futility" (Romans 8:20) and in "bondage to decay" (8:21). These phrases may echo the creation narrative in Genesis 3 about the sin of Adam: "Cursed is the ground because of you" (Genesis 3:17). What humans and all creation seek is "the freedom of the glory of the children of God" (8:21). Their search takes place "with eager longing" (8:19) and "with patience" marked by hope (8:25). Just because Christians possess "the first fruits of the Spirit" through their faith and baptism, they are not exempt from the "birthpangs" of the Messiah (see Mark 13:8)—the sufferings that will accompany the coming of the fullness of God's kingdom. Likewise, creation joins in the process: "The whole creation has been groaning in labor pains until now" (8:22). Thus Paul includes the cosmos in the already/not yet dynamic of God's kingdom.

THEOLOGICAL SIGNIFICANCE

Is the Bible friend or foe of the natural environment? The answer depends on what texts one reads, and the perspective from which they are read. From the first pages of the Bible we learn that humankind (*'adam*) has been formed from the earth (*'adamah*). And from Romans 8 we see all creation joining in sympathetic suffering with humans as they await the fullness of God's reign. The Old Testament offers both anthropocentric and theocentric views of creation, and combinations of the two. From the perspective of the New Testament, the christocentric vision of creation put forward in Colossians 1:15–20 resolves the tension or at least embraces both elements.

Because the world is God's creation, it is in that sense sacred. To defile and destroy God's creation is a sin on the part of humans. While recourse to the Bible cannot solve all the problems pertaining to our current environmental crisis, it does offer attitudes and perspectives that can help thoughtful humans to confront the environmental crisis without either deifying the earth or regarding it as something only to be "subdued" and exploited by humans.

MORAL THEOLOGICAL REFLECTIONS
J. F. Keenan

Because the field of moral theological reflection on the natural environment is so new, rather than providing any sustained reflection on one overriding point, we will consider briefly a series of issues.

ANTHROPOCENTRISM, THEOCENTRISM, AND ECOCENTRISM

There is a debate today about whether our point of departure should be the perspective of humans, God, or the world. The latter two approaches are somewhat dishonest intellectually. Eventually, our perspective must be a human one. No matter how much we try to refine it, it is still the human point of view. This does not mean that we cannot attempt to ask critical questions about the adequacy or the inclusiveness of our human perspective. But we cannot relinquish our own perspective and claim to assume another one. If we claim otherwise, we fall into a self-deception. It is as if we are speaking for God or for the world instead of for ourselves.

Proponents of theocentrism and ecocentrism nonetheless offer us ways of enhancing our anthropocentric perspective. From the theocentric argument, we can take an understanding of ourselves as creatures living with other creatures and having only one Creator to whom we are accountable for not only ourselves but all creation. From the ecocentric position, we should take our self-understanding not as related to nature but, as Klaus Demmer writes, as constituted in and through nature. We were created in nature. Our entire self-understanding is through and about our nature.

This debate about perspective indicates the incipient nature of our discourse. The debate is helpful because it prompts us to scrutinize effectively the assumptions that we have long held about our place in the universe. By turning ourselves to both God and the world, we find ourselves critically engaged and somewhat suspicious about our own nature and perspective.

RESURRECTION OF THE BODY

All early creedal formulas confessed the resurrection of the body (not the dead). In *Fragmentation and Redemption*, historian Caroline Bynum reminds us that for this reason early Christians went to the catacombs, not to flee from persecution but to worship near the remains of those who were in glory with Christ.[2] This same reverence for the body is also found in the regard that Christians have developed for the relics of the saints.

Christian ethicist William F. May looks at our contemporary Christian concepts of the human body and reverence for the dead human body.[3] He specifically examines the importance of corporeality that Christianity upholds. Arguing that the body is a constitutive extension of the person, he claims that the body (like the person) demands to be respected even after death. Against that view, Lori Andrews (philosopher and bioethicist) and Joel Feinberg (a noted American liberal philosopher) see only utility in the human body. Andrews argues that our body is our property, and that we therefore own our body parts and can dispose of them simply by autonomous choices.[4] Feinberg simply calls May a romantic for attaching moral respectability to any human body that is not alive.[5]

Christians cannot accept this objectification of our bodies. Our fidelity to the created material world does not mean that we are in control of it. Nor does it mean that the world is something that we own. Nor does it mean something to which we are related. Rather, we can only understand ourselves as-in-this-world. We are constituted in nature. Our future hope is not found by objectifying nature any more than if we objectify the human body. For Christians, the body and by extension the whole material world are precisely where we encounter God. The body and the world are the context for our encounter with the holy. This highlights the importance of materiality and warrants the skepticism about spiritualism, which, although frequently associated with religion, is regularly attacked by church leaders.

SACRAMENTALITY

The sacraments are ways by which we celebrate the mediation of God's grace in the world. Through them we perceive the worthiness of the physical to mediate the divine. By our use of bread and wine, oil and water, ashes and candles, we see in the physical world the expression of the divine presence.

Likewise through language we find the physical as the appropriate metaphor for discussing the foundations of Christian faith. For instance, the body becomes a central way for describing the basic tenets of Christian faith. We understand the event of Jesus Christ as the incarnation, the nature of the Church as the Body of Christ, the central sacrament of our faith as the body and blood of Christ, and our eschatological hope as the resurrection of the body. Our Christology, ecclesiology, sacramental life, and eschatology all depend on the body.

In *Holy Feast and Holy Fast*, historian Caroline Bynum highlights how Christian spirituality celebrates the material world.[6] Those in the monastic tradition saw in eating, for instance, a training ground for the feasting that would be celebrated in the kingdom of God. They recognized that eating gave them a sense of foretaste, and they developed habits of fasting and feasting in order to understand the kingdom as now but not yet. The wider Church assumed these practices by cultivating *Mardi Gras*, Lent, Friday abstinence from meat, fasting before communion, and days of feasting that included Sundays in Lent. Through eating and not eating we express an appreciation for the material in itself as well as an appropriate way to encounter the divine.

Not surprisingly, many monasteries, with their intense interest in the way the divine is found in our world, have been known to cultivate gardens, study herbs, discover medicines, cultivate botany, distill liquors, harvest grains, bake breads, expand husbandry, and so on. Small wonder that the entire world of genetics was broken open by a monk, Gregor Mendel, working on plants at a monastery.

CELEBRATING THE WORLD

Christians have a variety of ways of celebrating the world in which they live. Sacramental signs are some, and eating is another. Christian spirituality is at its best when it embraces the natural world within which it exists and thrives. We can turn to Benedictine spirituality to find its modest though evident embrace of the world. Likewise, Franciscan spirituality sees in the birds of the air and the fishes of the sea worthy hearers of the gospel. In *Brother Moon and Sister Sun,* Francis of Assisi found a universe that was itself as all encompassing as the love of God.

In the *Spiritual Exercises* of Ignatius of Loyola, retreatants are led through a series of four weeks of prayer and grace. In the first week they find the most introspective period in which they are called to see themselves in a world filled with sin where most people are in danger of eternal damnation. These "pre-conversion" reflections are meant to lead the retreatants to turn away from a life of sin. After the experience of conversion in the first week, retreatants make a general confession and begin discerning what their specific vocation is, while simultaneously meditating on the life, death, and resurrection of Jesus. No longer inconsiderate sinners but rather ardent disciples, retreatants no longer look at their relationship with the world as threatening or compromising. Rather, they come to view the world as the place for living out their response to God's call. This shift in perspective on the world is a gradual one. By the second week, retreatants begin to move out of their introspection and into the world where Christ is leading his disciples. By the end of the retreat in the fourth week, they embrace the world as the place for attaining the love of God. Before conversion, the world was an impediment; after conversion, it becomes the home of the converted. This shift in perspective is best seen at the tomb of Ignatius in the Jesuits' Mother Church, the Gesù in Rome. Above the statue of Ignatius, the Trinity blesses the world, which is represented by the world's largest piece of lapis lazuli.

HUMILITY

We have seen that mercy, reconciliation, and hope are distinctive Christian virtues. Now in the context of environmental ethics, we can consider humility. *Humility* is knowing the truth of one's place. As a virtue, it goes against extremes. One extreme is pride, which, in the context of the world, is domination. At the other extreme is self-deprecation, making oneself so weak as not to exercise oneself responsibly.

To be humble is to know one's power in the universe and to respect one's own place in that universe and the place of others. This theme is expressed beautifully in Mary's *Magnificat* (see Luke 1:46–55). In terms of ecology, humility means first that we see ourselves as created. As humble creatures we rejoice in our Creator and see that we are called to work responsibly in the created universe to bring it to fruition.

Humility therefore empowers us, but it does so modestly and responsibly. Rather than moving us away from the world, humility moves us to recognize our responsible place within it, and helps us to see how we are constituted in the world. It warns us against attitudes of dominion, but it also keeps us from being detached from the world. It prompts us to see our profound dependence on the world in which we are made.

AWE

Ever since Jews and Christians first heard about Adam and Eve awakening in the Garden, Noah entering the ark, and Moses crossing the Red Sea and ascending Mount Sinai, they have known that the world is a place for awe. *Awe* is a necessarily religious attitude. It is prayerful respect for the material world.

However, this religious awe is not based on a naïve, romantic notion of nature. Unlike some contemporary figures who see the world as better off without humanity, believers fall in awe of a world in which the human encounters the divine in and through the world. This awe is also not a fascination with power. We find, for instance, in the Elijah's encounter with the Lord a profound appreciation of how the divine is expressed in the world. As Elijah stood on the mountain, he fell down in awe not before the strong wind that rent the mountains and broke the rocks in pieces, or before the earthquake, or before the fire, but rather before the still small voice (see 1 Kings 19:9–18).

Awe is the ability to discern the presence of the divine in the natural. It is for this reason that perhaps the most fitting expression of awe in the Christian tradition is the encounter of Jesus' first followers (see Matthew 28:1–8; Mark 16:1–8; Luke 24:1–12; John 20:1–10) with the empty tomb. In their encounter with absence, the early Christians recognized a promise unfolding.

SOLIDARITY AND RECONCILIATION

When one people conquers another, they are only able to do so to the extent that they think of the enemy people not as fellow human beings but as objects for their own use. Violence, domination, and objectification go hand in hand, and one cannot be successful without the other two.

We are learning through history the danger of disassociating ourselves from any other human beings in particular or from the world as a whole. Just as humans have waged war against one another and dominated and objectified other peoples, similarly humans have violently abused the world in which they live. Violence, domination, and objectification are founded on and promote alienation. *Solidarity*, on the other hand, promotes bonds of fidelity both among humans and within the world.

We saw earlier that alienation is sin. Alienation from God's covenant leads to an alienation from the moral universe. Standing in fidelity with the covenant, however, means human prosperity and flourishment. Solidarity occasions a grasp of the world in which interdependency is viewed as a good to be pursued rather than as an evil to be destroyed.

Because we live in the world, we live in history. And history cannot allow us to pursue solidarity without also attending to *reconciliation* for past dispositions of alienation. Our appreciation of a kingdom that is at once present and yet forthcoming is also an appreciation for what, by grace, we have attained and what, by sin, we have lost. Because solidarity is based on a constant appreciation for an ongoing conversion in our lives, it does not allow us to escape the call to the ongoing task of reconciliation (see 2 Corinthians 5:16–21).

Just as we are called to celebrate and responsibly care for the world, and to identify ourselves in and through nature, so we are called to recognize the harm that we have brought to the world and our need to repair it. These two dispositions of being in solidarity with the world and being reconciled to the world are not separate. Rather, they are mutually defining. The more we stand in solidarity with the world, the more we can recognize the harm we have brought to the world. The more we are reconciled to the world, the more we can strengthen our solidarity with it.

Questions for Reflection and Discussion

1. Why were people in biblical times especially concerned about their natural environment?

2. In what sense does the risen Christ mitigate the tension between the theocentric and anthropocentric approaches to nature in the Bible?

3. How might cultivating the virtue of humility help humankind to deal better with our ecological crisis?

Notes

1. Lynn White, "The Historical Roots of Our Ecological Crisis," in *Machina ex Deo: Essays in the Dynamism of Western Culture* (Cambridge, MA-London: MIT Press, 1968), pp. 75–94.

2. Caroline W. Bynum, *Fragmentation and Redemption* (New York: Zone Books, 1991).

3. William F. May, "Attitudes toward the Newly Dead," in *Hastings Center Report* 1 (1973), pp. 3–13.

4. Lori Andrews, "My body, My Property," in *Hastings Center Report* 16/5 (1986), pp. 28–38.

5. Joel Feinberg, "The Mistreatment of Dead Bodies," in *Hastings Center Report* 15 (1985), pp. 31–37.

6. Caroline W. Bynum, *Holy Feast and Holy Fast: The Religious Significance of Food to Medieval Women* (Berkeley: University of California Press, 1987).

Select Bibliography

Andrews, Lori. "My Body, My Property." *Hastings Center Report* 16/5 (1986), pp. 28–38.

Brown, William P. *The Ethos of the Cosmos: The Genesis of Moral Imagination in the Bible*. Grand Rapids: Eerdmans, 1999.

Bynum, Caroline W. *Fragmentation and Redemption*. New York: Zone Books, 1991.

_____. *Holy Feast and Holy Fast: The Religious Significance of Food to Medieval Women*. Berkeley: University of California Press, 1987.

Campbell, Courtney. "Body, Self, and the Property Paradigm." In *Hastings Center Report* 22 (1992), pp. 34–43.

Edwards, Dennis. *Jesus the Wisdom of God: An Ecological Theology*. Maryknoll, NY: Orbis, 1995.

Feinberg, Joel. "The Mistreatment of Dead Bodies." In *Hastings Center Report* 15 (1985), pp. 31–37.

Kass, Leon. "Thinking About the Body." In *Hastings Center Report* 15 (1985), pp. 20–30.

May, William F. "Attitudes toward the Newly Dead." In *Hastings Center Report* 1 (1973), pp. 3–13.

_____. "Religious Justifications for Donating Body Parts." In *Hastings Center Report* 15 (1985), pp. 38–42.

Rhoads, David. "Reading the New Testament in the Environmental Age." In *Currents in Theology and Mission* 24 (1997), pp. 259–266.

Tucker, Eugene. "Rain on a Land Where No One Lives: The Hebrew Bible on the Environment." In *Journal of Biblical Literature* 116 (1997), pp. 3–17.

White, Lynn. "The Historical Roots of Our Ecological Crisis." In *Machina ex Deo: Essays in the Dynamism of Western Culture*. Cambridge, MA-London: MIT Press, 1968, pp. 75–94.

FINAL THOUGHTS

This work began from the premise that there is a need for building bridges between New Testament studies and moral theology. It arose from a course that we have taught several times at Weston Jesuit School of Theology, in which each of us lectured on a particular theme, treating it as we do here from our own competencies. Our students, having listened to the two presentations, were then asked to consider questions that we provided (similar to those at the end of each chapter) so as to further the work of building bridges between the two disciplines in their essays and discussions. We hope that readers of this book will find themselves now involved in the important work of building bridges between New Testament studies and moral theology.

Key to our bridge building has been the language of virtue, which flows easily and powerfully from both disciplines. Whether we discuss the Old Testament Torah, the Prophetic and Wisdom literatures, the Synoptic Gospels, or the Pauline Epistles, virtue language naturally arises from the Bible. Why? Because the Bible reveals to us not only God's call to us but also the transforming power of that call. We are transformed precisely as persons, and the common language that has been used cross-culturally to describe transformed persons has always been virtue.

Virtue is a concept that specifically qualifies character. Whether we talk about a people or an individual, the nature of the character being called is always given some normative description, and that description is in terms of virtue. We can read Micah, Isaiah, Jeremiah, Ezekiel, Job, Matthew, Acts, or Romans, and in every instance we inevitably encounter God inviting us into a deeper relationship whereby we are transformed into God's people and God's children.

These descriptions are hardly meaningless. To talk about fidelity is notably different from talking about self-love, and to talk about justice is different from talking about reconciliation. The distinctive content of each virtue provides us with a particular dimension of the overall anthropological profile that we ought to compose. Inevitably the virtues that we propose as cross-culturally cardinal (justice, fidelity, self-care, and prudence) then become normative for understanding the type of person each of us is called to become.

To suggest that mercy, reconciliation, and hope are distinctively Christian virtues is to make an even more demanding claim. Just as Richard Hays offered three lenses through which every scriptural passage must inevitably be read (see pp. 29–30), we are proposing that our ability to understand any scriptural passage depends not on impersonal lenses but on a triad of character traits that are necessary to understand Scripture. An exegete, a minister, a preacher, or an elder cannot understand and actualize Scripture without these virtues.

Yet, our bridge building is only at an incipient stage. We have offered in these pages a variety of insights in the hope that readers will find them beneficial. From the perspectives of our respective disciplines, we have tried to take readers deeper into an appreciation of the central themes found in the study of the New Testament: the kingdom of God, discipleship, the Sermon on the Mount, love, and sin. Then we have sought to bring biblical investigation and moral theological reflection to bear on both general ethical issues—such as politics, social justice, embodiment, and sexual ethics—and on specific topics—such as marriage and divorce, celibacy, homosexuality, abortion, and ecology.

These themes and issues are hardly exhaustive, however. Similarly, our engagement of them is sometimes too brief. We could have developed more the notion of discipleship proposed by Dietrich Bonhoeffer. We could have raised questions about feminist perspectives on abortion. We could have engaged John or Paul even more. But we are not putting forward here a definitive work on all these themes and issues. Rather, we are offering a heuristic, a general set of indicators that could further collaborative work between New Testament scholars and moral theologians, between biblical theologians and Christian ethicists, and their students.

Our heuristic is written in the language of virtue. In focusing on the virtues, we have tried to convey an approach that we find promising and fruitful, and to develop a conceptual framework and language that might better the dialogue between scholars in the fields of Scripture and moral theology. Because that language is so context dependent, moreover, we believe that this project could well be transposed into other cultural settings where specific virtues could be thickened or leavened by the concerns of those local cultures. As such then we think that the combination of our bridge motif, the selection of our themes and issues, and our use of virtue ethics offers a variety of tools to further the project of developing a more biblically based moral theology.

GLOSSARY

agent: person or subject who performs human actions.

anonymous Christian: the name given by some Christian theologians to non-Christians who act in ways that are consistent with the principles of Christianity.

anthropocentric: from the Greek word *anthrōpos*, meaning "human being." It refers to a philosophical or theological approach that focuses mainly on human beings and takes them as the norm.

anthropology: in philosophy and theology this term is often used to refer to human existence or the human condition rather than to the social science. It may concern how the human person is analyzed (body, soul, spirit) and/or how the person stands in relation to God.

apocalyptic kingdom: the reign of God (and of Christ) that is to be revealed at the end of human history, at the time of the general resurrection of the dead and the last judgment.

Aristotelian ethics: the approach to ethics developed by the Greek philosopher Aristotle (384–322 B.C.), who gave particular attention to the human person, the virtues, and their cultivation in the quest for human happiness.

ascetical theology: the branch of Christian theology that deals with the virtues and holiness, and their attainment.

Benedictine spirituality: the way of life proper to the order of monks founded by St. Benedict around A.D. 530, and characterized by focus on biblical study, community life, hospitality, liturgy, and appreciation of nature.

Biblical Theology Movement: a trend in Protestant theology after World War II (mainly in the United States) that gave special prominence to biblical texts and concepts, while maintaining a critical appreciation of their historical settings.

catacombs: subterranean burial places for early Christians, the most extensive of which were at Rome.

Christ event, the: the life, death, and resurrection of Jesus viewed as one entity and constituting the core of Christian faith. This is also known as the "paschal mystery."

Christian idealism: an approach that aims not at an unreal or unattainable "utopian" end point of human existence, but rather at the kingdom of God, which though already emerging is not yet fully present.

Christology: the study of how the person, titles, and significance of Jesus Christ have been and are now understood.

compendium: a brief treatment or concise treatise on an extensive subject such as philosophy, theology, ethics, or law.

confessors: those who hear confessions of sins and offer absolution or forgiveness based on appropriate penances (the prayers and works one performs) to atone for sins.

corporal works of mercy: good actions based on Matthew 25:31–46; that is, feeding the hungry, giving drink to the thirsty, clothing the naked, sheltering the homeless, caring for the sick, visiting the imprisoned, and burying the dead.

covenant: a treaty or alliance between leaders and/or peoples. The term is used frequently in the Old Testament to describe Israel's relationship to God (Yahweh).

creedal: pertaining to religious beliefs. A creedal formula is a concise statement of faith (e.g., 1 Corinthians 15:3–5, and the Apostles' Creed).

***Damascus Document,* the:** the rule for an ancient Jewish religious community active in Jesus' time. Copies of this work were found among the Dead Sea Scrolls at Qumran.

Decalogue: another name for the Ten Commandments; see Exodus 20:1–17 and Deuteronomy 5:6–21.

deductive application: the use of a moral principle or norm to answer directly questions about what is morally permissible. It differs from an inductive method whereby through analogy or comparison one measures one moral case or insight with another case or insight.

deontology: the approach to ethics that emphasizes duty, moral obligation, and right actions.

Deuteropauline epistles: the New Testament letters (Colossians, Ephesians, 2 Thessalonians, 1 and 2 Timothy, and Titus) ascribed to Paul but generally regarded as having been composed after Paul's death by students and admirers.

Diaspora: the collective term for Jews living outside the land of Israel and later applied to Christians living in the world.

dikaiosyne: the Greek word that is generally translated either as "justice" or as "righteousness." It is used with regard both to God and to humans.

discipleship: the process by which men and women come to follow Jesus, learn from him, and carry on his mission of teaching and healing.

ecclesiology: the study of the Church (*ekklesia*) with regard to its historical and theological foundations, structures, and mission.

ecocentric: the approach to the environment and to environmental ethics that focuses mainly on nature rather than on humans (anthropocentric) and God (theocentric).

effective history: the study of the impact or influence that a text or an idea has exercised over the centuries. Its German equivalent is *Wirkungsgeschichte.*

epitome: a summary or condensed account of a philosophical, ethical, or religious system.

eschatology: the branch of theology that deals with the end of human history and the final destiny of the person; that is, the "last things"—death, judgment, heaven, and hell.

ethics: the study of the principles of morality and the standards for right conduct or practices recognized by a particular group such as Stoics or Christians.

ethnography: the branch of anthropology that deals with the scientific description of individual cultures.

Evangelist: the author of one of the accounts (the Gospels) about Jesus' life and teachings; that is, Matthew, Mark, Luke, or John.

exegesis: the explanation and interpretation of biblical texts, with attention to their literary, historical, and theological significance.

existential encounter: a person-to-person encounter or "I" and "thou" relationship, conducted at a highly intentional and sensitive level.

Exodus event, the: the liberation of ancient Israel under the leadership of Moses from slavery in Egypt in the thirteenth century B.C.

feminist theology: an approach to theology that highlights the contributions that women have made throughout biblical and church history, and exposes the male-oriented emphasis in theology and church life.

fictive kinship: the idea that persons who are not biologically related can become "brothers" and "sisters" because of their common beliefs and way of life.

final (last) judgment: the "legal" procedure at the end of human history, with God and/or Christ presiding as judge, at which persons will be judged according to their deeds.

Franciscan spirituality: the way of life characteristic of the religious movement begun by St. Francis of Assisi in the thirteenth century that emphasizes dependence on God, material poverty, and respect for nature.

fundamentalism: the approach to the Bible that stresses the inerrancy of Scripture in matters not only of faith and morals but also of history and science.

gnostic individualism: an approach to life and ethics that presupposes a superior knowledge of spiritual matters on the part of its proponents.

hermeneutics: the interpretation of biblical texts, with regard to their meaning and their significance especially for people today.

heuristic probe: the investigation of a subject or issue that seeks to encourage and invite further exploration and discovery.

historical-critical method: the investigation of biblical texts that attends especially to their original historical settings and what they meant in those contexts.

historical Jesus, the: the life and teachings of the earthly Jesus as he was before his death and resurrection, and as reconstructed according to the criteria of historical research.

Holiness Code, the: the body of Old Testament laws in Leviticus 17–26, which are mainly concerned with religious and cultic matters.

hortatory: urging others to some course of action or conduct.

Humanae Vitae: the Latin title (meaning "Of Human Life") of the papal encyclical issued in 1968 by Pope Paul VI that reaffirmed the Catholic Church's condemnation of artificial means of contraception.

imitatio Christi: the approach to Christian life that takes Jesus Christ as its principal model and norm.

imitatio Dei: the approach to Christian life that takes God as its principal model and norm.

interim ethic: the theory (proposed by Albert Schweitzer) that Jesus intended his ethical teachings to be in force for only a short period, before the end of the world and the revelation of God's kingdom.

Jesus movement: the group of disciples formed by Jesus that spread his message before his death and formed the nucleus for the emergence of the early church.

kerygma: from the Greek word for "preaching, proclamation," it refers to the proclamation of Jesus' death and resurrection and of its saving effects (e.g., 1 Corinthians 15:3–5).

Levite: a descendant of the Israelite patriarch Levi. The Levites assisted the Jewish priests in the Jerusalem Temple.

liberal theology: the approach to theology that claims to be more progressive and attuned to the modern world than other approaches are.

liturgy: public worship and the rituals in which it is carried out.

Mammon: what one puts one's trust in, from the Semitic root 'mn ("believe"); in particular, money or other forms of wealth (see Matthew 6:24; Luke 16:13).

metaphysical unity: when discussing the nature of the human person as composed of body and soul, philosophers and theologians use this phrase to acknowledge that the soul is one with the body and vice versa.

methodology: the system of methods, principles, and rules for regulating a scientific discipline such as biblical exegesis.

moral identity: a way of describing the ethical and anthropological profile of a person.

moral pathology: the study of the origin, nature, and course of moral failures or sins.

moral theology: the branch of theology that deals with principles of ethical conduct.

natural law: the principles derived from nature and reason, and regarded as binding on all humans.

nature and species of sin: manuals of moral theology routinely described what was sin and then specifically categorized sins either according to the seven deadly sins or as violations of the Decalogue.

New Testament ethics: the moral teachings contained in the various books of the New Testament.

nexus: a means of connecting or linking two separate entities.

normative theological discipline: a branch of theology that claims to transcend mere historical description and to discover and set standards and norms for correct beliefs and actions today.

paradigm (paradigm case): a perfectly clear and uncontroversial example of a general point or reality.

paraenetic: urging or exhorting others to some course of action or conduct.

Pastoral Epistles: the three Pauline letters known as 1 and 2 Timothy and Titus. They concern the duties of "pastors" and the pastoral life of the Church.

paterfamilias: the male head of a Roman household or family, usually the father.

Pelagian (Pelagius): Pelagius was a British monk in the fifth century who maintained that righteousness could be attained by the exercise of human free will alone. A "Pelagian" approach to Christian ethics ignores the pivotal role of God and grace in Christian life, and concentrates on the role of the human person's willpower.

Penitentials: the books or codes compiled for confessors that specified the appropriate penances for various sins.

preferential option for the poor: the biblical theme that God is on the side of the poor, and hears their prayers. In social ethics this means the obligation to pay special attention to the needs of the poor in society.

Ptolemaic/Egyptian kingdom: the part of the empire founded by Alexander the Great (died 323 B.C.) that controlled the land of Israel from around 300 to 200 B.C.

Qumran: the site in the Holy Land where the largest and most important collection of Dead Sea Scrolls was found in 1947. The site was occupied in Jesus' time by a Jewish religious sect (Essenes).

Reformers: the leaders of the Protestant revolt against the Roman Catholic Church in sixteenth-century Europe. The most prominent figures were Martin Luther and John Calvin.

relational anthropological vision: almost all contemporary ethicists and moral theologians describe the human being as not only an individuated person but also one who is constitutively related to other humans, the world, and God.

restorative (redemptive) justice: the biblical approach to justice that moves beyond retribution and seeks the sinner's (or offender's) healing and reconciliation with God and the larger community.

Rule of the Community: a rule book for a Jewish religious community contemporary with Jesus that was discovered among the Dead Sea Scrolls at Qumran.

salvation: the act of rescuing or protecting from harm, loss, sickness, etc. In theology it refers to God's action through Christ to save people from the power of sin and to make possible for them eternal life with God.

sanctification: the act of making someone or something holy, consecrated, set apart, etc. In theology it refers to God's action through Christ to render believers holy.

Sayings Source Q: the collection of Jesus' sayings used independently by Matthew and Luke to supplement Mark's narrative. The symbol Q derives from the German word *Quelle* (meaning "source").

Second Vatican Council: the worldwide or ecumenical meeting of all Catholic bishops and their theological consultants that was held in Rome from 1962 to 1965.

ṣedeqah: the Hebrew word that is generally translated as "justice" or "righteousness." See the entry on its Greek equivalent *dikaiosyne*.

Seleucid/Syrian kingdom: the part of the empire founded by Alexander the Great (died 323 B.C.) whose center was in Syria and that controlled the land of Israel from around 200 to 165 B.C.

Septuagint, the: the oldest Greek version of the Old Testament, traditionally said to have been produced by 70 or 72 scholars at the request of the Egyptian ruler Ptolemy II in the third century B.C.

seven deadly sins: pride, envy, anger, sloth, avarice, gluttony, and lust.

Social Gospel Movement: an American Protestant movement in the late nineteenth and early twentieth century that stressed the social teachings of Jesus and their application to public life.

spiritual works of mercy: admonishing sinners, instructing the ignorant, counseling the doubtful, comforting the sorrowful, bearing wrongs patiently, forgiving injuries, and praying for the living and the dead.

spiritualism: the belief that the spirits of the dead can communicate with the living. In philosophy it can refer to the position that all reality is spiritual or that only spiritual realities are important.

spirituality: how one relates to God and so to others and to the world, and how one looks upon oneself in the light of that relationship to God. It generally involves meditation and prayer.

Stoics: an ancient school of philosophers founded by Zeno, who taught that people should be free from passion (whether joy or grief) and submit to suffering without complaint.

Synoptic Gospels: the term used to refer to the Gospels of Matthew, Mark, and Luke, because they present a "common view" (from the Greek *synopsis*) of Jesus (one that is different from John's Gospel).

teleological: moving toward a goal, end, or purpose (from the Greek *telos*).

telos: the Greek word for goal, end, or purpose.

Temple Scroll, the: a Jewish document found among the Dead Sea Scrolls at Qumran that describes the ideal temple and offers rules pertaining to worship there and to related topics.

theocentric: from the Greek word *theos* meaning "God," the term refers to an approach to life that focuses mainly on God rather than on human beings (anthropocentric) or nature (ecocentric).

theology: the study of divine things or religious truths, especially God, the divine attributes, God's relation to humans and to the world, and so on.

thicken: contemporary philosophers such as Michael Walzer and Martha Nussbaum differentiate between modestly formulated but universally held dispositions, concerns, and values (e.g., awareness of death, the need to nurture the young) and the way in which those dispositions, concerns, and values are developed or leavened in particular local cultures.

Torah: derived from the Hebrew word "teach, instruct," the word *Torah* is generally translated as "the (Mosaic) Law" and can refer to the Old Testament as a whole, the Pentateuch (Genesis to Deuteronomy), the 613 commandments in it, and/or the traditions about them collected in the Mishnah and the Talmuds.

typos: a Greek word that refers to a pattern, model, type, form, etc.

vigilance: the state of being always on guard or on watch. In the New Testament it is the attitude recommended for those who await the coming of God's kingdom.

virtue ethics: the approach to ethics that asks, "Who should we become?" It is concerned with these three basic questions: "Who are we?" "Who ought we to become?" and "How do we get there?"

INDEX

CPSIA information can be obtained at www.ICGtesting.com
Printed in the USA
LVOW07*0530130416

483385LV00004B/10/P